Advanced TypeScript Programming Projects

Build 9 different apps with TypeScript 3 and JavaScript frameworks such as Angular, React, and Vue

Peter O'Hanlon

BIRMINGHAM - MUMBAI

Advanced TypeScript Programming Projects

Commissioning Editor: Richa Tripathi
Acquisition Editor: Alok Dhuri
Content Development Editor: Tiksha Sarang
Senior Editor: Afshaan Khan
Technical Editor: Pradeep Sahu
Copy Editor: Safis Editing
Project Coordinator: Prajakta Naik
Proofreader: Safis Editing
Indexer: Pratik Shirodkar
Production Designer: Arvindkumar Gupta

First published: July 2019

Production reference: 1250719

Published by Packt Publishing Ltd.
Livery Place
35 Livery Street
Birmingham
B3 2PB, UK.

ISBN 978-1-78913-304-2

www.packtpub.com

To my wife, Jennifer, for all the love and patience she has shown while I have been locked away, slaving over a hot keyboard each day. As always, you are wise, kind, loving, and funny, and it is a true joy being your husband. To Catherine and Hannah, my daughters. The greatest pleasure a parent can have is seeing a child growing up to be even half as wonderful as I find you two. Wonderful is the right word, because you both fill me with wonder.
To Harvey – what can I say but "Woof!"

Packt>

Contributors

About the author

Peter O'Hanlon has been a professional developer for nearly 30 years. In this time, he has developed desktop and web applications of all types and sizes. During his development career, Peter has worked with languages such as C, C++, BASIC, Pascal, and JavaScript. For the last 18 years or so, Peter has concentrated on C# WPF, JavaScript, and now TypeScript. Over the years, Peter has been a Code Project MVP several times, a member of the Intel Innovator program, as well as competing in the Intel Ultimate Coder 2 contest. Peter is always keen to embrace new technologies and languages, which has led him to be actively involved in technologies such as augmented and mixed reality, computer vision, artificial intelligence, and gesture recognition.

About the reviewer

Nadun Indunil is a software engineer at Sysco Labs, Sri Lanka. As a software engineer, he is responsible for the development and management of AWS-related software and tools. He holds a BSc (Hons.) degree in engineering from the University of Moratuwa (Sri Lanka). Nadun is an AWS Certified Solutions Architect and an open source contributor. He has contributed to many open source JavaScript projects, and maintains a few as well.

> *I would like to express my special gratitude to Packt Publishing, who gave me the golden opportunity to do the review of Advanced TypeScript 3 Programming, which has helped me and taught me about so many new things. I am really thankful to them.*
>
> *Secondly, I would also like to thank my parents, friends, and fiancée, who helped me a lot in finalizing this project within the limited time frame.*

Packt is searching for authors like you

If you're interested in becoming an author for Packt, please visit `authors.packtpub.com` and apply today. We have worked with thousands of developers and tech professionals, just like you, to help them share their insight with the global tech community. You can make a general application, apply for a specific hot topic that we are recruiting an author for, or submit your own idea.

Table of Contents

Preface

This is a book about TypeScript; but then again, you got that from the title. But it's more than just a book about TypeScript. This is a book about how TypeScript can be used to go beyond basic examples. That means that this is a book about topics that are just that little bit harder than you might already have covered in your first forays into the world of TypeScript.

So, we could probably rephrase that opening sentence to "This is a book about TypeScript and some of the fun and cool ways that you can use TypeScript with technologies that are more advanced than ones I've been using before".

Upfront, I will say that this book is not a book about how to program in Angular, React, Vue, or ASP.NET Core. Those are big topics that deserve their own separate books (indeed, at the end of each chapter, I do my best to point you toward other resources that will help you learn these technologies on a much deeper level than the brief chapters we will have on them). Instead, for Angular and React, I try to limit the introduction of new features to no more than five new concepts per chapter. Where we are using a technology such as Bootstrap, which has a technology-specific implementation, we will use the library that is most appropriate, such as `reactstrap` for React. We do this because these libraries have been designed to work with the **user interface** (**UI**) framework in question.

When we were doing the initial research for this book, one of the questions that kept cropping up was, "what's hot right now? What are people using that's new and exciting?" This book aims to offer an introduction to some of those technologies, including GraphQL, microservices, and machine learning. Again, this book cannot teach everything about the relevant technology. What it does do is provide an introduction to the technology and show how we can leverage the power of TypeScript to make our lives so much easier when developing with it.

One thing we will find as we go through the book is that I tend to focus on **object-oriented programming** (**OOP**) pretty heavily. We will be building a lot of classes. There are many reasons for this, but the biggest reason for this focus is that in early chapters, we are going to be writing code that we can make use of in later chapters. I also wanted to write code that you could just drop into your own code base if you wanted to. With TypeScript, class-based development makes this make this so much simpler. This also gives us the opportunity to talk about techniques that we can apply to make code simpler, even when using more advanced technologies, so we cover principles such as classes having a single responsibility (known as the Single Responsibility Pattern), and pattern-based development, where we apply well-known software engineering patterns to complex problems to make the solution simple.

As well as TypeScript, we are going to be looking at using Bootstrap for the UI for most of the chapters. In the couple of chapters on Angular, we do look at using Angular Material instead of Bootstrap for laying out interfaces, because Material and Angular go hand in hand, and if you end up developing commercial Angular applications, then chances are that you are going to use Material.

The first chapter introduces us to features that we might not have used before, such as rest and spread, so we will cover them in more depth there. In later chapters, we will be using these features in a way that should become natural, so, rather than disturbing the flow of the code by calling out a particular item, we will tend to just use the features in a way that becomes second nature. The other side to this is that, as we progress through the book, we will find that features from earlier chapters will generally be touched on again, so that we don't just do something once and then forget about it.

Who this book is for

This book is intended for people who are comfortable with at least the basics of TypeScript. If you know how to use the TypeScript Compiler, tsc, to build a config file and compile code, and the basics of things such as type safety, functions, and classes in TypeScript, then you should be able to get something out of this book.

If you have a more advanced understanding of TypeScript, then there should be plenty of material on technologies that you've not used before that will be of interest.

What this book covers

Chapter 1, *Advanced TypeScript Features*, introduces us to features of TypeScript that we may not have encountered before, such as using Union and Intersection types, creating our own type declarations, and using Decorators to enable aspect-oriented programming, among other features. With this chapter, we are going to get familiar with a variety of TypeScript techniques that we will use on a daily basis as professional coders.

Chapter 2, *Creating a Markdown Editor with TypeScript*, is where we write our first practical project – a simple Markdown editor. We are going to create a simple parser that we are going to hook up, inside a web page, to a text block and use it to identify when the user has typed in a Markdown tag and reflect this in a preview area. While writing this code, we are going to see how we can use design patterns with TypeScript to build more robust solutions.

Chapter 3, *A React Bootstrap Personal Contacts Manager*, sees us building a personal contacts manager with the popular React library. While we are writing our application, we will see how React uses a special TSX file to mix TypeScript and HTML together to produce user components. We will also look at how to use binding and state in React to automatically update data models when the user changes values. The ultimate aim here is to create a UI that allows us to enter, save, and retrieve information using the browser's own IndexedDB database, and to see how we can apply validation to components to make sure that input is valid.

Chapter 4, *The MEAN Stack – Building a Photo Gallery*, is the first time we encounter the MEAN stack. The MEAN stack describes a specific number of cooperative technologies to build applications that run on both the client and the server. We use this stack to write a photo gallery application using Angular as our UI, with MongoDB being used to store images that the user uploads. As we create the application, we will use the power of Angular to create services and components. At the same time, we are going to see how we can use Angular Material to create attractive UIs.

Chapter 5, *Angular ToDo App with GraphQL and Apollo*, introduces us to the idea that we don't just need to use REST to communicate between a client and a server. One of the hot topics right now is the use of GraphQL to create applications that can consume and update data from multiple points using GraphQL servers and clients. The Angular application we write in this chapter will manage a list of to-do items for the user and will further demonstrate Angular features such as using templates to switch between read-only and editable features, as well as seeing what Angular provides out of the box to validate user input.

`Chapter` 6, *Building a Chat Room Application Using Socket.IO*, further explores the ideas that we don't need to rely on REST communications. We are going to look at how we can establish long-running client/server applications in Angular, where the connection between the client and the server appears to be kept permanently open so that messages can be passed backward and forward. Using the power of Socket.IO, we are going to write a chatroom application. To further enhance our code, we are going to use an external authentication provider to help us professionally secure our application so that we avoid embarrassing authentication failures such as storing passwords in plaintext.

`Chapter` 7, *Angular Cloud-Based Mapping with Firebase*, it has become impossible to ignore the growth of cloud-based services. In this, our last Angular application, we are going to use two separate cloud-based services. The first one we are going to use, Bing mapping, will show us how to sign up to a third-party, cloud-based mapping service and integrate it into our application. We will discuss the effect of scale on costs for this service. We will display a map where the user can save points of interest, with the data being stored in a separate cloud-based database using Google's Firebase cloud platform.

`Chapter` 8, *Building a CRM Using React and Microservices*, builds on our experiences with both React and the MEAN stack to introduce us to working with the equivalent React-based stack. When we first encountered MEAN, we used REST to talk to a single application endpoint. In this application, we are going to talk to multiple microservices to create a simplified React-based CRM system. We will discuss what microservices are and when we would want to use them, as well as seeing how we can design and document REST APIs using Swagger. The main takeaway from this chapter is that we introduce Docker to show how we can run up our services inside their own containers; containers are currently one of the favorite topics among developers when developing applications because of the way they simplify the rolling out of applications, and they aren't that hard to use.

`Chapter` 9, *Image Recognition with Vue.js and TensorFlow.js*, introduces us to using our web browser to host machine learning using TensorFlow.js. We will write an application using the popular Vue.js framework to identify images using pre-trained image models. We will extend this to see how to create pose detection applications that recognize which pose you are in and can be extended to tracking your poses using a web camera for purposes of sports coaching.

`Chapter` 10, *Building an ASP.NET Core Music Library*, is a big departure for us. We have written a number of applications now where TypeScript has represented the main coding language that we use to build our UIs. With ASP.NET Core, we are going to write a music library application where we can enter the name of an artist and search for details of their music using the free Discogs music API. We will be using a combination of C# and TypeScript to both run queries against Discog and to build up our UI.

To get the most out of this book

- You should have a basic knowledge of TypeScript in order to work with the content in this book. Knowledge of HTML and web pages would be useful as well.
- Where download code uses a package manager such as npm, you need to know how to restore the packages, because we haven't included them in the repository. To restore them, you can use npm install in the same directory that package.json is in, and that will restore the packages.
- In the last chapter, you won't have to explicitly download missing packages. Visual Studio will restore these packages when you build the project.

Download the example code files

You can download the example code files for this book from your account at www.packt.com. If you purchased this book elsewhere, you can visit www.packt.com/support and register to have the files emailed directly to you.

You can download the code files by following these steps:

1. Log in or register at www.packt.com.
2. Select the **SUPPORT** tab.
3. Click on **Code Downloads & Errata**.
4. Enter the name of the book in the **Search** box and follow the onscreen instructions.

Once the file is downloaded, please make sure that you unzip or extract the folder using the latest version of:

- WinRAR/7-Zip for Windows
- Zipeg/iZip/UnRarX for Mac
- 7-Zip/PeaZip for Linux

The code bundle for the book is also hosted on GitHub at https://github.com/PacktPublishing/Advanced-TypeScript-3-Programming-Projects. In case there's an update to the code, it will be updated on the existing GitHub repository.

We also have other code bundles from our rich catalog of books and videos available at https://github.com/PacktPublishing/. Check them out!

Download the color images

We also provide a PDF file that has color images of the screenshots/diagrams used in this book. You can download it here: `https://static.packt-cdn.com/downloads/9781789133042_ColorImages.pdf`.

Conventions used

There are a number of text conventions used throughout this book.

`CodeInText`: Indicates code words in text, database table names, folder names, filenames, file extensions, pathnames, dummy URLs, user input, and Twitter handles. Here is an example: "The following `tsconfig.json` file is used".

A block of code is set as follows:

```
{
  "compilerOptions": {
    "target": "ES2015",
    "module": "commonjs",
    "sourceMap": true,
    "outDir": "./script",
  }
}
```

When we wish to draw your attention to a particular part of a code block, the relevant lines or items are set in bold:

```
{
  "compilerOptions": {
    "target": "ES2015",
    "module": "commonjs",
    "sourceMap": true,
    "outDir": "./script",
  }
}
```

Any command-line input or output is written as follows:

```
npx create-react-app chapter03 --scripts-version=react-scripts-ts
```

Bold: Indicates a new term, an important word, or words that you see onscreen. For example, words in menus or dialog boxes appear in the text like this. Here is an example: "Typically, Angular is used to create **Single-Page Applications** (**SPAs**), whereby small sections of the client are updated rather than having to reload the whole page when a navigation event happens."

Warnings or important notes appear like this.

 Tips and tricks appear like this.

Get in touch

Feedback from our readers is always welcome.

General feedback: If you have questions about any aspect of this book, mention the book title in the subject of your message and email us at customercare@packtpub.com.

Errata: Although we have taken every care to ensure the accuracy of our content, mistakes do happen. If you have found a mistake in this book, we would be grateful if you would report this to us. Please visit www.packt.com/submit-errata, selecting your book, clicking on the Errata Submission Form link, and entering the details.

Piracy: If you come across any illegal copies of our works in any form on the Internet, we would be grateful if you would provide us with the location address or website name. Please contact us at copyright@packt.com with a link to the material.

If you are interested in becoming an author: If there is a topic that you have expertise in and you are interested in either writing or contributing to a book, please visit authors.packtpub.com.

Reviews

Please leave a review. Once you have read and used this book, why not leave a review on the site that you purchased it from? Potential readers can then see and use your unbiased opinion to make purchase decisions, we at Packt can understand what you think about our products, and our authors can see your feedback on their book. Thank you!

For more information about Packt, please visit packt.com.

Advanced TypeScript Features 1

In this chapter, we are going to look at aspects of TypeScript that go beyond the basics of the language. When used appropriately, these features provide a clean, intuitive way to work in TypeScript and will help you to craft professional-level code. Some of the things we cover here may not be new to you, but I am including them so that there is a common baseline of knowledge as we work through later chapters, as well as an understanding of why we will be using these features. We will also cover why we need these techniques; it is not merely enough to know how to apply something, we also need to know in what circumstances we should use them and what we need to consider when we do so. The focus of this chapter is not to create a dry, exhaustive list of each feature—instead, we are going to introduce the information we need to work through the rest of this book. These are practical techniques that we will apply again and again in our daily development.

As this is a book on web development, we are also going to be creating a lot of UIs, so we are going to look at how we can create attractive interfaces using the popular Bootstrap framework.

The following topics will be covered in this chapter:

- Using different types with union types
- Combining types with intersection types
- Simplifying type declarations with type aliases
- Deconstructing objects with REST properties
- Coping with a variable number of parameters using REST
- **Aspect-Oriented Programming** (**AOP**) using decorators
- Composing types using mixins
- Using the same code with different types and using generics
- Mapping values using maps
- Creating asynchronous code with promises and async/await
- Creating UIs with Bootstrap

Technical requirements

In order to complete this chapter, you are going to need Node.js installed. You can download and install Node.js from `https://nodejs.org/en/`.

You will also need the TypeScript compiler installed. There are two ways to do this through Node.js using the **Node Package Manager** (**NPM**). If you want the same version of TypeScript used in all of your applications and are happy that they will all run on the same version whenever you update it, use the following command:

```
npm install -g typescript
```

If you want the version of TypeScript to be local to a particular project, type the following in the project folder:

```
npm install typescript --save-dev
```

For a code editor, you can use any suitable editor or even a basic text editor. Throughout this book, I will be using Visual Studio Code, a free cross-platform **integrated development environment** (**IDE**), available at `https://code.visualstudio.com/`.

All code is available on GitHub at `https://github.com/PacktPublishing/Advanced-TypeScript-3-Programming-Projects/tree/master/Chapter01`.

Building future-proof TypeScript with tsconfig

As TypeScript has grown in popularity, it has benefited from a rapidly evolving open source architecture. The design goals behind the original implementation means that it has proven to be a popular choice for developers, from those who were new to JavaScript-based development to seasoned professionals. This popularity means that the language has quickly gained new features, some straightforward and others geared toward developers who are working on the cutting edge of the JavaScript ecosystem. This chapter aims to address the features that TypeScript has introduced to match either current or upcoming ECMAScript implementations that you might not have encountered previously.

As we progress through this chapter, I will occasionally call out features that require a newer ECMAScript standard. In some cases, TypeScript will already have provided a poly-filled implementation of a feature that works with earlier versions of ECMAScript. In other cases, the version we compile against will have a feature that could not be back-filled beyond a certain point so it will be worth using a more up-to-date setting.

While it's possible to compile TypeScript completely from the command line using nothing but parameters, I prefer to use `tsconfig.json`. You can either create this file manually or have TypeScript create it for you using the following command from the command line:

```
tsc --init
```

If you want to copy my settings, these are the ones I have set up by default. When we need to update references, I will point out the entries that need to be added:

```
{
  "compilerOptions": {
    "target": "ES2015",
    "module": "commonjs",
    "lib": [ "ES2015", "dom" ],
    "sourceMap": true,
    "outDir": "./script",
    "strict": true,
    "strictNullChecks": true,
    "strictFunctionTypes": true,
    "noImplicitThis": true,
    "alwaysStrict": true,
    "noImplicitReturns": true,
    "noFallthroughCasesInSwitch": true,
    "esModuleInterop": true,
    "experimentalDecorators": true,
  }
}
```

Introduction to advanced TypeScript features

With each release, TypeScript takes big strides forward, adding features and capabilities that build on the basics of the language that were introduced back in version 1. Since then, JavaScript has moved on and TypeScript has added features to target emerging standards, providing implementations for older implementations of JavaScript or by calling native implementations when targeting updated ECMA standards. In this first chapter, we are going to look at some of these features, which we will be using throughout this book.

Using different types with union types

The first feature that we are going to look at is one of my favorites, that is, the ability to use union types. These types are used when a function expects a single parameter to be one type or another. Suppose, for instance, that we have a validation routine that needs to check whether a value is in a particular range and this validation could receive the value either from a textbox as a `string` value, or as a `number` value from a calculation. As each of the techniques for solving this issue have a lot in common, we'll start off with a simple class that allows us to specify the minimum and maximum values that form our range and a function to actually perform the validation, as follows:

```
class RangeValidationBase {
    constructor(private start : number, private end : number) { }
    protected RangeCheck(value : number) : boolean {
        return value >= this.start && value <= this.end;
    }
    protected GetNumber(value : string) : number {
        return new Number(value).valueOf();
    }
}
```

If you haven't seen a `constructor` that looks like that before, that's the equivalent of writing the following:

```
private start : number = 0;
private end : number = 0;
constructor(start : number, end : number) {
    this.start = start;
    this.end = end;
}
```

If you need to check your parameters or manipulate them in some way, you should use this expanded format of parameters. If you are simply assigning the values to private fields, then the first format is a very elegant way to do this and saves cluttering up your code.

There are a few ways that we could solve the problem of ensuring we only perform our validation using `string` or `number`. The first way we could solve this problem would be by providing two separate methods that accept the relevant type, as follows:

```
class SeparateTypeRangeValidation extends RangeValidationBase {
    IsInRangeString(value : string) : boolean {
        return this.RangeCheck(this.GetNumber(value));
    }
    IsInRangeNumber(value : number) : boolean {
        return this.RangeCheck(value);
    }
}
```

While this technique would work, it's not very elegant and it certainly doesn't take advantage of the power of TypeScript. The second technique that we could use is to allow us to pass in the value without constraining it, as follows:

```
class AnyRangeValidation extends RangeValidationBase {
    IsInRange(value : any) : boolean {
        if (typeof value === "number") {
            return this.RangeCheck(value);
        } else if (typeof value === "string") {
            return this.RangeCheck(this.GetNumber(value));
        }
        return false;
    }
}
```

That's definitely an improvement over our original implementation because we have settled on one signature for our function, which means that calling the code is a lot more consistent. Unfortunately, we can still pass an invalid type into the method, so if we passed `boolean` in, for instance, this code would compile successfully but it would fail at runtime.

If we want to constrain our validation so that it only accepts strings or numbers, then we can use a union type. It doesn't differ much from the last implementation but it does give us the compile time type safety that we're after, as follows:

```
class UnionRangeValidation extends RangeValidationBase {
    IsInRange(value : string | number) : boolean {
        if (typeof value === "number") {
            return this.RangeCheck(value);
        }
        return this.RangeCheck(this.GetNumber(value));
    }
}
```

The signature that identifies the type constraints as being a union is `type | type` in the function name. This tells the compiler (and us) what the valid types are for this method. As we have constrained the input to be `number` or `string`, once we have ruled out that the type is not `number`, we don't need to check `typeof` to see whether it's a `string` so we have simplified the code even further.

 We can chain as many types together as we need in a union statement. There's no practical limit but we have to make sure that each type in the union list needs a corresponding `typeof` check if we are going to handle it properly. The order of the types does not matter either, so `number | string` is treated the same as `string | number`. Something to remember though is if the function has lots of types combined together, then it is probably doing too much and the code should be looked at to see whether it can be broken up into smaller pieces.

We can go further than this with union types. In TypeScript, we have two special types, `null` and `undefined`. These types can be assigned to anything unless we compile our code with the `–strictNullChecks` option or `strictNullChecks = true` if we're setting this as a flag in our `tsconfig.json` file. I like to set this value so that my code only handles null cases where it should, which is a great way to guard against side effects creeping in just because a function receives a null value. If we want to allow `null` (or `undefined`), we simply need to add these as a union type.

Combining types with intersection types

Sometimes, it's important for us to have the ability to handle a case where we can bring multiple types together and treat them as one type. Intersection types are the types that have all properties available from each type that is being combined. We can see what an intersection looks like with the following simple example. First of all, we are going to create classes for a `Grid` along with a `Margin` to apply to that `Grid`, as follows:

```
class Grid {
    Width : number = 0;
    Height : number = 0;
}
class Margin {
    Left : number = 0;
    Top : number = 0;
}
```

What we are going to create is an intersection that will end up with `Width` and `Height` from the `Grid` property, along with `Left` and `Top` from `Margin`. To do this, we are going to create a function that takes in `Grid` and `Margin` and returns a type that contains all of these properties, as follows:

```
function ConsolidatedGrid(grid : Grid, margin : Margin) : Grid & Margin {
    let consolidatedGrid = <Grid & Margin>{};
    consolidatedGrid.Width = grid.Width;
    consolidatedGrid.Height = grid.Height;
    consolidatedGrid.Left = margin.Left;
    consolidatedGrid.Top = margin.Top;
    return consolidatedGrid;
}
```

Note, we are going to come back to this function later in this chapter when we look at object spread to see how we can remove a lot of the boilerplate copying of properties.

The *magic* that makes this work is the way we define `consolidatedGrid`. We use & to join together the types we want to use to create our intersection. As we want to bring `Grid` and `Margin` together, we are using `<Grid & Margin>` to tell the compiler what our type will look like. We can see that we don't have to explicitly name this type; the compiler is smart enough to take care of this for us.

What happens if we have the same properties present in both types? Does TypeScript prevent us from mixing these types together? As long as the property is of the same type, then TypeScript is perfectly happy for us to use the same property name. To see this in action, we are going to expand our `Margin` class to also include `Width` and `Height` properties, as follows:

```
class Margin {
    Left : number = 0;
    Top : number = 0;
    Width : number = 10;
    Height : number = 20;
}
```

How we handle these extra properties really depends on what we want to do with them. In our example, we are going to add `Width` and `Height` of `Margin` to `Width` and `Height` of `Grid`. This leaves our function looking like this:

```
function ConsolidatedGrid(grid : Grid, margin : Margin) : Grid & Margin {
    let consolidatedGrid = <Grid & Margin>{};
    consolidatedGrid.Width = grid.Width + margin.Width;
    consolidatedGrid.Height = grid.Height + margin.Height;
    consolidatedGrid.Left = margin.Left;
```

```
        consolidatedGrid.Top = margin.Top;
        return consolidatedGrid;
    }
```

If, however, we wanted to try and reuse the same property name but the types of those properties were different, we can end up with a problem if those types have restrictions on them. To see the effect this has, we are going to expand our Grid and Margin classes to include Weight. Weight in our Grid class is a number and Weight in our Margin class is a string, as follows:

```
class Grid {
    Width : number = 0;
    Height : number = 0;
    Weight : number = 0;
}
class Margin {
    Left : number = 0;
    Top : number = 0;
    Width : number = 10;
    Height : number = 20;
    Weight : string = "1";
}
```

We are going to try and add the Weight types together in our ConsolidatedGrid function:

```
consolidatedGrid.Weight = grid.Weight + new
    Number(margin.Weight).valueOf();
```

At this point, TypeScript complains about this line with the following error:

```
error TS2322: Type 'number' is not assignable to type 'number & string'.
    Type 'number' is not assignable to type 'string'.
```

While there are ways to solve this issue, such as using a union type for Weight in Grid and parsing the input, it's generally not worth going to that trouble. If the type is different, this is generally a good indication that the behavior of the property is different, so we really should look to name it something different.

While we are working with classes in our examples here, it is worth pointing out that intersections are not just constrained to classes. Intersections apply to interfaces, generics, and primitive types as well.

There are certain other rules that we need to consider when dealing with intersections. If we have the same property name but only one side of that property is optional, then the finalized property will be mandatory. We are going to introduce a padding property to our `Grid` and `Margin` classes and make `Padding` optional in `Margin`, as follows:

```
class Grid {
    Width : number = 0;
    Height : number = 0;
    Padding : number;
}
class Margin {
    Left : number = 0;
    Top : number = 0;
    Width : number = 10;
    Height : number = 20;
    Padding?: number;
}
```

Because we have provided a mandatory `Padding` variable, we cannot change our intersection, as follows:

```
consolidatedGrid.Padding = margin.Padding;
```

As there is no guarantee that the margin padding will be assigned, the compiler is going to do its best to stop us. To solve this, we are going to change our code to apply the `margin` padding if it is set and fall back to the `grid` padding if it is not. To do this, we are going to make a simple fix:

```
consolidatedGrid.Padding = margin.Padding ? margin.Padding : grid.Padding;
```

This strange-looking syntax is called the ternary operator. This is a shorthand way of writing the following—if `margin.Padding` has a value, let `consolidatedGrid.Padding` equal that value; otherwise, let it equal `grid.Padding`. This could have been written as an if/else statement but, as this is a common paradigm in languages such as TypeScript and JavaScript, it is worth becoming familiar with.

Simplifying type declarations with type aliases

Something that goes hand in hand with intersection types and union types are type aliases. Rather than cluttering our code with references to `string | number | null`, TypeScript gives us the ability to create a handy alias that is expanded out by the compiler into the relevant code.

Suppose that we want to create a type alias that represents the union type of `string | number`, then we can create an alias that looks as follows:

```
type StringOrNumber = string | number;
```

If we revisit our range validation sample, we can change the signature of our function to use this alias, as follows:

```
class UnionRangeValidationWithTypeAlias extends RangeValidationBase {
    IsInRange(value : StringOrNumber) : boolean {
        if (typeof value === "number") {
            return this.RangeCheck(value);
        }
        return this.RangeCheck(this.GetNumber(value));
    }
}
```

The important thing to notice in this code is that we don't really create any new types here. The type alias is just a syntactic trick that we can use to make our code more readable and, more importantly, help us to create code that is more consistent when we are working in larger teams.

We can combine type aliases with types to create more complex type aliases as well. If we wanted to add `null` support to the previous type alias, we could add this type:

```
type NullableStringOrNumber = StringOrNumber | null;
```

As the compiler still sees the underlying type and uses that, we can use the following syntax to call our `IsInRange` method:

```
let total : string | number = 10;
if (new UnionRangeValidationWithTypeAlias(0,100).IsInRange(total)) {
    console.log(`This value is in range`);
}
```

Obviously, this doesn't give us very consistent-looking code, so we can change `string | number` to `StringOrNumber`.

Assigning properties using object spread

In the `ConsolidatedGrid` example from the *Intersection types* section, we assigned each property to our intersection individually. Depending on the effect that we are trying to achieve, there is another way that we could have created our `<Grid & Margin>` intersection type with less code. Using a spread operator, we could perform a shallow copy of the properties from one or more of our input types automatically.

First, let's see how we can rewrite our earlier example so that it automatically populates the margin information:

```
function ConsolidatedGrid(grid : Grid, margin : Margin) : Grid  & Margin {
    let consolidatedGrid = <Grid & Margin>{...margin};
    consolidatedGrid.Width += grid.Width;
    consolidatedGrid.Height += grid.Height;
    consolidatedGrid.Padding = margin.Padding ? margin.Padding :
    grid.Padding;
    return consolidatedGrid;
}
```

When we are instantiating our `consolidatedGrid` function, this code copies in the properties from `margin` and fills them in. The triple dots (`...`) tell the compiler to treat this as a spread operation. As we have already populated `Width` and `Height`, we use `+=` to simply add in the elements from the grid.

What happens if we wanted to apply both the values from `grid` and `margin` instead? To do this, we can change our instantiation to look like this:

```
let consolidatedGrid = <Grid & Margin>{...grid, ...margin};
```

This fills in the `Grid` values with the values from `grid` and then fills in the `Margin` values from `margin`. This tells us two things. The first is that the spread operation maps the appropriate property to the appropriate property. The second thing this tells us is that the order that it does this in is important. As `margin` and `grid` both have the same properties, the values set by `grid` are overwritten by the values set by `margin`. In order to set the properties so that we see the values from `grid` in `Width` and `Height`, we have to reverse the order of this line. In reality, of course, we can see the effect as follows:

```
let consolidatedGrid = <Grid & Margin>{...margin, ...grid };
```

At this stage, we should really take a look at the JavaScript that TypeScript produces out of this. This is what the code looks like when we compile it using ES5:

```
var __assign = (this && this.__assign) || function () {
    __assign = Object.assign || function(t) {
        for (var s, i = 1, n = arguments.length; i < n; i++) {
            s = arguments[i];
            for (var p in s) if (Object.prototype.hasOwnProperty.call(s,
            p))
                t[p] = s[p];
        }
        return t;
    };
    return __assign.apply(this, arguments);
};
function ConsolidatedGrid(grid, margin) {
    var consolidatedGrid = __assign({}, margin, grid);
    consolidatedGrid.Width += grid.Width;
    consolidatedGrid.Height += grid.Height;
    consolidatedGrid.Padding = margin.Padding ? margin.Padding :
    grid.Padding;
    return consolidatedGrid;
}
```

If, however, we compile the code using the version ES2015 or later, the __assign function is removed and our ConsolidatedGrid JavaScript looks as follows:

```
function ConsolidatedGrid(grid, margin) {
    let consolidatedGrid = Object.assign({}, margin, grid);
    consolidatedGrid.Width += grid.Width;
    consolidatedGrid.Height += grid.Height;
    consolidatedGrid.Padding = margin.Padding ? margin.Padding :
    grid.Padding;
    return consolidatedGrid;
}
```

What we are seeing here is that TypeScript works hard to ensure that it can produce code that works regardless of which version of ECMAScript we are targeting. We didn't have to worry whether the feature was available or not; we left it to TypeScript to fill in the blanks for us.

Deconstructing objects with REST properties

Where we used spread operators to build up an object, we can also deconstruct objects with something called a REST property. Deconstructing simply means that we are going to take a complex *thing* and break it down into simpler ones. In other words, destructuring happens when we assign the elements inside an array or an object's properties to individual variables. While we have always been able to break complex objects and arrays down into simpler types, TypeScript provides a clean and elegant way to break these types down using REST parameters, which can deconstruct both objects and arrays.

In order to understand what REST properties are, we first need to understand how to deconstruct an object or an array. We are going to start off by deconstructing the following object literal, as follows:

```
let guitar = { manufacturer: 'Ibanez', type : 'Jem 777', strings : 6 };
```

One way that we could deconstruct this is by using the following:

```
const manufacturer = guitar.manufacturer;
const type = guitar.type;
const strings = guitar.strings;
```

While this works, it's not very elegant and there's a lot of repetition. Fortunately, TypeScript adopts the JavaScript syntax for a simple deconstruction like this, which provides a much neater syntax:

```
let {manufacturer, type, strings} = guitar;
```

Functionally, this results in the same individual items as the original implementation. The name of the individual properties must match the names of the properties in the object we are deconstructing—that's how the language knows which variable matches with which property on the object. If we need to change the name of the property for some reason, we use the following syntax:

```
let {manufacturer : maker, type, strings} = guitar;
```

The idea behind a REST operator on an object is that it applies when you take a variable number of items, so we are going to deconstruct this object into the manufacturer and the other fields are going to be bundled into a REST variable, as follows:

```
let { manufacturer, ...details } = guitar;
```

The REST operator must appear at the end of the assignment list; the TypeScript compiler complains if we add any properties after it.

After this statement, `details` now contains the type and strings values. Where things get interesting is when we look at the JavaScript that has been produced. The form of destructuring in the previous example is the same in JavaScript. There is no equivalent to the REST property in JavaScript (certainly in versions up to ES2018), so TypeScript produces code for us that gives us a consistent way to deconstruct more complex types:

```
// Compiled as ES5
var manufacturer = guitar.manufacturer, details = __rest(guitar,
["manufacturer"]);
var __rest = (this && this.__rest) || function (s, e) {
    var t = {};
    for (var p in s) if (Object.prototype.hasOwnProperty.call(s, p) &&
    e.indexOf(p) < 0)
        t[p] = s[p];
    if (s != null && typeof Object.getOwnPropertySymbols === "function")
        for (var i = 0, p = Object.getOwnPropertySymbols(s); i < p.length;
        i++) if (e.indexOf(p[i]) < 0)
            t[p[i]] = s[p[i]];
    return t;
};
```

Array destructuring works in a similar fashion to object destructuring. The syntax is virtually identical to the object version; the differences being that it uses [ ] to destructure in place of { }, which the object version uses, and that the order of the variables is based on the position of the item in the array.

The original method of destructuring an array relied on the variable being associated with an item at a certain index in the array:

```
const instruments = [ 'Guitar', 'Violin', 'Oboe', 'Drums' ];
const gtr = instruments[0];
const violin = instruments[1];
const oboe = instruments[2];
const drums = instruments[3];
```

Using array destructuring, we can change this syntax to be much more concise, as follows:

```
let [ gtr, violin, oboe, drums ] = instruments;
```

Knowing that the TypeScript team are good at providing us with a consistent and logical experience, it should come as no surprise that we can also apply REST properties to arrays, using similar syntax:

```
let [gtr, ...instrumentslice] = instruments;
```

Yet again, there is no direct JavaScript equivalent, but the compiled TypeScript shows that JavaScript does provide the underlying fundamentals and the TypeScript designers have been able to elegantly roll this in using `array.slice`:

```
// Compiled as ES5
var gtr = instruments[0], instrumentslice = instruments.slice(1);
```

Coping with a variable number of parameters using REST

The final thing we need to look at with regard to REST is the idea of functions having REST parameters. These aren't the same as REST properties but the syntax is so similar that we should find it easy to pick up. The problem that REST parameters solves is to cope with a variable number of parameters being passed into a function. The way to identify a REST parameter in a function is that it is preceded by the ellipsis and that it is typed as an array.

In this example, we are going to log out a header followed by a variable number of `instruments`:

```
function PrintInstruments(log : string, ...instruments : string[]) : void {
    console.log(log);
    instruments.forEach(instrument => {
        console.log(instrument);
    });
}
PrintInstruments('Music Shop Inventory', 'Guitar', 'Drums', 'Clarinet',
'Clavinova');
```

As the REST parameter is an array, this gives us access to array functions, which means that we can perform actions such as `forEach` from it directly. Importantly, REST parameters are different from the arguments object inside a JavaScript function because they start at the values that have not been named in the parameters list, whereas the arguments object contains a list of all of the arguments.

As REST parameters were not available in ES5, TypeScript does the work necessary to provide JavaScript that simulates the REST parameter. First, we will see what this looks like when compiled as ES5, as follows:

```
function PrintInstruments(log) {
    var instruments = [];
    // As our rest parameter starts at the 1st position in the list of
    // arguments,
    // our index starts at 1.
    for (var _i = 1; _i < arguments.length; _i++) {
        instruments[_i - 1] = arguments[_i];
    }
    console.log(log);
    instruments.forEach(function (instrument) {
        console.log(instrument);
    });
}
```

When we look at the JavaScript produced from an ES2015 compilation (you will need to change the entry for target to ES2015 in the `tsconfig.json` file), we see that it looks exactly the same as our TypeScript code:

```
function PrintInstruments(log, ...instruments) {
    console.log(log);
    instruments.forEach(instrument => {
        console.log(instrument);
    });
}
```

At this point, I cannot stress enough how important it is to take a look at the JavaScript that is being produced. TypeScript is very good at hiding complexity from us, but we really should be familiar with what is being produced. I find it a great way to understand what is going on *under the covers*, where possible, to compile using different versions of the ECMAScript standard and see what code is being produced.

AOP using decorators

One of my favorite features in TypeScript is the ability to use decorators. Decorators were introduced as an experimental feature and are pieces of code that we can use to modify the behavior of individual classes without having to change the internal implementation of the class. With this concept, we can adapt the behavior of an existing class without having to subclass it.

If you have come to TypeScript from a language such as Java or C#, you might notice that decorators look a lot like a technique known as AOP. What AOP techniques provide us with is the ability to extract repetitive code by cutting across a piece of code and separating this out into a different location. This means that we do not have to litter our implementations with code that will largely be boilerplate code, but which absolutely must be present in the running application.

The easiest way to explain what a decorator is to start off with an example. Suppose we have a class where only users in certain roles can access certain methods, as follows:

```typescript
interface IDecoratorExample {
    AnyoneCanRun(args:string) : void;
    AdminOnly(args:string) : void;
}
class NoRoleCheck implements IDecoratorExample {
    AnyoneCanRun(args: string): void {
        console.log(args);
    }
    AdminOnly(args: string): void {
        console.log(args);
    }
}
```

Now, we are going to create a user who has the `admin` and `user` roles, meaning that there are no problems in calling both methods in this class:

```typescript
let currentUser = {user: "peter", roles : [{role:"user"}, {role:"admin"}]
};
function TestDecoratorExample(decoratorMethod : IDecoratorExample) {
    console.log(`Current user ${currentUser.user}`);
    decoratorMethod.AnyoneCanRun(`Running as user`);
    decoratorMethod.AdminOnly(`Running as admin`);
}
TestDecoratorExample(new NoRoleCheck());
```

This gives us our expected output, as follows:

```
Current user Peter
Running as user
Running as admin
```

If we were to create a user who only had the `user` role, we would expect that they should not be able to run the admin-only code. As our code has no role checking, the `AdminOnly` method will be run regardless of what roles the user has assigned. One way to fix this code would be to add code to check the entitlement and then add this inside each method.

First, we are going to create a simple function to check whether or not the current user belongs to a particular role:

```
function IsInRole(role : string) : boolean {
    return currentUser.roles.some(r => r.role === role);
}
```

Revisiting our existing implementation, we are going to change our functions to call this check and determine whether or not `user` is allowed to run that method:

```
AnyoneCanRun(args: string): void {
    if (!IsInRole("user")) {
        console.log(`${currentUser.user} is not in the user role`);
        return;
    };
    console.log(args);
}
AdminOnly(args: string): void {
    if (!IsInRole("admin")) {
        console.log(`${currentUser.user} is not in the admin role`);
    };
    console.log(args);
}
```

When we look at this code, we can see that there is a lot of repeated code in here. Worse still, while we have repeated code, there is a bug in this implementation. In the `AdminOnly` code, there is no return statement inside the `IsInRole` block so the code will still run the `AdminOnly` code, but it will tell us that the user is not in the `admin` role and will then output the message regardless. This highlights one of the problems with repeated code: it's very easy to introduce subtle (or not-so-subtle) bugs without realizing it. Finally, we are violating one of the basic principles of good **object-oriented** (OO) development practice. Our classes and methods are doing things that they should not be doing; the code should be doing one thing and one thing only, so checking roles does not belong there. In Chapter 2, *Creating a Markdown Editor with TypeScript*, we will cover this in more depth when we delve deeper into the OO development mindset.

Let's see how we can use a method decorator to remove the boilerplate code and address the single responsibility issue.

Before we write our code, we need to ensure that TypeScript knows that we are going to use decorators, which are an experimental ES5 feature. We can do this by running the following command from the command line:

```
tsc --target ES5 --experimentalDecorators
```

Or, we can set this up in our `tsconfig` file:

```
"compilerOptions": {
        "target": "ES5",
// other parameters....
        "experimentalDecorators": true
    }
```

With the decorator build features enabled, we can now write our first decorator to ensure that a user belongs to the `admin` role:

```
function Admin(target: any, propertyKey : string | symbol, descriptor :
PropertyDescriptor) {
        let originalMethod = descriptor.value;
        descriptor.value = function() {
            if (IsInRole(`admin`)) {
                originalMethod.apply(this, arguments);
                return;
            }
            console.log(`${currentUser.user} is not in the admin role`);
        }
        return descriptor;
    }
```

Whenever we see a function definition that looks similar to this, we know that we are looking at a method decorator. TypeScript expects exactly these parameters in this order:

```
function ...(target: any, propertyKey : string | symbol, descriptor :
PropertyDescriptor)
```

The first parameter is used to refer to the element that we are applying it to. The second parameter is the name of the element, and the last parameter is the descriptor of the method we are applying our decorator to; this allows us to alter the behavior of the method. We must have a function with this signature to use as our decorator:

```
let originalMethod = descriptor.value;
descriptor.value = function() {
    ...
}
return descriptor;
```

The internals of the decorator method are not as scary as they look. What we are doing is copying the original method from the descriptor and then replacing that method with our own custom implementation. This wrapped implementation is returned and will be the code that is executed when we encounter it:

```
if (IsInRole(`admin`)) {
    originalMethod.apply(this, arguments);
    return;
}
console.log(`${currentUser.user} is not in the admin role`);
```

In our wrapped implementation, we are performing the same role check. If the check passes, we apply the original method. By using a technique like this, we have added something that will avoid calling our methods if it does not need to in a consistent manner.

In order to apply this, we use @ in front of our decorator factory function name just before the method in our class. When we add our decorator, we must avoid putting a semicolon between it and the method, as follows:

```
class DecoratedExampleMethodDecoration implements IDecoratorExample {
    AnyoneCanRun(args:string) : void {
        console.log(args);
    }
    @Admin
    AdminOnly(args:string) : void {
        console.log(args);
    }
}
```

While this code works for the `AdminOnly` code, it is not particularly flexible. As we add more roles, we will end up having to add more and more virtually identical functions. If only we had a way to create a general-purpose function that we could use to return a decorator that would accept a parameter that sets the role we wanted to allow. Fortunately, there is a way that we can do this using something called a decorator factory.

Put simply, a TypeScript decorator factory is a function that can receive parameters and uses the parameters to return the actual decorator. It only needs a couple of minor tweaks to our code and we have a working factory where we can specify the role we want to guard:

```
function Role(role : string) {
    return function(target: any, propertyKey : string | symbol, descriptor
    : PropertyDescriptor) {
        let originalMethod = descriptor.value;
        descriptor.value = function() {
            if (IsInRole(role)) {
```

```
                    originalMethod.apply(this, arguments);
                    return;
            }
            console.log(`${currentUser.user} is not in the ${role} role`);
        }
        return descriptor;
    }
}
```

The only real differences here are that we have a function returning our decorator, which no longer has a name, and the factory function parameter is being used inside our decorator. We can now change our class to use this factory instead:

```
class DecoratedExampleMethodDecoration implements IDecoratorExample {
    @Role("user") // Note, no semi-colon
    AnyoneCanRun(args:string) : void {
        console.log(args);
    }
    @Role("admin")
    AdminOnly(args:string) : void {
        console.log(args);
    }
}
```

With this change, when we call our methods, only an admin will be able to access the AdminOnly method, while anyone who is a user will be able to call AnyoneCanRun. An important side note is that, our decorator only applies inside a class. We cannot use this on a standalone function.

The reason we call this technique a decorator is because it follows something called the **decorator pattern**. This pattern recognizes a technique that is used to add behavior to individual objects without affecting other objects from the same class and without having to create a subclass. A pattern is simply a formalized solution to problems that occur commonly in software engineering, so the names act as a useful shorthand for describing what is going on functionally. It will probably not come as much of a surprise to know that there is also a factory pattern. As we go through this book, we will encounter other examples of patterns, so we will be comfortable using them when we reach the end.

We can apply decorators to other items in a class as well. For instance, if we wanted to prevent an unauthorized user from even instantiating our class, we could define a class decorator. A class decorator is added to the class definition and expects to receive the constructor as a function. This is what our constructor decorator looks like when created from a factory:

```
function Role(role : string) {
    return function(constructor : Function) {
```

```
        if (!IsInRole (role)) {
            throw new Error(`The user is not authorized to access this
class`);
        }
    }
}
```

When we apply this, we follow the same format of using the @ prefix, so, when the code attempts to create a new instance of this class for a non-admin user, the application will throw an error, preventing this class from being created:

```
@Role ("admin")
class RestrictedClass {
    constructor() {
        console.log(`Inside the constructor`);
    }
    Validate() {
        console.log(`Validating`);
    }
}
```

We can see that we have not declared any of our decorators inside a class. We should always create them as a top-level function because their usage is not suited for decorating a class, so we will not see syntax such as @MyClass.Role("admin");.

Beyond constructor and method decorations, we can decorate properties, accessors, and more. We aren't going to go into these here, but they will be cropping up later on in this book. We will also be looking at how we can chain decorators together so we have a syntax that looks as follows:

```
@Role ("admin")
@Log("Creating RestrictedClass")
class RestrictedClass {
    constructor() {
        console.log(`Inside the constructor`);
    }
    Validate() {
        console.log(`Validating`);
    }
}
```

Composing types using mixins

When we first encounter classic OO theory, we come across the idea that classes can be inherited. The idea here is that we can create even more specialized classes from general-purpose classes. One of the more popular examples of this is that we have a vehicle class that contains basic details about a vehicle. We inherit from the `vehicle` class to make a `car` class. We then inherit from the `car` class to make a `sports car` class. Each layer of inheritance here adds features that aren't present in the class we are inheriting from.

In general, this is a simple concept for us to work with, but what happens when we want to bring two or more seemingly unrelated things together to make our code? Let's examine a simple example.

It is a common thing with database applications to store whether a record has been deleted without actually deleting the record, and the time that the last update occurred on the record. At first glance, it would seem that we would want to track this information in a person's data entity. Rather than adding this information into every data entity, we might end up creating a base class that includes this information and then inheriting from it:

```
class ActiveRecord {
    Deleted = false;
}
class Person extends ActiveRecord {
    constructor(firstName : string, lastName : string) {
        this.FirstName = firstName;
        this.LastName = lastName;
    }

    FirstName : string;
    LastName : string;
}
```

The first problem with this approach is that it mixes details about the status of a record with the actual record itself. As we continue further into OO designs over the next few chapters, we will keep reinforcing the idea that mixing items together like this is not a good idea because we are creating classes that have to do more than one thing, which can make them less robust. The other problem with this approach is that, if we wanted to add the date the record was updated, we are either going to have to add the updated date to `ActiveRecord`, which means that every class that extends `ActiveRecord` will also get the updated date, or we are going to have to create a new class that adds the updated date and add this into our hierarchy chain, which means that we could not have an updated field without a deleted field.

While inheritance definitely does have its place, recent years have seen the idea of composing objects together to make new objects gain in prominence. The idea behind this approach is that we build discrete elements that do not rely on inheritance chains. If we revisit our person implementation, we will build the same features using a feature called a mixin instead.

The first thing we need to do is define a type that will act as a suitable constructor for our mixin. We could name this type anything, but the convention that has evolved around mixins in TypeScript is to use the following type:

```
type Constructor<T ={}> = new(...args: any[]) => T;
```

This type definition gives us something that we can extend to create our specialized mixins. The strange-looking syntax effectively says that, given any particular type, a new instance will be created using any appropriate arguments.

Here is our record status implementation:

```
function RecordStatus<T extends Constructor>(base : T) {
    return class extends base {
        Deleted : boolean = false;
    }
}
```

The `RecordStatus` function extends the `Constructor` type by returning a new class that extends the constructor implementation. In this, we add our `Deleted` flag.

To *merge* or mix in these two types, we simply do the following:

```
const ActivePerson = RecordStatus(Person);
```

This has created something we can use to create a `Person` object with `RecordStatus` properties. It has not actually instantiated any objects yet. To do that, we instantiate the information in the same way we would with any other type:

```
let activePerson = new ActivePerson("Peter", "O'Hanlon");
activePerson.Deleted = true;
```

Now, we also want to add details about when the record was last updated. We create another mixin, as follows:

```
function Timestamp<T extends Constructor>(base : T) {
 return class extends base {
   Updated : Date = new Date();
 }
}
```

To add this to `ActivePerson`, we change the definition to include `Timestamp`. It does not matter which mixin we put first, whether it is `Timestamp` or `RecordStatus`:

```
const ActivePerson = RecordStatus(Timestamp(Person));
```

As well as properties, we can also add constructors and methods to our mixins. We are going to change our `RecordStatus` function to log out when the record was deleted. To do this, we are going to convert our `Deleted` property into a getter method and add a new method to actually perform the deletion:

```
function RecordStatus<T extends Constructor>(base : T) {
    return class extends base {
        private deleted : boolean = false;
        get Deleted() : boolean {
            return this.deleted;
        }
        Delete() : void {
            this.deleted = true;
            console.log(`The record has been marked as deleted.`);
        }
    }
}
```

A word of warning about using mixins like this. They are a great technique, and they provide the ability to neatly do some really useful things, but we cannot pass them as a parameter unless we relax the parameter restrictions to any. That means we cannot use code like this:

```
function DeletePerson(person : ActivePerson) {
    person.Delete();
}
```

If we look at mixins in the TypeScript documentation at `https://www.typescriptlang.org/docs/handbook/mixins.html`, we see that the syntax looks very different. Rather than dealing with that approach, with all of the inherent limitations it has, we will stick with the method here, which I was first introduced to at `https://basarat.gitbooks.io/typescript/docs/types/mixins.html`.

Using the same code with different types and using generics

When we first start developing classes in TypeScript, it is very common for us to repeat the same code again and again, only changing the type that we are relying on. For instance, if we wanted to store a queue of integers, we might be tempted to write the following class:

```
class QueueOfInt {
    private queue : number[]= [];

    public Push(value : number) : void {
        this.queue.push(value);
    }

    public Pop() : number | undefined {
        return this.queue.shift();
    }
}
```

Calling this code is as easy as this:

```
const intQueue : QueueOfInt = new QueueOfInt();
intQueue.Push(10);
intQueue.Push(35);
console.log(intQueue.Pop()); // Prints 10
console.log(intQueue.Pop()); // Prints 35
```

Later on, we decide that we also need to create a queue of strings, so we add code to do this as well:

```
class QueueOfString {
    private queue : string[]= [];

    public Push(value : string) : void {
        this.queue.push(value);
    }

    public Pop() : string | undefined {
        return this.queue.shift();
    }
}
```

It is easy to see that the more code we add like this, the more tedious our job becomes and the more error-prone. Suppose that we forgot to put the shift operation in one of these implementations. The shift operation allows us to remove the first element from the array and return it, which gives us the core behavior of a queue (a queue operates as **First In First Out** (or **FIFO**)). If we had forgotten the shift operation, we would have implemented a stack operation instead (**Last In First Out** (or **LIFO**)). This could lead to subtle and dangerous bugs in our code.

With generics, TypeScript provides us with the ability to create something called a generic, which is a type that uses a placeholder to denote what the type is that is being used. It is the responsibility of the code calling that generic to determine what type they are accepting. We recognize generics because they appear after the class name inside <>, or after things such as method names. If we rewrite our queue to use a generic, we will see what this means:

```
class Queue<T> {
    private queue : T[]= [];

    public Push(value : T) : void {
        this.queue.push(value);
    }

    public Pop() : T | undefined {
        return this.queue.shift();
    }
}
```

Let's break this down:

```
class Queue<T> {
}
```

Here, we are creating a class called Queue that accepts any type. The <T> syntax tells TypeScript that, whenever it sees T inside this class, it refers to the type that is passed in:

```
private queue : T[]= [];
```

Here is our first instance of the generic type appearing. Rather than the array being fixed to a particular type, the compiler will use the generic type to create the array:

```
public Push(value : T) : void {
    this.queue.push(value);
}

public Pop() : T | undefined {
    return this.queue.shift();
}
```

Again, we have replaced the specific type in our code with the generic instead. Note that TypeScript is happy to use this with the undefined keyword in the Pop method.

Changing the way we use our code, we can now just tell our Queue object what type we want to apply to it:

```
const queue : Queue<number> = new Queue<number>();
const stringQueue : Queue<string> = new Queue<string>();
queue.Push(10);
queue.Push(35);
console.log(queue.Pop());
console.log(queue.Pop());
stringQueue.Push(`Hello`);
stringQueue.Push(`Generics`);
console.log(stringQueue.Pop());
console.log(stringQueue.Pop());
```

What is particularly helpful is that TypeScript enforces the type that we assign wherever it is referenced, so if we attempted to add a string to our queue variable, TypeScript would fail to compile this.

While TypeScript does its best to protect us, we have to remember that it converts into JavaScript. This means that it cannot protect our code from being abused, so, while TypeScript enforces the type we assign, if we were to write external JavaScript that also called our generic types, there is nothing there to prevent adding an unsupported value. The generic is enforced at compile time only so, if we have code that is going to be called from outside our control, we should take steps to guard against incompatible types in our code.

We aren't limited to just having one type in the generic list. Generics allow us to specify any number of types in the definition as long as they have unique names, as follows:

```
function KeyValuePair<TKey, TValue>(key : TKey, value : TValue)
```

Keen-eyed readers will note that we have already encountered generics. When we created a mixin, we were using generics in our `Constructor` type.

What happens if we want to call a particular method from our generic? As TypeScript expects to know what the underlying implementation of the type is, it is strict about what we can do. This means that the following code is not acceptable:

```
interface IStream {
    ReadStream() : Int8Array; // Array of bytes
}
class Data<T> {
    ReadStream(stream : T) {
        let output = stream.ReadStream();
        console.log(output.byteLength);
    }
}
```

As TypeScript cannot guess that we want to use the `IStream` interface here, it is going to complain if we try to compile this. Fortunately, we can use a generic constraint to tell TypeScript that we have a particular type that we want to use here:

```
class Data<T extends IStream> {
    ReadStream(stream : T) {
        let output = stream.ReadStream();
        console.log(output.byteLength);
    }
}
```

The `<T extends IStream>` part tells TypeScript that we are going to use *any* class that is based on our `IStream` interface.

 While we can constrain generics to types, we are generally going to want to constrain our generics to interfaces. This gives us a lot of flexibility in the classes that we use in the constraint and does not impose limitations that we can only use classes that inherit from a particular base class.

To see this in action, we are going to create two classes that implement `IStream`:

```
class WebStream implements IStream {
    ReadStream(): Int8Array {
        let array : Int8Array = new Int8Array(8);
        for (let index : number = 0; index < array.length; index++){
            array[index] = index + 3;
        }
```

```
        return array;
    }
}
class DiskStream implements IStream {
    ReadStream(): Int8Array {
        let array : Int8Array = new Int8Array(20);
        for (let index : number = 0; index < array.length; index++){
            array[index] = index + 3;
        }
        return array;
    }
}
```

These can now be used as type constraints in our generic Data implementation:

```
const webStream = new Data<WebStream>();
const diskStream = new Data<DiskStream>();
```

We have just told webStream and diskStream that they are going to have access to our classes. To use them, we would still have to pass an instance, as follows:

```
webStream.ReadStream(new WebStream());
diskStream.ReadStream(new DiskStream());
```

While we declared our generic and its constraints at the class level, we don't have to do that. We can declare finer-grained generics, down to the method level, if we need to. In this case though, it makes sense to make it a class-level generic if we want to refer to that generic type in multiple places in our code. If the only place we wanted to apply a particular generic was at one or two methods, we could change our class signature to this:

```
class Data {
    ReadStream<T extends IStream>(stream : T) {
        let output = stream.ReadStream();
        console.log(output.byteLength);
    }
}
```

Mapping values using maps

A situation that often comes up is needing to store a number of items with an easily looked up key. For instance, suppose we had a music collection broken down into a number of genres:

```
enum Genre {
    Rock,
    CountryAndWestern,
```

```
        Classical,
        Pop,
        HeavyMetal
    }
```

Against each one of these genres, we are going to store the details of a number of artists or composers. One approach we could take would be to create a class that represents each genre. While we could do that, it would be a waste of our coding time. The way we are going to solve this problem is by using something called a **map**. A map is a generic class that takes in two types: the type of key to use for the map and the type of objects to store in it.

The key is a unique value that is used to allow us to store values or to quickly look things up—this makes maps a good choice for rapidly looking values up. We can have any type as a key and the value can be absolutely anything. For our music collection, we are going to create a class that uses a map with the genre as the key and a string array to represent the composer or artists:

```
class MusicCollection {
    private readonly collection : Map<Genre, string[]>;
    constructor() {
        this.collection = new Map<Genre, string[]>();
    }
}
```

In order to populate a map, we call the `set` method, as follows:

```
public Add(genre : Genre, artist : string[]) : void {
    this.collection.set(genre, artist);
}
```

Retrieving the values from the map is as simple as calling `Get` with the relevant key:

```
public Get(genre : Genre) : string[] | undefined {
    return this.collection.get(genre);
}
```

 We have to add the `undefined` keyword to the return value here because there is a possibility that the map entry does not exist. If we forgot to take the possibility of undefined into account, TypeScript helpfully warns us of this. Yet again, TypeScript works hard to provide that robust safety net for our code.

We can now populate our collection, as follows:

```
let collection = new MusicCollection();
collection.Add(Genre.Classical, [`Debussy`, `Bach`, `Elgar`, `Beethoven`]);
collection.Add(Genre.CountryAndWestern, [`Dolly Parton`, `Toby Keith`,
`Willie Nelson`]);
collection.Add(Genre.HeavyMetal, [`Tygers of Pan Tang`, `Saxon`, `Doro`]);
collection.Add(Genre.Pop, [`Michael Jackson`, `Abba`, `The Spice Girls`]);
collection.Add(Genre.Rock, [`Deep Purple`, `Led Zeppelin`, `The Dixie
Dregs`]);
```

If we want to add a single artist, our code becomes slightly more complex. Using set, we either add a new entry into our map or we replace the previous entry with our new one. As this is the case, we really need to check to see whether we have already added that particular key. To do this, we call the has method. If we have not added the genre, we are going to call set with an empty array. Finally, we are going to get the array out of our map using get so that we can push our values in:

```
public AddArtist(genre: Genre, artist : string) : void {
    if (!this.collection.has(genre)) {
        this.collection.set(genre, []);
    }
    let artists = this.collection.get(genre);
    if (artists) {
        artists.push(artist);
    }
}
```

One more thing we are going to do to our code is change the Add method. Right now, that implementation overwrites previous calls to Add for a particular genre, which means that calling AddArtist and then Add would end up overwriting the artist we added individually with the ones from the Add call:

```
collection.AddArtist(Genre.HeavyMetal, `Iron Maiden`);
// At this point, HeavyMetal just contains Iron Maiden
collection.Add(Genre.HeavyMetal, [`Tygers of Pan Tang`, `Saxon`, `Doro`]);
// Now HeavyMetal just contains Tygers of Pan Tang, Saxon and Doro
```

In order to fix the Add method, it is a simple change to iterate over our artists and call the AddArtist method, as follows:

```
public Add(genre : Genre, artist : string[]) : void {
    for (let individual of artist) {
        this.AddArtist(genre, individual);
    }
}
```

Now, when we finish populating the `HeavyMetal` genre, our artists consist of `Iron Maiden`, `Tygers of Pan Tang`, `Saxon`, and `Doro`.

Creating asynchronous code with promises and async/await

We often need to write code that behaves in an asynchronous fashion. By this, we mean that we need to start a task off and leave it running in the background while we do something else. An example of this could be when we have made a call out to a web service, which may take a while to return. For a long time, the standard way in JavaScript was to use a callback. A big problem with this approach is that the more callbacks we need, the more complex and potentially error-prone our code becomes. This is where promises come in.

A promise tells us that something will happen asynchronously; after the asynchronous operation finishes, we have the option to continue processing and work with the result of the promise, or to catch any exceptions that have been thrown by the exception.

Here's a sample that demonstrates this in action:

```
function ExpensiveWebCall(time : number) : Promise<void> {
    return new Promise((resolve, reject) => setTimeout(resolve, time));
}
class MyWebService {
    CallExpensiveWebOperation() : void {
        ExpensiveWebCall(4000).then(()=> console.log(`Finished web
        service`))
            .catch(()=> console.log(`Expensive web call failure`));
    }
}
```

When we write a promise, we optionally take in two parameters—a `resolve` function and a `reject` function that can be called to trigger the error handling. Promises supply two functions for us to cope with these values, so `then()` will be triggered by successfully completing the operation and a separate `catch` function that copes with the `reject` function.

Now, we are going to run this code to see its effect:

```
console.log(`calling service`);
new MyWebService().CallExpensiveWebOperation();
console.log(`Processing continues until the web service returns`);
```

When we run this code, we get the following output:

```
calling service
Processing continues until the web service returns
Finished web service
```

Between the `Processing continues until the web service returns` and `Finished web service` lines, there is a four-second delay that we would expect because the application is waiting for the promise to return before it writes out the text in the `then()` function. What this is demonstrating to us is that the code is behaving asynchronously here because it is not waiting for the web service call to come back when it executed the processing console log.

We might be tempted to think that this code is a bit too verbose, and that scattering `Promise<void>` is not the most intuitive way for others to understand that our code is asynchronous. TypeScript provides a syntactic equivalent that makes it much more apparent where our code is asynchronous. With the use of the `async` and `await` keywords, we easily turn our previous sample into something much more elegant:

```
function ExpensiveWebCall(time : number) {
    return new Promise((resolve, reject) => setTimeout(resolve, time));
}
class MyWebService {
    async CallExpensiveWebOperation() {
        await ExpensiveWebCall(4000);
        console.log(`Finished web service`);
    }
}
```

The `async` keyword tells us that our function is returning `Promise`. It also tells the compiler that we want to process the function differently. Where we find `await` inside an `async` function, the application will pause that function at that point until the operation that is being awaited returns. At that point, processing continues, mimicking the behavior we saw inside the `then()` function from `Promise`.

In order to catch errors in `async/await`, we really should wrap the code inside the function in a try...catch block. Where the error was explicitly caught by the `catch()` function, `async/await` does not have an equivalent way of handling errors, so it is up to us to deal with problems:

```
class MyWebService {
    async CallExpensiveWebOperation() {
        try {
            await ExpensiveWebCall(4000);
            console.log(`Finished web service`);
```

```
    } catch (error) {
        console.log(`Caught ${error}`);
    }
  }
}
```

Whichever approach you choose to take is going to be a personal choice. The use of `async`/`await` just means it wraps the `Promise` approach so the runtime behavior of the different techniques is exactly the same. What I do recommend though is, once you decide on an approach in an application, be consistent. Don't mix styles as that will make it much harder for anyone reviewing your application.

Creating UIs with Bootstrap

In the remaining chapters, we are going to be doing a lot of work in the browser. Creating an attractive UI can be a difficult thing to do, especially in an era when we may also be targeting mobile devices in different layout modes. In order to make things easier for ourselves, we are going to rely quite heavily on Bootstrap. Bootstrap was designed to be a mobile device first UI framework that smoothly scales up to PC browsers. In this section, we are going to lay out the base template that contains the standard Bootstrap elements, and then have a look at how to lay out a simple page using features such as the Bootstrap grid system.

We are going to start with the starter template from Bootstrap (`https://getbootstrap.com/docs/4.1/getting-started/introduction/#starter-template`). With this particular template, we avoid the need to download and install the various CSS stylesheets and JavaScript files; instead, we rely on well-known **Content Delivery Networks** (**CDNs**) to source these files for us.

Where possible, I would recommend using CDNs to source external JavaScript and CSS files. This provides many benefits including not needing to maintain these files ourselves and getting the benefit of browser caching when the browser has encountered this CDN file elsewhere.

The starter template looks as follows:

```
<!doctype html>
<html lang="en">
    <head>
        <!-- Required meta tags -->
        <meta name="viewport" content="width=device-width, initial-scale=1,
```

```
        shrink-to-fit=no">
        <link
rel="stylesheet"href="https://stackpath.bootstrapcdn.com/bootstrap
        /4.1.3/css/bootstrap.min.css" integrity="sha384-
        MCw98/SFnGE8fJT3GXwEOngsV7Zt27NXFoaoApmYm81iuXoPkFOJwJ8ERdknLPMO"
        crossorigin="anonymous">
        <title>
            <
        <Template Bootstrap>
            >
        </title>
    </head>
    <body>
        <!--
            Content goes here...
            Start with the container.
            -->
        <script src="https://code.jquery.com/jquery-3.3.1.slim.min.js"
            integrity="sha384-
        q8i/X+965DzO0rT7abK41JStQIAqVgRVzpbzo5smXKp4YfRvH+8abtTE1Pi6jizo"
            crossorigin="anonymous"></script>
        <script
src="https://cdnjs.cloudflare.com/ajax/libs/popper.js/1.14.3/umd/popper.min
.js"
            integrity="sha384-
        ZMP7rVo3mIykV+2+9J3UJ46jBk0WLaUAdn689aCwoqbBJiSnjAK/l8WvCWPIPm49"
            crossorigin="anonymous"></script>
        <script
src="https://stackpath.bootstrapcdn.com/bootstrap/4.1.3/js/bootstrap.min.js
"
            integrity="sha384-
        ChfqqxuZUCnJSK3+MXmPNIyE6ZbWh2IMqE241rYiqJxyMiZ6OW/JmZQ5stwEULTy"
            crossorigin="anonymous"></script>
    </body>
</html>
```

The starting point for laying out content is the container. This goes in the preceding content section. The following code shows the `div` section:

```
<div class="container">
</div>
```

The `container` class gives us that familiar Twitter look where it has a fixed size for each screen size. If we need to fill the full window, we can change this to `container-fluid`.

Inside the container, Bootstrap attempts to lay items out in a grid pattern. Bootstrap operates a system where each row of the screen can be represented as up to 12 discrete columns. By default, these columns are evenly spread out across the page so we can make complicated layouts just by choosing the appropriate number of columns to occupy for each part of our UI. Fortunately for us, Bootstrap provides an extensive set of predefined styles that help us to make layouts for different types of devices, whether they are PCs, mobile phones, or tablets. These styles all follow the same naming convention of `.col-`
`<<size-identifier>>-<<number-of-columns>>`:

Type	Extra small devices	Small devices	Medium devices	Large devices
Dimensions	Phones < 768px	Tablets >= 768px	Desktops >= 992px	Desktops >= 1200px
Prefix	.col-xs-	.col-sm-	.col-md-	.col-lg-

The way that the number of columns works is that each row should ideally add up to 12 columns. So, if we wanted to have a row made of content covering three columns, then six columns, and finally another three columns, we would define our rows to look like this inside our container:

```
<div class="row">
  <div class="col-sm-3">Hello</div>
  <div class="col-sm-6">Hello</div>
  <div class="col-sm-3">Hello</div>
</div>
```

That styling defines how this would appear on small devices. It is possible to override the styles for larger devices. For instance, if we wanted large devices to use columns of five, two, and five, we could apply this styling:

```
<div class="row">
  <div class="col-sm-3 col-lg-5">Hello</div>
  <div class="col-sm-6 col-lg-2">Hello</div>
  <div class="col-sm-3 col-lg-5">Hello</div>
</div>
```

This is the beauty of a responsive layout system. It allows us to generate content that is appropriate for our devices.

Let's take a look at how to add some content to our page. We are going to add `jumbotron` to our first column, some text into our second column, and a button in our third column:

```
<div class="row">
  <div class="col-md-3">
    <div class="jumbotron">
      <h2>
        Hello, world!
```

```
        </h2>
        <p>
          Lorem ipsum dolor sit amet, consectetur adipiscing elit. Phasellus
          eget mi odio. Praesent a neque sed purus sodales interdum. In augue
sapien,
          molestie id lacus eleifend...
        </p>
        <p>
          <a class="btn btn-primary btn-large" href="#">Learn more</a>
        </p>
      </div>
    </div>
    <div class="col-md-6">
      <h2>
        Heading
      </h2>
      <p>
        Lorem ipsum dolor sit amet, consectetur adipiscing elit. Phasellus
        eget mi odio. Praesent a neque sed purus sodales interdum. In augue
sapien,
        molestie id lacus eleifend...
      </p>
      <p>
        <a class="btn" href="#">View details</a>
      </p>
    </div>
    <div class="col-md-3">
      <button type="button" class="btn btn-primary btn-lg btn-block active">
        Button
      </button>
    </div>
  </div>
</div>
```

Again, we are using CSS styling to control what our display looks like. By giving a `div`
section a styling of `jumbotron`, Bootstrap immediately applies that styling for us. We
controlled exactly what our button looks like by choosing to make it the primary button
(`btn-primary`) and so on.

`jumbotron` normally stretches across the width of all of the columns. We put it inside a
three-column `div` just so we can see that the width and styling is controlled by the grid
layout system and that `jumbotron` does not have some special properties that force it to lay
out across the page.

When I want to rapidly prototype a layout, I always follow a two-stage process. The first step is to draw on a piece of paper what I want my UI to look like. I could do this using a wireframe tool but I like the ability to quickly draw things out. Once I have got a general idea of what I want my layout to look like, I use a tool such as Layoutit! (`https://www.layoutit.com/`) to put the ideas on to the screen; this also gives me the option to export the layout so that I can further refine it by hand.

Summary

In this chapter, we had a look at features of TypeScript that help us to build future-proof TypeScript code. We looked at how to set the appropriate ES levels to simulate or use modern ECMAScript features. We looked at how to use union and intersection types as well as how to create type aliases. We then looked into object spread and REST properties before we covered AOP with decorators. We also covered how to create and use map types, as well as using generics and promises.

As preparation for the UIs we will be producing in the rest of this book, we briefly looked at using Bootstrap to lay out UIs and covered the basics of the Bootstrap grid layout system.

In the next chapter, we are going to build a simple markdown editor using a simple Bootstrap web page hooked up to our TypeScript. We will see how techniques such as design patterns and single responsibility classes help us to create robust professional code.

Questions

1. We have written an application that allows users to convert from Fahrenheit into Celsius and from Celsius into Fahrenheit. The calculations are performed in the following classes:

```
class FahrenheitToCelsius {
    Convert(temperature : number) : number {
        return (temperature - 32) * 5 / 9;
    }
}

class CelsiusToFahrenheit {
    Convert(temperature : number) : number {
        return (temperature * 9/5) + 32;
    }
}
```

We want to write a method that accepts a temperature and an instance of either of these types, which will then perform the relevant calculation. What technique would we use to write this method?

2. We have written the following class:

```
class Command {
    public constructor(public Name : string = "", public Action :
Function = new Function()){}
}
```

We want to use this in another class where we will add a number of commands. Name of the command is going to be the key that we can use to look up Command later on in our code. What would we use to provide this key-value functionality and how would we add records to it?

3. How would we automatically log that we were adding entries to the command we added in *Question 2* without adding any code inside our Add methods?

4. We have created a Bootstrap web page where we want to display a row with six medium columns of equal size. How would we do this?

Creating a Markdown Editor with TypeScript

It is hard to deal with content on the internet without encountering markdown. Markdown is a simplified way to create content using plain text that is easily converted into simple HTML. In this chapter, we are going to investigate what it takes to create a parser that will convert a subset of the markup format into HTML content. We will automatically convert relevant tags into the first three header levels, the horizontal rule, and paragraphs.

By the end of this chapter, we will have covered how to create a simple Bootstrap web page and reference the JavaScript generated from our TypeScript, as well as hooking up to a simple event handler. We will also cover how to create classes using simple design patterns and how to design classes with single responsibilities, which are techniques that serve us well as professional developers.

The following topics will be covered in this chapter:

- Creating a Bootstrap page that overrides the Bootstrap styling
- Choosing which tags we are going to use in our markdown
- Defining requirements
- Mapping our markdown tag types to HTML tag types
- Storing our converted markdown in a custom class
- Using the visitor pattern to update our document
- Using the chain-of-responsibility pattern to apply tags
- Hooking this back to our HTML

Technical requirements

The code for this chapter can be downloaded from `https://github.com/PacktPublishing/Advanced-TypeScript-3-Programming-Projects/tree/master/Chapter02`.

Understanding the project overview

Now that we have a grasp of some of the concepts that we are going to cover throughout the rest of this book, we are going to start putting them into practice by creating a project that parses a very simple markdown format while the user types into a text area and displays the resulting web page alongside it. Unlike full markdown parsers, we are going to concentrate on formatting the first three header types, the horizontal rule, and paragraphs. The markup is restricted to breaking lines down by newline characters and looking at the start of a line. It then determines whether or not a particular tag is present and, if not, it assumes the current line is a paragraph. The reason we have chosen this implementation is because it is a simple task to pick up immediately. While it is simple, it offers sufficient depth to show that we are going to tackle topics that require us to give real thought to how we will structure the application.

The **user interface** (**UI**), uses Bootstrap, and we will look at how to hook up to a change event handler and how to get and update HTML content from the current web page. This is what our project will look like when we have finished:

Now that we have our overview, we can move on to getting started with creating the HTML project.

Getting started with a simple HTML project

This project is a simple HTML and TypeScript file combination. Create a directory to hold the HTML and TypeScript files. Our JavaScript will reside in a script folder under this directory. The following `tsconfig.json` file is used:

```json
{
  "compilerOptions": {
    "target": "ES2015",
    "module": "commonjs",
    "sourceMap": true,
    "outDir": "./script",
    "strict": true,
    "strictNullChecks": true,
    "strictFunctionTypes": true,
    "noImplicitThis": true,
    "alwaysStrict": true,
    "noImplicitReturns": true,
    "noFallthroughCasesInSwitch": true,
    "esModuleInterop": true,
    "experimentalDecorators": true,
  }
}
```

Writing a simple markdown parser

When I was thinking about the project that we are going to tackle in this chapter, I had a clear objective in mind. While we are writing this code, we are going to try out things such as patterns and good **object-oriented** (**OO**) practices, such as classes having a single responsibility. If we can apply these techniques right from the start, we will soon get into the habit of using them and this will translate into useful development skills.

As professional developers, before we write any code, we should gather the requirements that we are going to use and ensure that we are making no assumptions about what our application will do. We may think that we know what we want our application to do, but if we make a list of our requirements, we'll make sure that we understand everything that we are meant to deliver and we'll come up with a handy checklist to tick features off as we complete them.

So, here is my list:

- We are going to create an application to parse markdown
- The user will type into a text area
- Every time the text area changes, we will parse the entire document again
- We will break the document down based on where the user presses the *Enter* key
- The opening characters will determine whether or not the line is markdown
- Entering # followed by a space is replaced by an H1 heading
- Entering ## followed by a space is replaced by an H2 heading
- Entering ### followed by a space is replaced by an H3 heading
- Entering --- is replaced by a horizontal rule
- If the line does not start with markdown, the line is treated as a paragraph
- The resulting HTML will be displayed in a label
- If the content in the markdown text area is empty, the label will contain an empty paragraph
- The layout will be done in Bootstrap and the content will stretch to 100% height

Given those requirements, we have a good idea of what we are going to deliver, so we are starting off by creating our UI.

Building our Bootstrap UI

In `Chapter 1`, *Advanced TypeScript Features*, we looked at the basics of creating a UI using Bootstrap. We will take the same basic page and adjust it to fit our needs with a couple of little tweaks. Our starting point is this page, which stretches across the full width of the screen by setting the container to use `container-fluid`, and divides the interface into two equal parts by setting `col-lg-6` on both sides:

```html
<div class="container-fluid">
  <div class="row">
    <div class="col-lg-6">
    </div>
    <div class="col-lg-6">
    </div>
  </div>
</div>
```

When we add our text area and label components to our form, we find that rendering them in this row does not automatically expand them to fill the height of the screen. We need to make a couple of adjustments. First, we need to manually set the style of the html and body tags to fill the available space. To do this, we add the following in the header:

```
<style>
  html, body {
    height: 100%;
  }
</style>
```

With that in place, we can take advantage of a new feature in Bootstrap 4, which is applying h-100 to these classes to fill 100% of the space. We are also going to take this opportunity to add the text area and label, as well as giving them IDs that we can look up from our TypeScript code:

```
<div class="container-fluid h-100">
  <div class="row h-100">
    <div class="col-lg-6">
      <textarea class="form-control h-100" id="markdown"></textarea>
    </div>
    <div class="col-lg-6 h-100">
      <label class="h-100" id="markdown-output"></label>
    </div>
  </div>
</div>
```

Before we finish off our page, we are going to start writing TypeScript code that we can use in our application. Add a file called MarkdownParser.ts to hold our TypeScript code and add the following code to it:

```
class HtmlHandler {
    public TextChangeHandler(id : string, output : string) : void {
        let markdown = <HTMLTextAreaElement>document.getElementById(id);
        let markdownOutput =
<HTMLLabelElement>document.getElementById(output);
        if (markdown !== null) {
            markdown.onkeyup = (e) => {
                if (markdown.value) {
                    markdownOutput.innerHTML = markdown.value;
                }
                else
                    markdownOutput.innerHTML = "<p></p>";
            }
        }
    }
}
```

We created this class so that we could get the text area and the label based on their IDs. Once we have these, we are going to hook into the text area, key up the event, and write the keypress value back to the label. Notice how, even though we are not in a web page at this point, TypeScript implicitly gives us access to standard web page behaviors. This allows us to retrieve the text area and label based on the IDs we previously entered, and to cast them to the appropriate type. With this, we gain the ability to do things such as subscribe to events or access an element's `innerHTML`.

For the sake of simplicity, we are going to use the `MarkdownParser.ts` file for all of our TypeScript in this chapter. Normally, we would separate the classes into their own files, but this single-file structure should be simpler to review as we progress through the code. In future chapters, we will be moving away from a single file because those projects are much more complex.

Once we have these interface elements, we hook up to the keyup event. When the event is fired, we look to see if we have any text in the text area and set the HTML of the label with the content (if it is present), or the empty paragraph (if it is not present). The reason we have written this code is because we want to use it to ensure that we properly link up our generated JavaScript and the web page.

We use the keyup event—rather than the keydown or keypress events—because the key is not added into the text area until the keypress event is completed.

We can now revisit our web page and add the missing bits so that we can update our label when our text area changes. Just before the `</body>` tag, add the following to reference the JavaScript file that TypeScript produces, in order to create an instance of our `HtmlHandler` class and hook the `markdown` and `markdown-output` elements together:

```
<script src="script/MarkdownParser.js">
</script>
<script>
  new HtmlHandler().TextChangeHandler("markdown", "markdown-output");
</script>
```

As a quick review, this is what the HTML file looks like at this point:

```
<!doctype html>
<html lang="en">
 <head>
 <meta name="viewport" content="width=device-width, initial-scale=1,
shrink-to-fit=no">
```

```html
    <link rel="stylesheet"
href="https://stackpath.bootstrapcdn.com/bootstrap/4.1.3/css/bootstrap.min.
css" integrity="sha384-
MCw98/SFnGE8fJT3GXwEOngsV7Zt27NXFoaoApmYm81iuXoPkFOJwJ8ERdknLPMO"
crossorigin="anonymous">
    <style>
    html, body {
    height: 100%;
    }
    </style>
    <title>Advanced TypeScript - Chapter 2</title>
    </head>
    <body>
    <div class="container-fluid h-100">
    <div class="row h-100">
    <div class="col-lg-6">
    <textarea class="form-control h-100" id="markdown"></textarea>
    </div>
    <div class="col-lg-6 h-100">
    <label class="h-100" id="markdown-output"></label>
    </div>
    </div>
    </div>
    <script src="https://code.jquery.com/jquery-3.3.1.slim.min.js"
integrity="sha384-
q8i/X+965DzO0rT7abK41JStQIAqVgRVzpbzo5smXKp4YfRvH+8abtTE1Pi6jizo"
crossorigin="anonymous"></script>
    <script
src="https://cdnjs.cloudflare.com/ajax/libs/popper.js/1.14.3/umd/popper.min
.js" integrity="sha384-
ZMP7rVo3mIykV+2+9J3UJ46jBk0WLaUAdn689aCwoqbBJiSnjAK/l8WvCWPIPm49"
crossorigin="anonymous"></script>
    <script
src="https://stackpath.bootstrapcdn.com/bootstrap/4.1.3/js/bootstrap.min.js
" integrity="sha384-
ChfqqxuZUCnJSK3+MXmPNIyE6ZbWh2IMqE241rYiqJxyMiZ6OW/JmZQ5stwEULTy"
crossorigin="anonymous"></script>

    <script src="script/MarkdownParser.js">
    </script>
    <script>
    new HtmlHandler().TextChangeHandler("markdown", "markdown-output");
    </script>
    </body>
</html>
```

If we run our application at this point, typing in the text area automatically updates the label. The following screenshot shows what our application looks like in action:

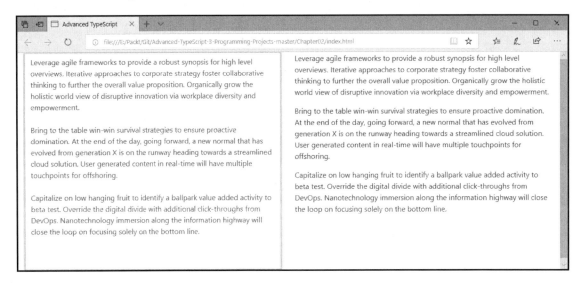

Now we know that we can automatically update our web page, we have no more changes that need to be made to it. All the code that we are about to write will be done entirely in the TypeScript file. Going back to our list of requirements, we have done enough to satisfy the last three requirements.

Mapping our markdown tag types to HTML tag types

In our requirements, we set out a master list of tags that our parser is going to handle. In order to identify these tags, we are going to add an enumeration consisting of the tags we are making available to our users:

```
enum TagType {
    Paragraph,
    Header1,
    Header2,
    Header3,
    HorizontalRule
}
```

From our requirements, we also know that we need to translate between these tags and their equivalent opening and closing HTML tags. The way that we are going to do this is to map `tagType` to an equivalent HTML tag. To do this, we are going to create a class that has the sole responsibility of handling this mapping for us. The following code shows this:

```
class TagTypeToHtml {
    private readonly tagType : Map<TagType, string> = new Map<TagType,
string>();
    constructor() {
        this.tagType.set(TagType.Header1, "h1");
        this.tagType.set(TagType.Header2, "h2");
        this.tagType.set(TagType.Header3, "h3");
        this.tagType.set(TagType.Paragraph, "p");
        this.tagType.set(TagType.HorizontalRule, "hr")
    }
}
```

At first, the use of `readonly` on a type can appear confusing. What this keyword means is that, after the class has been instantiated, `tagType` cannot be recreated elsewhere in the class. This means that we can set up our mappings in the constructor safe, knowing that we are not going to call `this.tagType = new Map<TagType, string>();` later on.

We also need a way to retrieve opening and closing tags from this class. We're going to start by creating a method to get the opening tag from `tagType`, as follows:

```
public OpeningTag(tagType : TagType) : string {
    let tag = this.tagType.get(tagType);
    if (tag !== null) {
        return `<${tag}>`;
    }
    return `<p>`;
}
```

This method is pretty straightforward. It starts by trying to get `tagType` from the map. With the code we currently have, we will always have an entry in the map, but we could extend the enumeration in the future and forget to add the tag to the list of tags. That is why we check to see if the tag is present; if it is, we return the tag enclosed in <>. If the tag is not present, we return a paragraph tag as a default.

Now, let's look at `ClosingTag`:

```
public ClosingTag(tagType : TagType) : string {
    let tag = this.tagType.get(tagType);
    if (tag !== null) {
        return `</${tag}>`;
    }
    return `</p>`;
}
```

Looking at these two methods, we can see that they are almost identical. When we think about the problem of creating our HTML tag, we realize that the only difference between an opening and a closing tag is that the closing tag has a / in it. With that in mind, we can change the code to use a helper method that accepts whether the tag starts with < or </:

```
private GetTag(tagType : TagType, openingTagPattern : string) : string {
    let tag = this.tagType.get(tagType);
    if (tag !== null) {
        return `${openingTagPattern}${tag}>`;
    }
    return `${openingTagPattern}p>`;
}
```

All that remains is for us to add methods to retrieve the opening and closing tags:

```
public OpeningTag(tagType : TagType) : string {
    return this.GetTag(tagType, `<`);
}

public ClosingTag(tagType : TagType) : string {
    return this.GetTag(tagType, `</`);
}
```

Pulling this all together, the code for our `TagTypeToHtml` class now looks like this:

```
class TagTypeToHtml {
    private readonly tagType : Map<TagType, string> = new Map<TagType,
string>();
    constructor() {
        this.tagType.set(TagType.Header1, "h1");
        this.tagType.set(TagType.Header2, "h2");
        this.tagType.set(TagType.Header3, "h3");
        this.tagType.set(TagType.Paragraph, "p");
        this.tagType.set(TagType.HorizontalRule, "hr")
    }

    public OpeningTag(tagType : TagType) : string {
        return this.GetTag(tagType, `<`);
```

```
    }

    public ClosingTag(tagType : TagType) : string {
        return this.GetTag(tagType, `</`);
    }

    private GetTag(tagType : TagType, openingTagPattern : string) : string
{
        let tag = this.tagType.get(tagType);
        if (tag !== null) {
            return `${openingTagPattern}${tag}>`;
        }
        return `${openingTagPattern}p>`;
    }
}
```

The single responsibility of our `TagTypeToHtml` class is
mapping `tagType` to an HTML tag. Something that we are going to keep
coming back to throughout this chapter is that we want classes to have a
single responsibility. In OO theory, this is known as one of the principles
of **SOLID** (short for **Single Responsibility Principle, Open/Closed
Principle, Liskov Substitution Principle, Interface Segregation
Principle, Dependency Inversion Principle**) design. The acronym refers
to a set of complementary development techniques to create more robust
code.

This handy acronym serves to guide us on how to structure classes and
the most important part, in my opinion, is the Single Responsibility
Principle, which states that a class should do one thing and one thing
only. While I would certainly recommend reading about this topic (and
we will touch on other aspects of it as we progress), in my opinion, the
most important part of SOLID design is that classes are responsible for
one thing and one thing only; everything else flows out of that principle.
Classes that only do one thing are generally much easier to test and they
are a lot easier to understand. That does not mean that they should only
have one method. They can have many methods, as long as they are all
related to the purpose of the class. We will cover this topic again and
again throughout the book because it is so important.

Representing our converted markdown using a markdown document

While we are parsing our content, we need a mechanism to actually store the text that we are creating during the parsing process. We could just use a global string and update it directly, but that would become problematic if we decided to asynchronously add to it later on. The main reason for not using a string is down to Single Responsibility Principle again. If we were using a simple string, then each piece of code that we add to the text would end up having to write to the string in the correct way, which means that they would be mixing reading the markdown with writing to the HTML output. When we discuss it like that, it becomes apparent that we need to have a separate means of writing the HTML content out.

What this means for us is that we are going to want code that can accept a number of strings to form the content (these could include our HTML tags, so we don't want to just accept a single string). We also want a means of getting our document when we have finished building it up. We are going to start by defining an interface, which will act as the contract that consuming code will implement. Of particular interest here is that we are going to allow our code to accept any number of items in our Add method, so we will be using a REST parameter here:

```
interface IMarkdownDocument {
    Add(...content : string[]) : void;
    Get() : string;
}
```

Given this interface, we can create our MarkdownDocument class as follows:

```
class MarkdownDocument implements IMarkdownDocument {
    private content : string = "";
    Add(...content: string[]): void {
        content.forEach(element => {
            this.content += element;
        });
    }
    Get(): string {
        return this.content;
    }
}
```

This class is incredibly straightforward. For each piece of content passed in to our `Add` method, we add it to a member variable called `content`. As this is declared as private, our `Get` method returns the same variable. This is why I like having classes with a single responsibility—in this case, they are just updating the content; they tend to be a lot cleaner and easier to understand than convoluted classes that do many different things. The main thing is that we can do whatever we like to keep our content updated internally, as we have hidden *how* we maintain the document from the consuming code.

As we are going to be parsing our document one line at a time, we are going to use a class to represent the current line that we are processing:

```
class ParseElement {
    CurrentLine : string = "";
}
```

Our class is very simple. Again, we have decided not to go with a simple string to pass around our code base because this class makes our intent clear—we want to parse the current line. If we had just used a string to represent the line, it would be too easy to pass the wrong thing when we wanted to use the line.

Updating markdown document using visitors

In `Chapter 1`, *Advanced TypeScript Features*, we briefly touched on patterns. Simply put, patterns in the software development process are general solutions to particular problems. This simply means that we use the name of a pattern to convey to others that we are solving a problem using particular and well-established code examples. For instance, if we say to another developer that we are solving a problem using a mediator pattern, as long as the other developer is aware of patterns, they will have a pretty good idea as to how we will be structuring our code.

When I was planning this code out, I made a conscious decision early on that we would be using something called the visitor pattern with our code. Before we look at the code we are going to create, we will have a look at what this pattern is and why we are going to use it.

Understanding the visitor pattern

The visitor pattern is what is known as a **behavioral pattern**. The term behavioral pattern is simply a classification of a group of patterns that are concerned with the way that classes and objects communicate. What the visitor pattern gives us is the ability to separate an algorithm from the object that the algorithm works on. This sounds a lot more complicated than it really is.

One of the motivations behind us using the visitor pattern is that we want to take the common `ParseElement` class and apply different operations on it, depending on what the underlying markdown is, which ultimately leads to us building up the `MarkdownDocument` class. The idea here is that if the content the user types in is something we would represent in HTML as a paragraph, we want to add different tags to those used, for example, when the content represents a horizontal rule. The convention for the visitor pattern is that we have two interfaces, `IVisitor` and `IVisitable`. At their most basic, these interfaces look like this:

```
interface IVisitor {
    Visit(......);
}
interface IVisitable {
    Accept(IVisitor, .....);
}
```

The idea behind these interfaces is that the object will be visitable, so when it needs to perform the relevant operations, it accepts the visitor so that it can visit the object.

Applying the visitor pattern to our code

Now that we know what the visitor pattern is, let's take a look at how we are going to apply it to our code:

1. First, we are going to create the `IVisitor` and `IVisitable` interfaces as follows:

```
interface IVisitor {
    Visit(token : ParseElement, markdownDocument :
IMarkdownDocument) : void;
}
interface IVisitable {
    Accept(visitor : IVisitor, token : ParseElement,
markdownDocument : IMarkdownDocument) : void;
}
```

2. When our code reaches the point where `Visit` is called, we are going to use the `TagTypeToHtml` class to add the relevant opening HTML tag, the line of text, and then the matching closing HTML tag to our `MarkdownDocument`. As this is common to each of our tag types, we can implement a base class that encapsulates this behavior, as follows:

```
abstract class VisitorBase implements IVisitor {
    constructor (private readonly tagType : TagType, private
readonly TagTypeToHtml : TagTypeToHtml) {}
```

```
        Visit(token: ParseElement, markdownDocument:
    IMarkdownDocument): void {
    markdownDocument.Add(this.TagTypeToHtml.OpeningTag(this.tagType),
    token.CurrentLine,
                this.TagTypeToHtml.ClosingTag(this.tagType));
        }
    }
```

3. Next, we need to add the concrete visitor implementations. This is as simple as creating the following classes:

```
    class Header1Visitor extends VisitorBase {
        constructor() {
            super(TagType.Header1, new TagTypeToHtml());
        }
    }
    class Header2Visitor extends VisitorBase {
        constructor() {
            super(TagType.Header2, new TagTypeToHtml());
        }
    }
    class Header3Visitor extends VisitorBase {
        constructor() {
            super(TagType.Header3, new TagTypeToHtml());
        }
    }
    class ParagraphVisitor extends VisitorBase {
        constructor() {
            super(TagType.Paragraph, new TagTypeToHtml());
        }
    }
    class HorizontalRuleVisitor extends VisitorBase {
        constructor() {
            super(TagType.HorizontalRule, new TagTypeToHtml());
        }
    }
```

At first, this code may seem like overkill, but it serves a purpose. If we take `Header1Visitor`, for instance, we have a class that has the single responsibility of taking the current line and adding it to our markdown document wrapped in H1 tags. We could litter our code with classes that were responsible for checking whether the line started with #, and then remove the # from the start, prior to adding the H1 tags and the current line. However, that makes the code harder to test and more likely to break, especially if we want to change the behavior. Also, the more tags we add, the more fragile this code will become.

The other side of the visitor pattern code is the `IVisitable` implementation. For our current code, we know that we want to visit the relevant visitor whenever we call `Accept`. What this means to our code is that we can have a single visitable class that implements our `IVisitable` interface. This is shown in the following code:

```
class Visitable implements IVisitable {
    Accept(visitor: IVisitor, token: ParseElement, markdownDocument:
IMarkdownDocument): void {
        visitor.Visit(token, markdownDocument);
    }
}
```

For this example, we have put the simplest visitor pattern implementation in place that we could. There are many variants of the visitor pattern, so we have gone with an implementation that respects the design philosophy of the pattern without slavishly sticking to it. That's the beauty of patterns—while they give us a guide as to how to do something, we should not feel that we have to blindly follow a particular implementation if modifying it slightly differently suits our needs.

Deciding which tags to apply by using the chain-of-responsibility pattern

Now that we have the means to transform a simple line into an HTML encoded line, we need a way to decide which tags we should apply. Right from the start, I knew that we would be applying yet another pattern, one that is eminently suitable for asking the question, *"Should I handle this tag?"* If no, then I will forward this on so that something else can decide whether or not it should handle the tag.

We are going to use another behavioral pattern to handle this—the chain-of-responsibility pattern. This pattern lets us chain together a series of classes by creating a class that accepts the next class in the chain, along with a method to handle a request. Depending on the internal logic of the request handler, it may pass processing onto the next class in the chain.

If we start off with our base class, we can see what this pattern gives us and how we are going to use it:

```
abstract class Handler<T> {
    protected next : Handler<T> | null = null;
    public SetNext(next : Handler<T>) : void {
        this.next = next;
    }
    public HandleRequest(request : T) : void {
        if (!this.CanHandle(request)) {
            if (this.next !== null) {
                this.next.HandleRequest(request);
            }
            return;
        }
    }
    protected abstract CanHandle(request : T) : boolean;
}
```

The next class in our chain is set using `SetNext`. `HandleRequest` works by calling our abstract `CanHandle` method to see whether the current class can handle the request. If it cannot handle the request and if `this.next` is not `null` (note the use of union types here), we forward the request onto the next class. This is repeated until we can either handle the request or `this.next` is `null`.

We can now add a concrete implementation of our `Handler` class. First, we will add our constructor and member variables, as follows:

```
class ParseChainHandler extends Handler<ParseElement> {
    private readonly visitable : IVisitable = new Visitable();
    constructor(private readonly document : IMarkdownDocument,
        private readonly tagType : string,
        private readonly visitor : IVisitor) {
        super();
    }
}
```

Our constructor accepts the instance of the markdown document; the `string` that represents our `tagType`, for example, #; and the relevant visitor will visit the class if we get a matching tag. Before we see what the code for `CanHandle` looks like, we need to take a slight detour and introduce a class that will help us parse the current line and see if the tag is present at the start.

We are going to create a class that exists purely to parse the string, and looks to see if it starts with the relevant markdown tag. What is special about our `Parse` method is that we are returning something called a **tuple**. We can think of a tuple as a fixed-size array that can have different types at different positions in the array. In our case, we are going to return a `boolean` type and a `string` type. The `boolean` type indicates whether or not the tag was found, and the `string` type will return the text without the tag at the start; for example, if the `string` was # `Hello` and the tag was `#`, we would want to return `Hello`. The code that checks for the tag is very straightforward; it simply looks to see if the text starts with the tag. If it does, we set the `boolean` part of our tuple to `true` and use `substr` to get the remainder of our text. Consider the following code:

```
class LineParser {
    public Parse(value : string, tag : string) : [boolean, string] {
        let output : [boolean, string] = [false, ""];
        output[1] = value;
        if (value === "") {
            return output;
        }
        let split = value.startsWith(`${tag}`);
        if (split) {
            output[0] = true;
            output[1] = value.substr(tag.length);
        }
        return output;
    }
}
```

Now that we have our `LineParser` class, we can apply that in our `CanHandle` method as follows:

```
protected CanHandle(request: ParseElement): boolean {
    let split = new LineParser().Parse(request.CurrentLine, this.tagType);
    if (split[0]){
        request.CurrentLine = split[1];
        this.visitable.Accept(this.visitor, request, this.document);
    }
    return split[0];
}
```

Here, we are using our parser to build a tuple where the first parameter states whether or not the tag was present, and the second parameter contains the text without the tag if the tag was present. If the markdown tag was present in our string, we call the `Accept` method on our `Visitable` implementation.

Strictly speaking, we could have directly called
`this.visitor.Visit(request, this.document);`, however, that
provides us with more knowledge about how to perform the visit into this
class than I would like. By using the `Accept` approach, if we make our
visitors more complex, we avoid having to revisit this method as well.

This is what our `ParseChainHandler` looks like now:

```
class ParseChainHandler extends Handler<ParseElement> {
    private readonly visitable : IVisitable = new Visitable();
    protected CanHandle(request: ParseElement): boolean {
        let split = new LineParser().Parse(request.CurrentLine,
this.tagType);
        if (split[0]){
            request.CurrentLine = split[1];
            this.visitable.Accept(this.visitor, request, this.document);
        }
        return split[0];
    }
    constructor(private readonly document : IMarkdownDocument,
        private readonly tagType : string,
        private readonly visitor : IVisitor) {
        super();
    }
}
```

We have a special case that we need to handle. We know that the paragraph has no tag
associated with it—if there are no matches through the rest of the chain, by default, it's a
paragraph. This means that we need a slightly different handler to cope with paragraphs,
shown as follows:

```
class ParagraphHandler extends Handler<ParseElement> {
    private readonly visitable : IVisitable = new Visitable();
    private readonly visitor : IVisitor = new ParagraphVisitor()
    protected CanHandle(request: ParseElement): boolean {
        this.visitable.Accept(this.visitor, request, this.document);
        return true;
    }
    constructor(private readonly document : IMarkdownDocument) {
        super();
    }
}
```

With this infrastructure in place, we are now ready to create the concrete handlers for the appropriate tags as follows:

```
class Header1ChainHandler extends ParseChainHandler {
    constructor(document : IMarkdownDocument) {
        super(document, "# ", new Header1Visitor());
    }
}

class Header2ChainHandler extends ParseChainHandler {
    constructor(document : IMarkdownDocument) {
        super(document, "## ", new Header2Visitor());
    }
}

class Header3ChainHandler extends ParseChainHandler {
    constructor(document : IMarkdownDocument) {
        super(document, "### ", new Header3Visitor());
    }
}

class HorizontalRuleHandler extends ParseChainHandler {
    constructor(document : IMarkdownDocument) {
        super(document, "---", new HorizontalRuleVisitor());
    }
}
```

We now have a route through from the tag, for example, `---`, to the appropriate visitor. We have now linked our chain-of-responsibility pattern to our visitor pattern. We have one final thing that we need to do: set up the chain. To do this, let's use a separate class that builds our chain:

```
class ChainOfResponsibilityFactory {
    Build(document : IMarkdownDocument) : ParseChainHandler {
        let header1 : Header1ChainHandler = new
Header1ChainHandler(document);
        let header2 : Header2ChainHandler = new
Header2ChainHandler(document);
        let header3 : Header3ChainHandler = new
Header3ChainHandler(document);
        let horizontalRule : HorizontalRuleHandler = new
HorizontalRuleHandler(document);
        let paragraph : ParagraphHandler = new ParagraphHandler(document);

        header1.SetNext(header2);
        header2.SetNext(header3);
        header3.SetNext(horizontalRule);
```

```
        horizontalRule.SetNext(paragraph);

        return header1;
    }
}
```

This simple-looking method accomplishes a lot for us. The first few statements initialize the chain-of-responsibility handlers for us; first for the headers, then for the horizontal rule, and finally for the paragraph handler. Remembering that this is only part of what we need to do here, we then go through the headers and the horizontal rule and set up the next item in the chain. Header 1 will forward calls on to header 2, header 2 forwards to header 3, and so on. The reason we don't set any further chained items after the paragraph handler is because that is the last case we want to handle. If the user isn't typing `header1`, `header2`, `header3`, or `horizontalRule`, then we're going to treat this as a paragraph.

Bringing it all together

The last class that we are going to write is used to take the text that the user is typing in and split it into individual lines, and create our `ParseElement`, chain-of-responsibility handlers, and `MarkdownDocument` instance. Each line is then forwarded to `Header1ChainHandler` to start the processing of the line. Finally, we get the text from the document and return it so that we can display it in the label:

```
class Markdown {
    public ToHtml(text : string) : string {
        let document : IMarkdownDocument = new MarkdownDocument();
        let header1 : Header1ChainHandler = new
ChainOfResponsibilityFactory().Build(document);
        let lines : string[] = text.split(`\n`);
        for (let index = 0; index < lines.length; index++) {
            let parseElement : ParseElement = new ParseElement();
            parseElement.CurrentLine = lines[index];
            header1.HandleRequest(parseElement);
        }
        return document.Get();
    }
}
```

Now that we can generate our HTML content, we have one change left to do. We are going to revisit the `HtmlHandler` method and change it so that it calls our `ToHtml` markdown method. At the same time, we are going to address an issue with our original implementation where refreshing the page loses our content until we press a key. To handle this, we are going to add a `window.onload` event handler:

```
class HtmlHandler {
 private markdownChange : Markdown = new Markdown;
    public TextChangeHandler(id : string, output : string) : void {
        let markdown = <HTMLTextAreaElement>document.getElementById(id);
        let markdownOutput =
<HTMLLabelElement>document.getElementById(output);
        if (markdown !== null) {
            markdown.onkeyup = (e) => {
                this.RenderHtmlContent(markdown, markdownOutput);
            }
            window.onload = (e) => {
                this.RenderHtmlContent(markdown, markdownOutput);
            }
        }
    }

    private RenderHtmlContent(markdown: HTMLTextAreaElement,
markdownOutput: HTMLLabelElement) {
        if (markdown.value) {
            markdownOutput.innerHTML =
this.markdownChange.ToHtml(markdown.value);
        }
        else
            markdownOutput.innerHTML = "<p></p>";
    }
}
```

Now, when we run our application, it displays the rendered HTML content, even when we refresh our page. We have successfully created a simple markdown editor that satisfies the points that we laid out in our requirements, gathering stage.

I cannot stress enough how important the requirements, gathering stage is. All too often, poor requirements lead to us having to make assumptions about the behavior of an application. These assumptions can lead to delivering an application that users do not want. If you find yourself making an assumption, go back and ask your users exactly what they want. As we built our code here, we referred back to our requirements to make sure that we were building exactly what we were meant to build.

A final point about requirements—they change. It is common for requirements to evolve or get removed while we are writing an application. When they do change, we make sure that the requirements are updated, that we are making no assumptions, and that we check the work that has already been produced to make sure that it matches the updated requirements. This is what we do because we are professionals.

Summary

In this chapter, we have built an application that responded to what the user was typing into a text area, and updated a label with converted text. The conversion of this text was handled by classes, each of which had a single responsibility. The reason we concentrated on producing classes that only did one thing was to learn, right from the start, how to use industry best practices to make our code cleaner and less prone to errors, since a well-designed class that only does one thing is less likely to have problems than classes that do lots of different things.

We introduced the visitor and chain-of-responsibility patterns in order to see how we could separate the text processing into deciding whether a line contained markdown and adding the appropriate HTML-encoded text. We started introducing patterns because patterns occur in so many different software development problems. Not only do they provide clear details about how to solve a problem; they also provide a clear language so that if someone says that a piece of code needs a particular pattern, there is no ambiguity for other developers about what that code needs to do.

In the next chapter, we are going to look at our first application using React.js, for when we build a personal contacts manager.

Questions

1. The application currently only reacts to the user changing the content using the keyboard. It is possible that the user could use the context menu to paste the text in. Enhance the `HtmlHandler` method to cope with the user pasting text in.
2. We added H1 to H3 support. HTML also supports H4, H5, and H6. Add support for these tags.
3. In the `CanHandle` code, we are calling the `Visitable` code. Change the base `Handler` class so that it calls the `Accept` method.

Further reading

For further information about using design patterns, I would recommend the book *TypeScript Design Patterns* (https://www.packtpub.com/application-development/typescript-design-patterns) by Vilic Vane, published by Packt.

3
A React Bootstrap Personal Contacts Manager

In this chapter, we are going to learn how to build a personal contacts manager using React, which is a library for building **user interfaces** (**UIs**) out of small components. By learning React, you will gain the ability to use one of the most popular libraries currently in use, as well as begin to understand how and when to use the power of binding to simplify your code.

Exploring React will help us to understand how to write a modern application for the client side and also study its requirements.

To help us to develop the application, the following topics will be covered in this chapter:

- Creating a mock layout to check our layouts
- Creating our React application
- Analyzing and formatting code with `tslint`
- Adding Bootstrap support
- Using tsx components in React
- The `App` component in React
- Displaying our personal details UI
- Using binding to simplify our updates
- Creating validators and applying them as validation
- Applying validation in a React component
- Creating and sending data to an IndexedDB database

Technical requirements

As we are using an IndexedDB database to store data, a modern web browser such as Chrome (version 11 or later) or Firefox (version 4 or later) will be required. The finished project can be downloaded from `https://github.com/PacktPublishing/Advanced-TypeScript-3-Programming-Projects/tree/master/chapter03`. After downloading the project, you will have to install the package requirements using `npm install`.

Understanding the project overview

We are going to build a personal contacts manager database using React. The data is stored locally on the client using the standard IndexedDB database. When we have finished, our application will look like the following:

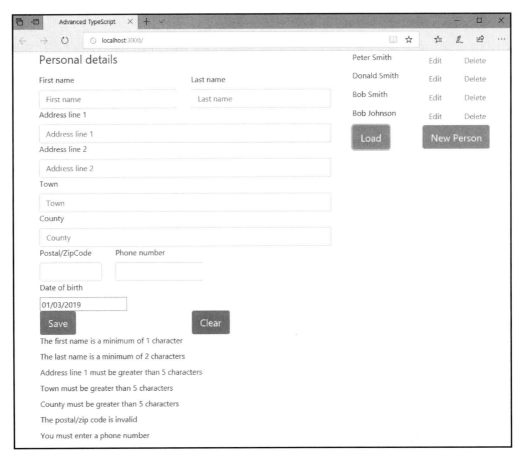

You should be able to complete the steps in this chapter, working alongside the code in the GitHub repository, in approximately two hours.

Getting started with the components

This chapter relies on Node.js, which is available at `https://nodejs.org/`. As we progress through the chapter, we will install the following components:

- `@types/bootstrap` (4.1.2 or later)
- `@types/reactstrap` (6.4.3 or later)
- `bootstrap` (4.1.3 or later)
- `react` (16.6.3 or later)
- `react-dom` (16.6.3 or later)
- `react-script-ts` (3.1.0 or later)
- `reactstrap` (6.5.0 or later)
- `create-react-app` (2.1.2 or later)

Creating a React Bootstrap project with TypeScript support

As we discussed in `Chapter 2`, *Creating a Markdown Editor with TypeScript*, it is a good idea to start off by gathering the requirements of the application that we are going to write. Here are the requirements for this chapter:

- The user will be able to create new details of a person or edit them
- These details will be saved to a client-side database
- The user will be able to load the list of all people
- The user will be able to delete the personal details of a person
- The personal details will consist of the first and last names, the address (made up of two address lines, the town, the county, and the zip code), the phone number, and the date of birth
- The personal details will be saved to the database

- The first name will be at least one character and the last name will be at least two characters
- Address line 1, town, and county will be at least five characters
- The zip code will conform to the American standard for most zip codes
- The phone number will conform to the standard American phone format
- The user can clear details with the click of a button

Creating our mock layout

Once we have our requirements, it is normally a good idea to draw up some rough drafts of what we think the layout of our application should be. What we want to do is to create a layout that shows we are using a web browser layout in a sketch format. The reason we want it to look as though it is sketched is because of the way we interact with our clients. We want them to get an idea about the rough layout of our application without getting caught up in details such as exactly how wide a particular button is.

What is particularly useful is the ability to use a tool such as `https://ninjamock.com/` to create a wireframe sketch of our interface. These sketches can be shared online with clients or other team members who can directly add comments. The following sketch diagram demonstrates what we want our interface to look like when we are finished:

Creating our application

Before we can begin writing our code, we need to install React. While it is possible to create the infrastructure we need for React manually, most people use the `create-react-app` command to create a React application. We aren't going to do this any differently, so we are also going to use the `create-react-app` command. React does not use TypeScript by default so we are going to add a little bit extra to the command we use to create our application to give us all the TypeScript capacity that we need. We use `create-react-app`, giving it the name of our application and an extra `scripts-version` parameter that hooks in TypeScript for us:

```
npx create-react-app chapter03 --scripts-version=react-scripts-ts
```

 If you have installed Node.js packages before, you may think that there is a mistake in the preceding command and that we should be using `npm` to install `create-react-app`. However, we are using `npx` in place of `npm` because `npx` is an enhanced version of the **Node Package Manager** (**NPM**). With `npx`, we missed out the need to run `npm install create-react-app` to install the `create-react-app` package before manually running `create-react-app` to start the process. The use of `npx` does help to speed up our development workflow.

Once our application has been created, we open the `Chapter03` directory and run the following command:

```
npm start
```

Assuming that we have a default browser set, it should be opened to `http://localhost:3000`, which is the default web page for this application. This will serve up a standard web page that just happens to contain a default React sample. What we are going to do now is edit the `public/index.html` file and set a title for it. We are going to set our title to `Advanced TypeScript - Personal Contacts Manager`. While the contents of this file appear to be sparse, they contain everything that we need on our HTML side, namely, a `div` element called `root`. This is the hook that our React code will hang off, as we will discuss later. We can live edit our application so that any changes we make will be compiled and served back to the browser automatically:

```
<!DOCTYPE html>
<html lang="en">
  <head>
    <meta charset="utf-8">
    <meta name="viewport" content="width=device-width, initial-scale=1,
shrink-to-fit=no">
```

```
    <meta name="theme-color" content="#000000">
    <link rel="manifest" href="%PUBLIC_URL%/manifest.json">
    <link rel="shortcut icon" href="%PUBLIC_URL%/favicon.ico">
    <title>Advanced TypeScript - Personal Contacts Manager</title>
  </head>
  <body>
    <noscript>
      You need to enable JavaScript to run this app.
    </noscript>
    <div id="root"></div>
  </body>
</html>
```

Formatting our code using tslint

Once we have created our application, we are using something called `tslint`, which analyzes our code by looking for potential problems. Note that support for this was automatically added when we created our application. The `tslint` version that runs applies a very aggressive set of rules against which we check our code. I have gone with the full set of `tslint` rules in my code base; however, if you want to relax the rules a bit, you just need to change the `tslint.json` file to something like the following:

```
{
  "extends": [],
  "defaultSeverity" : "warning",
  "linterOptions": {
    "exclude": [
      "config/**/*.js",
      "node_modules/**/*.ts",
      "coverage/lcov-report/*.js"
    ]
  }
}
```

Adding Bootstrap support

One of the things we need to do with our application is bring in support for Bootstrap. This is not something that is provided *out of the box* with React, so we need to add this capacity using other packages:

1. Install Bootstrap as follows:

```
npm install --save bootstrap
```

2. With this in place, we are now free to use a React-ready Bootstrap component. We are going to use the `reactstrap` package because this package targets Bootstrap 4 in a React-friendly fashion:

```
npm install --save reactstrap react react-dom
```

3. `reactstrap` is not a TypeScript component, so we need to install the `DefinitelyTyped` definition for this and for Bootstrap:

```
npm install --save @types/reactstrap
npm install --save @types/bootstrap
```

4. With this in place, we can now add the Bootstrap CSS files. To do this, we are going to update the `index.tsx` file by adding a reference to our locally installed Bootstrap CSS file, by adding the following `import` to the very top of the file:

```
import "bootstrap/dist/css/bootstrap.min.css";
```

Here, we are using the local Bootstrap file for convenience. As we discussed in Chapter 1, *Advanced TypeScript Features*, we want to change this to use a CDN source for the production version of this application.

5. To tidy up, remove the following line from `src/index.tsx` and then remove the matching `.css` file from the disk:

```
import './index.css'
```

React using tsx components

One question that you might have right now is why does the index file have a different extension? That is, why is it `.tsx` and not `.ts`? To answer these questions, we have to change our mental image of the extension slightly and talk about why React uses `.jsx` files and not `.js` (the `.tsx` version is the TypeScript equivalent of `.jsx`).

These JSX files are extensions of JavaScript that get transpiled to JavaScript. If you were to try and run them *as is* in JavaScript, then you would get runtime errors if they contained any of these extensions. In traditional React, there is a transpilation phase that takes the JSX file and converts it to JavaScript by expanding out the code to standard JavaScript. Effectively, this is a form of the compilation phase that we get from TypeScript anyway. With TypeScript React, we get the same end result where the TSX file ultimately ends up as a JavaScript file.

So, the question now is why do we actually need these extensions? To answer this, we are going to analyze the `index.tsx` file. This is what the file looks like with our Bootstrap CSS file added:

```
import "bootstrap/dist/css/bootstrap.min.css";
import * as React from 'react';
import * as ReactDOM from 'react-dom';
import App from './App';

import registerServiceWorker from './registerServiceWorker';

ReactDOM.render(
  <App />,
  document.getElementById('root') as HTMLElement
);
registerServiceWorker();
```

The `import` statements should be familiar to us by now and `registerServiceWorker` is the behavior that is added to the code to provide a faster production application by serving assets from a cache, rather than reloading them time and time again. One of the key tenets of React is that it should be as fast as possible and that's where `ReactDOM.render` comes in. If we read this piece of code, things should become clear. What it is doing is looking for the element marked as root in the HTML page we serve up—we saw this in the `index.html` file. The reason we use the `as HTMLElement` syntax here is that we want to let TypeScript know what type this is (this parameter either has to derive from an element or be null—yes, that does mean that underlying this is a union type).

Now, the reason we need a special extension is because of the piece of code that says `<App />`. What we are doing here is inlining a piece of XML code into our statement. In this particular instance, we are telling our `render` method to render out a component called App, that has been defined in the `App.tsx` file.

How React uses a virtual DOM to be more responsive

I glossed over why the `render` method is used, so now is the time to address React's secret weapon, that is, the virtual **Document Object Model (DOM)**. If you've been developing web applications for a while, you are probably aware of the DOM. If you have never encountered this, the DOM is an entity that describes exactly what a web page will look like. Web browsers rely very heavily on the DOM, and, as it has grown organically over the years, it can be pretty unwieldy. There is only so much that browser manufacturers can do to try and speed up the DOM. If they want to be able to serve up old web pages, then they have to support the full DOM.

The virtual DOM is a light weight copy of the standard DOM. The reason it is lighter in weight is that it misses out a major feature of the standard DOM; that is, it doesn't have to render out to the screen. When React runs the `render` method, it traverses each `.tsx` (or `.jsx` in JavaScript) file and executes the rendering code there. It then compares this rendered code to a copy of the last render that was run to work out exactly what has changed. Only those changed elements are updated on the screen. This comparison stage is the reason we have to use a virtual DOM. It's much faster to tell what elements need updating using this approach, and only those elements that get changed need to be updated.

Our React App component

We have already touched on the use of components in React. By default, we will always have an `App` component. This is the component that will be rendered to the root element in our HTML. Our components derive from `React.Component`, so the start of our `App` component looks like the following:

```
import * as React from 'react';
import './App.css';

export default class App extends React.Component {

}
```

Of course, our component requires a well-known method to trigger the rendering of the component. It will not come as much of a surprise to learn that the method is called `render`. As we are using Bootstrap to display our UI, we want to be rendering out a component that relates to our `Container` div. To do this, we are going to use a `Container` component from `reactstrap` (and introduce the core component that we are going to use to display our interface):

```
import * as React from 'react';
import './App.css';
import Container from 'reactstrap/lib/Container';
import PersonalDetails from './PersonalDetails';
export default class App extends React.Component {
  public render() {
    return (
      <Container>
        <PersonalDetails />
      </Container>
    );
  }
}
```

Displaying the personal details interface

We are going to create a class called `PersonalDetails`. This class is going to render out the core of our interface inside the `render` method. Again, we are using `reactstrap` to lay out the various parts of the interface. Before we break down the intricacies of what our `render` method does, let's take a look at what this all looks like:

```
import * as React from 'react';
import Button from 'reactstrap/lib/Button';
import Col from 'reactstrap/lib/Col';
import Row from 'reactstrap/lib/Row';

export default class PersonalDetails extends React.Component {

  public render() {
    return (
      <Row>
        <Col lg="8">
          <Row>
            <Col><h4 className="mb-3">Personal details</h4></Col>
          </Row>
          <Row>
            <Col><label htmlFor="firstName">First name</label></Col>
```

```
                <Col><label htmlFor="lastName">Last name</label></Col>
            </Row>
            <Row>
                <Col>
                    <input type="text" id="firstName" className="form-control"
placeholder="First name" />
                </Col>
                <Col><input type="text" id="lastName" className="form-control"
placeholder="Last name" /></Col>
            </Row>
... Code omitted for brevity
        <Col>
            <Col>
                <Row>
                    <Col lg="6"><Button size="lg"
color="success">Load</Button></Col>
                    <Col lg="6"><Button size="lg" color="info">New
Person</Button></Col>
                </Row>
            </Col>
        </Col>
    </Row>
    );
  }
}
```

As you can see, there's a lot going on in this method; however, the vast majority of it is repeated code used to replicate the row and column Bootstrap elements. If we take a look at the layout for the postcode and phoneNumber elements, for instance, we can see that we are laying out two rows with two explicit columns in each. In Bootstrap terms, one of these Col elements is a large size of three and the other one is a large size of four (we will leave it to Bootstrap to factor in the empty column that remains):

```
<Row>
  <Col lg="3"><label htmlFor="postcode">Postal/ZipCode</label></Col>
  <Col lg="4"><label htmlFor="phoneNumber">Phone number</label></Col>
</Row>
<Row>
  <Col lg="3"><input type="text" id="postcode" className="form-control"
/></Col>
  <Col lg="4"><input type="text" id="phoneNumber" className="form-control"
/></Col>
</Row>
```

Looking at the label and input elements, we can see that there are two unfamiliar elements. Surely, the correct key in a label is `for` and we should use `class` to refer to a CSS class in our input? The reason we have replacement keys here is that `for` and `class` are JavaScript keywords. As React allows us to mix the code and markup language inside a render, React has to use different keywords. This means that we use `htmlFor` to replace `for` and `className` to replace `class`. Going back to when we talked about the virtual DOM, this gives us a major hint that these HTML elements are copies that serve a similar purpose, rather than the elements themselves.

Simplify updating values with binding

One feature of many modern frameworks is the use of binding to remove the need to manually update inputs or trigger events. The idea behind using a binding is that the framework establishes a connection between a UI element and the code, such as a property, watches for changes to the underlying values, and then triggers updates when it detects a change. When done correctly, this removes a lot of drudgery from writing our code and, more importantly, helps to reduce errors.

Supplying state to bind against

The idea behind binding with React is that we have a state that we need to bind to. In the case of creating data that we want to display on the screen, our state can be as simple as an interface describing the properties that we want to use. For a single contact, this translates to our state looking like this:

```
export interface IPersonState {
  FirstName: string,
  LastName: string,
  Address1: string,
  Address2: StringOrNull,
  Town: string,
  County: string,
  PhoneNumber: string;
  Postcode: string,
  DateOfBirth: StringOrNull,
  PersonId : string
}
```

Note that we have created a union type called `StringOrNull` as a convenience. We will place this in a file called `Types.tsx` so that it looks like this:

```
export type StringOrNull = string | null;
```

What we want to do now is tell our component what state it is going to use. The first thing to do is update our class definition so that it looks like this:

```
export default class PersonalDetails extends React.Component<IProps,
IPersonState>
```

This follows the convention where the properties are passed into our class from the parent and the state comes from our local component. This separation of properties and state is important to us because it provides us with a way for the parent to communicate with the component (and for the component to communicate back with the parent), while still being able to manage the data and behaviors that our component wants as the state.

Here, our properties are defined in an interface called `IProps`. Now that we have told React what the *shape* of our state is going to be internally, React and TypeScript use this to create a `ReadOnly<IPersonState>` property. Therefore, it is important to ensure that we are using the right state. If we use the wrong type for our state, TypeScript will inform us of this.

Note that there is a caveat to that preceding statement. If we have two interfaces of exactly the same shape, then TypeScript treats them as equivalent to each other. So, even though TypeScript is expecting `IState`, if we supply something called `IMyOtherState` that has exactly the same properties, then TypeScript will happily let us use that in its place. The question, of course, is why would we want to duplicate the interface in the first place? I cannot think of many cases where we would want to do that, so the idea of using the right state is accurate for almost all the cases we are ever likely to encounter.

Our `app.tsx` file is going to create a default for the state and pass this to our component as its property. The default state is the one that will be applied when the user presses clear to clear the currently edited entry, or **New Person** to start adding a new person. Our `IProps` interface looks like this:

```
interface IProps {
  DefaultState : IPersonState
}
```

Something that may seem slightly confusing at first is a potential contradiction between my earlier statement the idea that the properties and state are different—with state being something that is local to the component and yet we are passing state down as part of the properties. I deliberately use state as part of the name to reinforce the fact that this represents the state. The values that we are passing in can be called anything at all. They do not have to represent any state; they could simply be functions that the component calls to trigger some response in the parent. Our component will receive this property and it will be its responsibility to convert any part that it needs into state.

With this in place, we are ready to change our App.tsx file to create our default state and to pass this into our PersonalDetails component. As we can see in the following code, the property from the IProps interface becomes a parameter in the <PersonalDetails .. line. The more items we add to our properties interface, the more parameters we will have to add to this line:

```
import * as React from 'react';
import Container from 'reactstrap/lib/Container';
import './App.css';
import PersonalDetails from './PersonalDetails';
import { IPersonState } from "./State";

export default class App extends React.Component {
  private defaultPerson : IPersonState = {
    Address1: "",
    Address2: null,
    County: "",
    DateOfBirth : new Date().toISOString().substring(0,10),
    FirstName: "",
    LastName: "",
    PersonId : "",
    PhoneNumber: "",
    Postcode: "",
    Town: ""
  }
  public render() {
    return (
      <Container>
        <PersonalDetails DefaultState={this.defaultPerson} />
      </Container>
    );
  }
}
```

Date handling with JavaScript can be off-putting when we want to hook the date into a date picker component. The date picker expects to receive the date in the format of YYYY-MM-DD. So, we use the `new Date().toISOString().substring(0,10)` syntax to get today's date, which includes a time component, and only retrieve the YYYY-MM-DD portion from this. Even though the date picker expects the date to be in this format, it does not say that this is the format that will be displayed on the screen. The format on your screen should respect the local settings of the user.

What was interesting about the changes we made to support passing in properties is that we have already seen binding in action here. Inside the `render` method, where we set `Default={this.defaultPerson}`, we are using binding. With the use of `{ }` here, we are telling React that we want to bind to something, whether it's to a property or an event. We will encounter binding a lot in React.

Now we are going to add a constructor to `PersonalDetails.tsx` to support the property that is being passed in from `App.tsx`:

```
private defaultState: Readonly<IPersonState>;
constructor(props: IProps) {
  super(props);
  this.defaultState = props.DefaultState;
  this.state = props.DefaultState;
}
```

We are doing two things here. First, we are setting up a default state to go back to if we need to, which we received from our parent; second, we are setting up the state for this page. We didn't have to create a state property in our code as this is provided for us by `React.Component`. This is the final part of learning how we have tied our property from the parent to the state.

Changes to state will not be reflected back in the parent props. If we wanted to explicitly set a value back in the parent component, this would require us to trigger a change to `props.DefaultState`. I advise against doing this directly if you can possibly avoid it.

Right. Let's set up our first name and last name elements to work with the binding from our state. The idea here is that if we update the state of the first or last names in our code, this will automatically be updated in our UI. So, let's change the entries as required:

```
<Row>
  <Col><input type="text" id="firstName" className="form-control"
value={this.state.FirstName} placeholder="First name" /></Col>
  <Col><input type="text" id="lastName" className="form-control"
value={this.state.LastName} placeholder="Last name" /></Col>
</Row>
```

Now, if we run our application, we have entries that are bound to the underlying state. There is, however, an issue with this code. If we try to type into either textbox, we will see that nothing happens. The actual text entry is rejected. That does not mean we have done anything wrong, rather we only have part of the overall picture here. What we need to understand is that React provides us with a read-only version of the state. If we want our UI to update our state, we have to explicitly opt into this by reacting to changes and then setting the state as appropriate. First, we are going to write an event handler to handle setting the state when the text changes:

```
private updateBinding = (event: any) => {
  switch (event.target.id) {
    case `firstName`:
      this.setState({ FirstName: event.target.value });
      break;
    case `lastName`:
      this.setState({ LastName: event.target.value });
      break;
  }
}
```

With this in place, we can now update our input to trigger this update using the onChange attribute. Again, we are going to use binding to match the onChange event to the code that is triggered as a result:

```
<Row>
  <Col>
    <input type="text" id="firstName" className="form-control"
value={this.state.FirstName} onChange={this.updateBinding}
placeholder="First name" />
  </Col>
  <Col><input type="text" id="lastName" className="form-control"
value={this.state.LastName} onChange={this.updateBinding} placeholder="Last
name" /></Col>
</Row>
```

From this code, we can clearly see that `this.state` provides us with access to the underlying state that we set up in our component and that we need to change it using `this.setState`. The syntax of `this.setState` should look familiar as it matches the key to the value, which we have encountered many times before in TypeScript. At this stage, we can now update the rest of our entry components to support this two-way binding. First, we expand our `updateBinding` code as follows:

```
private updateBinding = (event: any) => {
  switch (event.target.id) {
    case `firstName`:
      this.setState({ FirstName: event.target.value });
      break;
    case `lastName`:
      this.setState({ LastName: event.target.value });
      break;
    case `addr1`:
      this.setState({ Address1: event.target.value });
      break;
    case `addr2`:
      this.setState({ Address2: event.target.value });
      break;
    case `town`:
      this.setState({ Town: event.target.value });
      break;
    case `county`:
      this.setState({ County: event.target.value });
      break;
    case `postcode`:
      this.setState({ Postcode: event.target.value });
      break;
    case `phoneNumber`:
      this.setState({ PhoneNumber: event.target.value });
      break;
    case `dateOfBirth`:
      this.setState({ DateOfBirth: event.target.value });
      break;
  }
}
```

We aren't going to code dump all of the changes that we need to make to our actual inputs. We just need to update each input to match the value to the appropriate state element, and then add the same `onChange` handler in each case.

> As `Address2` can be null, we are using the `!` operator on our binding so that it looks slightly different: `value={this.state.Address2!}`.

Validating user inputs and the use of validators

At this stage, we really should think about validating inputs from the user. We are going to introduce two types of validation in our code. The first is the minimum length validation. In other words, we are going to ensure that some of the entries have to have a minimum number of entries before they can be considered to be valid. The second type of validation uses something called a regular expression to validate it. What this means is that it takes the input and compares it against a set of rules to see whether there is a match; the expressions can look a little bit odd if you are new to regular expressions, so we will break them down to see exactly what rules we are applying.

We are going to break our validation down into three parts:

1. The classes that provide the checking features, such as applying a regular expression. We will call these validators.
2. The classes that apply the validation items to the different parts of the state. We will call these classes validations.
3. The component that will call the validation items and update the UI with the details of a failed validation. This will be a new component called `FormValidation.tsx`.

We will start by creating an interface called `IValidator`. This interface is going to accept a generic parameter so that we can apply it to pretty much anything that we want. As a validation will tell us whether the input is valid, it will have a single method called `IsValid` that accepts the relevant input and then returns a `boolean` value:

```
interface IValidator<T> {
  IsValid(input : T) : boolean;
}
```

The first validator that we are going to write checks to see whether a string has a minimum number of characters, which we will set through the constructor. We will also guard against situations where the user fails to supply an input, by returning `false` from `IsValid` when the input is null:

```
export class MinLengthValidator implements IValidator<StringOrNull> {
  private minLength : number;
  constructor(minLength : number) {
    this.minLength = minLength;
  }
  public IsValid(input : StringOrNull) : boolean {
    if (!input) {
      return false;
    }
    return input.length >= this.minLength;
  }
}
```

The other validator that we are going to create is slightly more complicated. This validator accepts a string, which it uses to create something called a regular expression. A regular expression is effectively a mini language that provides a set of rules to test our input string against. In this case, the rules that form our regular expression are passed into our constructor. The constructor will then instantiate an instance of the JavaScript regular expression engine (`RegExp`). In a similar way to the minimum length validation, we ensure that we return `false` if there is no input. If we have an input, then we return the result of our regular expression test:

```
import { StringOrNull } from 'src/Types';

export class RegularExpressionValidator implements IValidator<StringOrNull>
{
  private regex : RegExp;
  constructor(expression : string) {
    this.regex = new RegExp(expression);
  }
  public IsValid (input : StringOrNull) : boolean {
    if (!input) {
      return false;
    }
    return this.regex.test(input);
  }
}
```

Now that we have our validators, we are going to examine how we are going to apply them. It probably will not come as a surprise that the first thing that we are going to do is define an interface that forms the *contract* of what we want our validation to do. Our `Validate` method is going to accept the `IPersonState` state from our component, validate items from this, and then return an array of validation failures:

```
export interface IValidation {
  Validate(state : IPersonState, errors : string[]) : void;
}
```

I have decided to break the validation down into the following three areas:

1. Validating the address
2. Validating the name
3. Validating the phone number

Validating the address

Our address validation is going to use the `MinLengthValidator` and `RegularExpressionValidator` validators:

```
export class AddressValidation implements IValidation {
  private readonly minLengthValidator : MinLengthValidator = new
MinLengthValidator(5);
  private readonly zipCodeValidator : RegularExpressionValidator
    = new RegularExpressionValidator("^[0-9]{5}(?:-[0-9]{4})?$");
}
```

The minimum length validation is simple enough, but the regular expression can be intimidating if you have never seen this type of syntax before. Before we look at our validation code, we will break down what the regular expression is doing.

The first character, ^, tells us that our validation is going to start at the very beginning of the string. If we left this character out, it would mean that our match could occur anywhere in the text. The use of `[0-9]` tells the regular expression engine that we want to match against a number. Strictly speaking, as US zip codes start with five numbers, we need to tell the validator that we want to match against five numbers, which we do by telling the engine how many we want: `[0-9]{5}`. If we only wanted to match against major area codes such as 10023, we could almost end our expression here. Zip codes, however, have an optional four-digit portion as well that is separated from the main part by a hyphen. Therefore, we have to tell the regular expression engine that we have an optional part that we want to apply.

We know that the format of the optional part of the zip code is a hyphen with four digits. This means that the next part of the regular expression has to consider the test as being one test. This means that we cannot test for a hyphen and then separately test for the numbers; we either have the -1234 format or we don't have anything. This tells us that we want to group the items we want to test together. The way that we group things together in a regular expression is to put the expression inside brackets. So, if we apply the same logic that we had before, we would probably think that this part of the validation was `(-[0-9]{4})`. As a first pass, that is pretty close to what we want. The rule, here, is to treat this as a group where the first character must be a hyphen and then there must be four numbers. There are two things that we need to sort out with this part of the expression. The first thing is that this test is not optional at the moment. In other words, the input 10012-1234 is valid, while 10012 is no longer valid. The second problem is that we have created something called a capture group in our expression, which we do not need.

A capture group is a numbered group that represents the number of the match. This can be useful if we want to match the same text in a number of places in a document; however, as we only want one match, it is something we can avoid.

We will fix both issues with the optional part of the validation now. The first thing we are going to do is remove the capture group. This is done by using an `?:` operator that tells the engine that this group is a non-capture group. The next thing we are going to take care of is applying a `?` operator that says that we want this match to happen zero times or one time only. In other words, we have made this an optional test. At this point, we can successfully test both 10012 and 10012-1234, but we do have one more thing that we need to take care of. We need to make sure that the input only matches this input. In other words, we don't want to allow any stray characters at the end; otherwise, the user would be able to type in 10012-12345 and the engine would think that we had a valid input. What we need to do is add the `$` operator at the end of the expression, which states that the expression is expecting the end of the line at that point. At this point, our regular expression is `^[0-9]{5}(?:-[0-9]{4})?$`, which matches the validation that we are expecting to apply to the zip code.

I have chosen to explicitly specify that a number is represented as `[0-9]` because it is a clear indicator for someone new to regular expressions that this represents a number between 0 and 9. There is an equivalent shorthand that can be used to represent a single digit, and that is to use `\d` in its place. With this, we can rewrite this rule to `^\d{5}(?:-\d{4})?$`. The use of `\d` in this represents a single **American Standard Code for Information Interchange (ASCII)** digit.

Going back to our address validation, the actual validation itself is extremely straightforward because we took the time to write validators that did the hard work for us. All we need to do is apply the minimum length validator against the first line of the address, the town, and the county, and the regular expression validator is applied to the zip code. Each failing validation item is added to the list of errors:

```
public Validate(state: IPersonState, errors: string[]): void {
  if (!this.minLengthValidator.IsValid(state.Address1)) {
    errors.push("Address line 1 must be greater than 5 characters");
  }
  if (!this.minLengthValidator.IsValid(state.Town)) {
    errors.push("Town must be greater than 5 characters");
  }
  if (!this.minLengthValidator.IsValid(state.County)) {
    errors.push("County must be greater than 5 characters");
  }
  if (!this.zipCodeValidator.IsValid(state.Postcode)) {
    errors.push("The postal/zip code is invalid");
  }
}
```

Validating the name

The name validation is the simplest piece of validation we are going to write. This validation assumes that we have a minimum of one letter for the first name and two letters for the last name:

```
export class PersonValidation implements IValidation {
  private readonly firstNameValidator : MinLengthValidator = new
MinLengthValidator(1);
  private readonly lastNameValidator : MinLengthValidator = new
MinLengthValidator(2);
  public Validate(state: IPersonState, errors: string[]): void {
    if (!this.firstNameValidator.IsValid(state.FirstName)) {
      errors.push("The first name is a minimum of 1 character");
    }
    if (!this.lastNameValidator.IsValid(state.FirstName)) {
      errors.push("The last name is a minimum of 2 characters");
    }
  }
}
```

Validating the phone number

The phone number validation is going to be broken down into two parts. First, we validate that there is an entry for the phone number. Then, we validate to ensure that it is in the correct format using a regular expression. Before we analyze the regular expression, let's see what this validation class looks like:

```
export class PhoneValidation implements IValidation {

  private readonly regexValidator : RegularExpressionValidator = new
RegularExpressionValidator(`^(?:\\((?:[0-9]{3})\\)|(?:[0-9]{3}))[-.
]?(?:[0-9]{3})[-. ]?(?:[0-9]{4})$`);
  private readonly minLengthValidator : MinLengthValidator = new
MinLengthValidator(1);

  public Validate(state : IPersonState, errors : string[]) : void {
    if (!this.minLengthValidator.IsValid(state.PhoneNumber)) {
      errors.push("You must enter a phone number")
    } else if (!this.regexValidator.IsValid(state.PhoneNumber)) {
      errors.push("The phone number format is invalid");
    }
  }
}
```

The regular expression initially looks more complicated than the zip code validation; however, once we break it down, we will see that it has lots of familiar elements. It uses ^ to capture from the start of the line, $ to capture right to the end, and ?: to create non-capture groups. We also see that we have set number matches such as [0-9]{3} to represent three numbers. If we break this down section by section, we will see that this really is a straightforward piece of validation.

The first part of our phone number either takes the format of (555) or 555 optionally followed by a hyphen, period, or space. At first glance, (?:\\((?:[0-9]{3})\\)|(?:[0-9]{3}))[-.]? is the most intimidating part of the expression. As we know, the first part either has to be something such as (555) or 555; that means that we have either *this expression* or *this expression* test. We have already seen that (and) mean something special to the regular expression engine so we must have some mechanism available to us to say that we are looking at the actual brackets rather than the expression that the brackets represent. That is what the \\ part means in the expression.

The use of \ in a regular expression escapes the next character so that it is treated literally, rather than as an expression that forms a rule that will be matched. Additionally, as TypeScript already treats \ as an escape character, we have to escape the escape character as well so that the expression engine sees the correct value.

When we want a regular expression to say a value must be this or that, we group the expression and then use | to break it apart. Looking at our expression there, we see that we are looking for the (*nnn*) part first and, if that is not matched, we look at the *nnn* part instead.

We also said that this value could be followed by a hyphen, period, or space. We use [-.] to match a single character from that list. To make this test optional, we put ? at the end.

With this knowledge, we see that the next part of the regular expression, (?:[0-9]{3})[-.]?, is looking for three numbers optionally followed by a hyphen, period, or space. The final part, (?:[0-9]{4}), states that the number must end in four digits. We now know that we can match numbers such as (555) 123-4567, 123.456.7890, and (555) 543 9876.

For our purpose, simple zip code and phone number validations such as these work perfectly. In larger-scale applications, we do not want to rely on these as validation. These only test the data that looks to be in a particular format; they don't actually check to see whether they belong to real addresses or phones. If we reached a stage with our application where we actually wanted to verify that these existed, we would have to hook up to the services that did these checks.

Applying validation in a React component

In our mock layout, we identified that we wanted our validation to appear below the `Save` and `Clear` buttons. While we could do this inside our main component, we are going to separate our validation out into a separate validation component. The component will receive the current state of our main component, apply the validation whenever the state changes, and return whether we can save our data.

In a similar way to how we created our `PersonalDetails` component, we are going to create properties to pass into our component:

```
interface IValidationProps {
  CurrentState : IPersonState;
  CanSave : (canSave : boolean) => void;
}
```

We are going to create a component in `FormValidation.tsx`, that will apply the different `IValidation` classes that we have just created. The constructor simply adds the different validators into an array that we will shortly iterate over and apply the validation for:

```
export default class FormValidation extends
React.Component<IValidationProps> {
  private failures : string[];
  private validation : IValidation[];

  constructor(props : IValidationProps) {
    super(props);
    this.validation = new Array<IValidation>();
    this.validation.push(new PersonValidation());
    this.validation.push(new AddressValidation());
    this.validation.push(new PhoneValidation());
  }

  private Validate() {
    this.failures = new Array<string>();
    this.validation.forEach(validation => {
      validation.Validate(this.props.CurrentState, this.failures);
    });

    this.props.CanSave(this.failures.length === 0);
  }
}
```

In the `Validate` method, we apply each piece of validation inside `forEach` before we call the `CanSave` method from our properties.

Before we add our `render` method, we are going to revisit `PersonalDetails` and add our `FormValidation` component:

```
<Row><FormValidation CurrentState={this.state} CanSave={this.userCanSave}
/></Row>
```

The `userCanSave` method looks like this:

```
private userCanSave = (hasErrors : boolean) => {
  this.canSave = hasErrors;
}
```

So, whenever the validation is updated, our `Validate` method calls back to `userCanSave`, which has been passed in as a property.

The last thing we need to do to get our validation running is to call the `Validate` method from the `render` method. We do this because the render cycle is called whenever the state of the parent changes. When we have a list of validation failures, we need to add them into our DOM as elements that we want to render back to the interface. A simple way to do this is to create a map of all of the failures and provide an iterator as a function that will loop over each failure and write it back as a row to the interface:

```
public render() {
  this.Validate();
  const errors = this.failures.map(function it(failure) {
    return (<Row key={failure}><Col><label>{failure}</label></Col></Row>);
  });
  return (<Col>{errors}</Col>)
}
```

At this point, whenever we change the state inside the application, our validation will automatically be triggered and any failures will be written in the browser as a `label` tag.

Creating and sending data to the IndexedDB database

It would make for a very poor experience when using the application if we could not save details for use the next time we came back to it. Fortunately, newer web browsers provide support for something called IndexedDB, which is a web browser-based database. Using this as our data store means that the details will be available when we reopen the page.

While we are working with the database, we have two distinct areas that we need to bear in mind. We require code to build the database table and we require code to save the records in a database. Before we start writing the database table, we are going to add the ability to describe what our database looks like, which will be used to build the database.

Next, we will create a fluent interface to add the information that `ITable` exposes:

```
export interface ITableBuilder {
  WithDatabase(databaseName : string) : ITableBuilder;
  WithVersion(version : number) : ITableBuilder;
  WithTableName(tableName : string) : ITableBuilder;
  WithPrimaryField(primaryField : string) : ITableBuilder;
  WithIndexName(indexName : string) : ITableBuilder;
}
```

The idea behind fluent interfaces is that they allow us to chain methods together so that they can be read in an easier fashion. They encourage the idea of keeping method operations together, making it easier to read what is happening to an instance because the operations are all grouped together. This interface is fluent because the methods return ITableBuilder. The implementations of these methods use return this; to allow the chaining of operations together.

 With fluent interfaces, not all methods need to be fluent. If you create a non-fluent method on an interface, that becomes the end of the call chain. This is sometimes used for classes that need to set some properties and then build an instance of a class that has those properties.

The other side of building the table is the ability to get the values from the builder. As we want to keep our fluent interface purely dealing with adding the details, we are going to write a separate interface to retrieve these values and build our IndexedDB database:

```
export interface ITable {
   Database() : string;
   Version() : number;
   TableName() : string;
   IndexName() : string;
   Build(database : IDBDatabase) : void;
}
```

While both of these interfaces serve different purposes and will be used by classes in different ways, they both refer to the same underlying code. When we write the class that exposes these interfaces, we are going to implement both the interfaces in the same class. The reason for doing this is so that we can segregate how they behave depending on which interface our calling code sees. Our table building class definition looks as follows:

```
export class TableBuilder implements ITableBuilder, ITable {
   }
```

Of course, if we tried to build this right now, it would fail because we haven't implemented either of our interfaces. The code for the ITableBuilder portion of this class looks like this:

```
private database : StringOrNull;
private tableName : StringOrNull;
private primaryField : StringOrNull;
private indexName : StringOrNull;
private version : number = 1;
public WithDatabase(databaseName : string) : ITableBuilder {
   this.database = databaseName;
   return this;
}
```

```
public WithVersion(versionNumber : number) : ITableBuilder {
  this.version = versionNumber;
  return this;
}
public WithTableName(tableName : string) : ITableBuilder {
  this.tableName = tableName;
  return this;
}
public WithPrimaryField(primaryField : string) : ITableBuild
  this.primaryField = primaryField;
  return this;
}
public WithIndexName(indexName : string) : ITableBuilder {
  this.indexName = indexName;
  return this;
}
```

For the most part, this is simple code. We have defined a number of member variables to hold the details, and each method is responsible for populating a single value. Where the code does get interesting is in the return statement. By returning this, we have the ability to chain each method together. Before we add our ITable support, let's explore how we use this fluent interface by creating a class to add the personal details table definition:

```
export class PersonalDetailsTableBuilder {
  public Build() : TableBuilder {
    const tableBuilder : TableBuilder = new TableBuilder();
    tableBuilder
      .WithDatabase("packt-advanced-typescript-ch3")
      .WithTableName("People")
      .WithPrimaryField("PersonId")
      .WithIndexName("personId")
      .WithVersion(1);
    return tableBuilder;
  }
}
```

What this code does is create a table builder that sets the database name to packt-advanced-typescript-ch3 and adds the People table to it, setting the primary field as PersonId and creating an index in this named personId.

Now that we have seen the fluent interface in action, we need to complete the TableBuilder class by adding the missing ITable methods:

```
public Database() : string {
  return this.database;
}
```

```
public Version() : number {
  return this.version;
}

public TableName() : string {
  return this.tableName;
}

public IndexName() : string {
  return this.indexName;
}

public Build(database : IDBDatabase) : void {
  const parameters : IDBObjectStoreParameters = { keyPath :
this.primaryField };
  const objectStore = database.createObjectStore(this.tableName,
parameters);
  objectStore!.createIndex(this.indexName, this.primaryField);
}
```

The `Build` method is the most interesting one in this part of the code. This is where we physically create the table using the methods from the underlying IndexedDB database. `IDBDatabase` is the connection to the actual IndexedDB database, which we are going to retrieve when we start writing the core database functionality. We use this to create the object store that we will use to store our people records. Setting `keyPath` allows us to give the object store a field that we want to search in, so it will match the name of a field. When we add indexes, we can tell the object store what fields we want to be able to search in.

Adding active record support to our state

Before we look at our actual database code, we need to introduce one last piece of the puzzle—the object that we are going to store. While we have been working with state, we have been using `IPersonState` to represent the state of a person and, as far as the `PersonalDetails` component goes, that is sufficient. While working with the database, we want to expand this state. We are going to introduce a new `IsActive` parameter that will determine whether a person is shown on the screen. We don't need to change the implementation of `IPersonState` to add this capability; we are going to use an intersection type to handle this instead. The first thing we have to do is add a class that has this active flag and then create our intersection type:

```
export interface IRecordState {
  IsActive : boolean;
}
```

```
export class RecordState implements IRecordState {
  public IsActive: boolean;
}

export type PersonRecord = RecordState & IPersonState;
```

Working with the database

Now that we have the ability to build the table and a representation of the state that we want to save into the table, we can turn our attention to connecting to the database and actually manipulating data in it. The first thing that we are going to do is define our class as a generic type that can work with any type that extends the RecordState class we just implemented:

```
export class Database<T extends RecordState> {

}
```

The reason we need to specify the type that we accept in this class is that most of the methods in it are going to either accept instances of that type as a parameter or return instances of that type to be worked with in the calling code.

As IndexedDB has become the standard client-side database, it has become something that can be directly accessed from the window object. TypeScript provides strong interfaces to support the database, so it is exposed as an IDBFactory type. This is important to us because it gives us access to operations such as opening the database. Effectively, this is the route that our code has to begin at to start manipulating data.

Whenever we want to open the database, we give it a name and version. If the database name does not exist, or we are attempting to open a newer version, then our application code needs to upgrade the database. This is where the TableBuilder code comes into play. As we have specified that TableBuilder implements an ITable interface to provide the ability to read values and build the underlying database table, we are going to use that (the table instance is passed into the constructor, as we will see shortly).

Working with IndexedDB can seem slightly strange at first because it emphasizes the use of event handlers a lot. For instance, when we attempt to open the database, if the code decides that an upgrade is needed, it triggers the upgradeneeded event, which we handle using onupgradeneeded. This use of events allows our code to behave asynchronously because the execution continues without waiting for the operation to complete. Then, when the event handler is triggered, it takes over the processing. We will be seeing a lot of this when we add our data methods to this class.

With this information in mind, we can write our `OpenDatabase` method to open the database with the value from the `Version` method. The first time we hit this code, we are going to need to write the database table. Even though this is a new table, it is treated as an upgrade so the `upgradeneeded` event is triggered. Again, we can see the benefit of having the ability to build the database in the `PersonalDetailsTableBuilder` class because we keep our database code free from knowing how to build the table. By doing this, we can reuse this class for writing other types to the database if we need to. When the database opens, the `onsuccess` handler will be triggered, and we will set an instance-level `database` member that we can use later on:

```
private OpenDatabase(): void {
    const open = this.indexDb.open(this.table.Database(),
this.table.Version());
    open.onupgradeneeded = (e: any) => {
        this.UpgradeDatabase(e.target.result);
    }
    open.onsuccess = (e: any) => {
        this.database = e.target.result;
    }
}

private UpgradeDatabase(database: IDBDatabase) {
    this.database = database;
    this.table.Build(this.database);
}
```

Now that we have the ability to build and open the table that is in place, we are going to write a constructor that accepts the `ITable` instance, which we will use to build the table:

```
private readonly indexDb: IDBFactory;
private database: IDBDatabase | null = null;
private readonly table: ITable;

constructor(table: ITable) {
    this.indexDb = window.indexedDB;
    this.table = table;
    this.OpenDatabase();
}
```

We have one last helper method to write for this class before we start writing the code that works with the data. In order to write data to the database, we have to create a transaction and retrieve an instance of the object store from it. Effectively, the object store represents a single table in our database. Essentially, we require an object store if we want to read or write data. As this is so common, we create a `GetObjectStore` method that returns the object store. For convenience, we are going to allow our transaction to treat every operation as read or write, which we specify when we call the transaction:

```
private GetObjectStore(): IDBObjectStore | null {
    try {
        const transaction: IDBTransaction =
this.database!.transaction(this.table.TableName(), "readwrite");
        const dbStore: IDBObjectStore =
transaction.objectStore(this.table.TableName());
        return dbStore;
    } catch (Error) {
        return null;
    }
}
```

As we go through the code, you will see that I have chosen to name the methods `Create`, `Read`, `Update`, and `Delete`. It is fairly common to name the first two methods `Load` and `Save`; however, I chose these method names deliberately, because when working with data in databases, we often use the term *CRUD operation*, where **CRUD** refers to **Create**, **Read**, **Update**, and **Delete**. By adopting this naming convention, I hope that this solidifies this connection for you.

The first (and simplest) method that we are going to add will allow us to save a record to the database. The `Create` method takes in an individual record, gets the object store, and adds the record to the database:

```
public Create(state: T): void {
    const dbStore = this.GetObjectStore();
    dbStore!.add(state);
}
```

When I was originally writing the code for this chapter, I wrote the Read and Write methods to use callback methods. The idea behind the callback method was simply to accept a function that our methods could *call back to* when the success event handlers were triggered. When we look at a lot of IndexedDB samples, we can see that they tend to adopt this type of convention. Before we look at the finalized version, let's take a look at what the Read method originally looked like:

```
public Read(callback: (value: T[]) => void) {
    const dbStore = this.GetObjectStore();
        const items : T[] = new Array<T>();
        const request: IDBRequest = dbStore!.openCursor();
        request.onsuccess = (e: any) => {
            const cursor: IDBCursorWithValue = e.target.result;
            if (cursor) {
                const result: T = cursor.value;
                if (result.IsActive) {
                    items.push(result);
                }
                cursor.continue();
            } else {
                // When cursor is null, that is the point that we want to
                // return back to our calling code.
                callback(items);
            }
        }
    }
}
```

The method opens by getting the object store and using it to open something called a cursor. A cursor provides us with the ability to read a record and move onto the next one; so, when the cursor is opened, the success event is triggered, which means that we enter the onsuccess event handler. As this happens asynchronously, the Read method completes, so we will rely on the callback to transfer the actual values back to the class that called it. The rather strange-looking callback: (value: T[]) => void is the actual callback that we will use to return the array of T items back to the calling code.

Inside the success event handler, we get the result from the event, which will be a cursor. Assuming that the cursor is not null, we get the result from the cursor and add the record to our array if the state of our record is active; this is why we apply the generic constraint to our class—so that we can access the IsActive property. We then call continue on the cursor, which moves on to the next record. The continue method results in success being fired again, which means that we re-enter the onsuccess handler, resulting in the same code happening for the next record. When there are no more records, the cursor will be null so the code will call back to the calling code with the array of items.

I mentioned that this was the initial implementation of this code. While callbacks are useful, they don't really take advantage of the power that TypeScript gives us. What this misses is the ability to use promises in our code base. As we are relying on a promise, we are going to gather all of the records together before we return them to the calling code. This means that we will have some minor structural differences to the logic inside our `success` handler:

```
public Read() : Promise<T[]> {
    return new Promise((response) => {
        const dbStore = this.GetObjectStore();
        const items : T[] = new Array<T>();
        const request: IDBRequest = dbStore!.openCursor();
        request.onsuccess = (e: any) => {
            const cursor: IDBCursorWithValue = e.target.result;
            if (cursor) {
                const result: T = cursor.value;
                if (result.IsActive) {
                    items.push(result);
                }
                cursor.continue();
            } else {
                // When cursor is null, that is the point that we want to
                // return back to our calling code.
                response(items);
            }
        }
    });
}
```

As this is returning a promise, we drop the callback from the method signature and return a promise of an array of `T`. One of the things we have to be aware of is that the scope of the array we are going to use to store the results in has to be outside the `success` event handler; otherwise, we would reallocate it every time we hit `onsuccess`. What is interesting about this code is how similar it is to the callback version. All we have done is change the return type while dropping the callback from the method signature. The response part of our promise acts in place of the callback.

In general, if our code accepts a callback, we can convert it to a promise by returning a promise with the callback moved from the method signature into the promise itself.

The logic for our cursor is the same as we rely on the cursor check to see whether we have a value, and, if we do, we push it onto our array. When there are no more records, we call the response on our promise so that the calling code can work with it in the `then` part of the promise. To illustrate this, let's examine the `loadPeople` code in `PersonalDetails`:

```
private loadPeople = () => {
  this.people = new Array<PersonRecord>();
  this.dataLayer.Read().then(people => {
    this.people = people;
    this.setState(this.state);
  });
}
```

The `Read` method is the most complicated part of our CRUD operation. The next method that we are going to write is the `Update` method. When the record has been updated, we want to reload the records in our list so that changes to the first or last names are updated on the screen. The object store operation that updates our record is `put`. If it completes successfully, it raises the success event, which leads our code to call the `resolve` property on our promise. As we are returning a `Promise<void>` type, we have the ability to use the `async`/`await` syntax when calling this:

```
public Update(state: T) : Promise<void> {
    return new Promise((resolve) =>
    {
        const dbStore = this.GetObjectStore();
        const innerRequest : IDBRequest = dbStore!.put(state);
        innerRequest.onsuccess = () => {
          resolve();
        }
    });
}
```

Our final database method is the `Delete` method. The syntax of the `Delete` method is very similar to that of the `Update` method—the only real difference is that it just takes the index, which tells it what row to `delete` in the database:

```
public Delete(idx: number | string) : Promise<void> {
    return new Promise((resolve) =>
    {
        const dbStore = this.GetObjectStore();
        const innerRequest : IDBRequest = dbStore!.delete(idx.toString());
        innerRequest.onsuccess = () => {
          resolve();
        }
    });
}
```

Accessing the database from PersonalDetails

We can now add database support to our `PersonalDetails` class. The first thing we are going to do is update the member variables and constructor to bring in the database support and store the list of people we want to display:

1. First, we add the members:

```
private readonly dataLayer: Database<PersonRecord>;
private people: IPersonState[];
```

2. Next, we update the constructor to hook up to the database and create `TableBuilder` using `PersonalDetailsTableBuilder`:

```
const tableBuilder : PersonalDetailsTableBuilder = new
PersonalDetailsTableBuilder();
this.dataLayer = new Database(tableBuilder.Build());
```

3. One thing that we still have to do is add the ability to show people into our `render` method. In a similar way to displaying the validation failures using `map`, we are going to apply `map` to the `people` array:

```
let people = null;
if (this.people) {
  const copyThis = this;
  people = this.people.map(function it(p) {
  return (<Row key={p.PersonId}><Col lg="6"><label >{p.FirstName}
{p.LastName}</label></Col>
  <Col lg="3">
    <Button value={p.PersonId} color="link"
onClick={copyThis.setActive}>Edit</Button>
  </Col>
  <Col lg="3">
    <Button value={p.PersonId} color="link"
onClick={copyThis.delete}>Delete</Button>
  </Col></Row>)
  }, this);
}
```

4. This is then rendered out with the following:

```
<Col>
  <Col>
  <Row>
    <Col>{people}</Col>
  </Row>
  <Row>
```

```
        <Col lg="6"><Button size="lg" color="success"
onClick={this.loadPeople}>Load</Button></Col>
        <Col lg="6"><Button size="lg" color="info"
onClick={this.clear}>New Person</Button></Col>
      </Row>
      </Col>
    </Col>
```

The **Load** button is one of a number of places that the `loadPeople` method is called from in this class. We will see it in use when we update and then delete the records.

When working with database code, it is common to encounter situations where the deletion of a record should not physically delete the record from the database. We might not want to physically delete it because another record points to that one, and so deleting it will break the other record. Alternatively, we might have to keep it in place for auditing purposes. In those cases, it is common to do something called a soft delete (a hard delete being the one where the record is deleted from the database). With a soft delete, there is a flag on a record that indicates whether the record is active. While `IPersonState` does not provide this flag, the `PersonRecord` type does because it is an intersection of `IPersonState` and `RecordState`. Our `delete` method is going to change `IsActive` to `false` and update the database with that value. The code that loads the people already understands that it is retrieving records where `IsActive` is `true`, so these deleted records will disappear as soon as the list is reloaded. This means that, while we wrote a Delete method in our database code, we aren't actually going to be using it. It's there as a handy reference and you might want to change the code to do a hard delete but this isn't necessary for our purpose.

The **Delete** button is going to trigger the delete operation. As there can be a number of items in this list, and we cannot assume that the user is going to select a person before deleting them, we need to find that person from the list of people before we attempt to delete them. Looking back at the code to render out the people, we can see that the ID of the person is passed across to the event handler. Before we write our event handler, we are going to write the method that asynchronously deletes the person from the database. The first thing we are going to do in this method is find the person using the `find` array method:

```
private async DeletePerson(person : string) {
  const foundPerson = this.people.find((element : IPersonState) => {
    return element.PersonId === person;
  });
  if (!foundPerson) {
    return;
  }
}
```

Assuming that we find the person from the array, we need to get the person into a state where we can set `IsActive` to `false`. We start off by creating a new instance of `RecordState`, as follows:

```
const personState : IRecordState = new RecordState();
personState.IsActive = false;
```

We have an intersection type, `PersonRecord`, made up of the intersection of the person and record states. We are going to spread `foundPerson` and `personState` to give us our `PersonRecord` type. With this in place, we are going to call our `Update` database method. What we want to do, when our update has completed, is reload the list of people and clear the item currently in the editor—just in case it's the one that we have just deleted; we don't want the user to be able to reinstate the record simply because they save it again with `IsActive` set to `true`. We are going to use the fact that we can use `await` on code written as a promise to wait until the record has been updated before we carry on with the processing:

```
const state : PersonRecord = {...foundPerson, ...personState};
await this.dataLayer.Update(state);
this.loadPeople();
this.clear();
```

The `clear` method simply changes the state back to our default state. That's the whole reason we passed it into this component, so that we can easily clear the values back to their default state:

```
private clear = () => {
  this.setState(this.defaultState);
}
```

Using our `delete` event handler, the full code for this is as follows:

```
private delete = (event : any) => {
  const person : string = event.target.value;
  this.DeletePerson(person);
}

private async DeletePerson(person : string) {
  const foundPerson = this.people.find((element : IPersonState) => {
    return element.PersonId === person;
  });
  if (!foundPerson) {
    return;
  }
  const personState : IRecordState = new RecordState();
  personState.IsActive = false;
```

```
    const state : PersonRecord = {...foundPerson, ...personState};
    await this.dataLayer.Update(state);
    this.loadPeople();
    this.clear();
}
```

The last database operations we need to hook up to are triggered from the **Save** button. What happens with the save depends on whether we have previously saved the record, which can be identified by whether `PersonId` is empty. Before we attempt to save the record, we have to determine whether it can be saved. This comes down to checking whether the validation says we can save or not. If there are outstanding validation failures, we are going to alert the users that they cannot save the record:

```
private savePerson = () => {
  if (!this.canSave) {
    alert(`Cannot save this record with missing or incorrect items`);
    return;
  }
}
```

Similarly to how we used the deletion technique, we are going to create our `PersonRecord` type by bringing the state together with `RecordState`. This time, we set `IsActive` to `true` so that it is picked up as a live record:

```
const personState : IRecordState = new RecordState();
personState.IsActive = true;
const state : PersonRecord = {...this.state, ...personState};
```

When we insert our record, we need to assign it a unique value for `PersonId`. For simplicity, we are just going to use it with the current date and time. When we add the person to the database, we reload the list of people and clear the current record from the editor so that the user cannot insert a duplicate just by clicking on **Save** again:

```
if (state.PersonId === "") {
  state.PersonId = Date.now().toString();
  this.dataLayer.Create(state);
  this.loadPeople();
  this.clear();
}
```

The code to update the person leverages the features of a promise so that the list of people is updated immediately after it has finished saving. We do not need to clear the current record in this case because if the user clicks on **Save** again, there is no possibility that we are going to create a new record—but we will simply update the current one:

```
else {
    this.dataLayer.Update(state).then(rsn => this.loadPeople());
}
```

The completed method for saving is as follows:

```
private savePerson = () => {
  if (!this.canSave) {
    alert(`Cannot save this record with missing or incorrect items`);
    return;
  }
  if (state.PersonId === "") {
    state.PersonId = Date.now().toString();
    this.dataLayer.Create(state);
    this.loadPeople();
    this.clear();
  }
  else {
    this.dataLayer.Update(state).then(rsn => this.loadPeople());
  }
}
```

There is one last method that we need to cover. What you may have noticed is that we have no way of selecting and displaying a user in the textboxes when we click on the **Edit** button. Logic dictates that pressing the button should trigger an event that passes PersonId to an event handler, which we can use to find the relevant person from the list; we have already seen this type of behavior when using the **Delete** button, so we have a good idea of what the selection portion of the code will look like. Once we have the person, we call setState to update the state, which will update the display through the power of binding:

```
private setActive = (event : any) => {
  const person : string = event.target.value;
  const state = this.people.find((element : IPersonState) => {
    return element.PersonId === person;
  });
  if (state) {
    this.setState(state);
  }
}
```

We now have all the code we need to build our contact manager with React. We have satisfied the requirements that we set out at the start of the chapter and our display looks close enough to our mock layout.

Enhancements

The `Create` method has a potential problem in that it assumes that it succeeds immediately. It does not handle the `success` event for the operation. Additionally, there is a further issue in that `add` operations have a `complete` event because the `success` event may fire before the record has been successfully written to the disk, and, if the transaction fails, the `complete` event is not raised. You can convert the `Create` method so that it uses a promise and resumes processing when the `success` event is raised. Then, update the insert portion of the component to reload once this has been completed.

The deletion resets the state even if the user wasn't editing the record that was deleted. So, enhance the delete code to only reset the state if the record being edited is the same as the one that was deleted.

Summary

This chapter introduced us to the popular React framework and discussed how we can use it with TypeScript to build a modern client side application to add contact information. We started by defining the requirements and creating a mock layout of our application before we created the basic implementation using `create-react-app` with the `react-scripts-ts` script version. To leverage Bootstrap 4 in a React-friendly way, we added in the `reactstrap` package.

After discussing how React uses the special JSX and TSX formats to control the way it renders, we moved on to customizing the `App` component and adding our own custom TSX components. With these components, we looked at passing properties and setting up state, which we then used to create two-way bindings. With the bindings, we discussed how to validate user inputs by creating reusable validators that were then applied to validation classes. As part of the validation, we added two regular expressions, which we analyzed to understand how they were constructed.

Finally, we examined how to save personal information in the IndexedDB database. The first part of this was to understand how to build the database and tables using table builders, which was complemented by looking at how to work with the database. We looked at how to convert a callback-based method to use the promises API to provide asynchronous support as well as the difference between soft and hard deletes of data.

In the next chapter, we are going to move on to using Angular with MongoDB, Express, and Node.js, which are collectively known as the MEAN stack, to build a photo gallery application.

Questions

1. What gives React the ability to mix visual elements with code inside the `render` method?
2. Why does React use `className` and `htmlFor`?
3. We saw that phone numbers can be validated using the regular expression `^(?:\\((?:[0-9]{3})\\)|(?:[0-9]{3}))[-. ]?(?:[0-9]{3})[-. ]?(?:[0-9]{4})$`. We also discussed that there was an alternative way of representing a single digit. How could we convert this expression to give exactly the same result with the alternative representation?
4. Why do we create validators separately from validation code?
5. What is the difference between a soft delete and a hard delete?

Further reading

- React is a big topic. In order to find out more about the ideas behind it, I recommend *React and React Native – Second Edition* (https://www.packtpub.com/application-development/react-and-react-native-second-edition).
- For more information on using React with TypeScript, I recommend *Learn React with TypeScript 3* by Carl Rippon (https://www.packtpub.com/web-development/learn-react-typescript-3).
- Packt also publishes the excellent book *JavaScript Regular Expressions* by Loiane Groner and Gabriel Manricks (https://www.packtpub.com/web-development/javascript-regular-expressions), if you want to take your regular expression knowledge to the next level.

4
The MEAN Stack - Building a Photo Gallery

Nowadays, it's almost impossible to write Node.js applications and not hear about the MEAN stack. MEAN is the acronym used to describe a set of common technologies used on both the client and server side to build web applications with persistent server-side storage. The technologies that make up the **MEAN** stack are **MongoDB**, **Express** (sometimes known as **Express.js**), **Angular**, and **Node.js**.

We are ready to build on the knowledge we developed in the previous chapters to write a photo gallery application using the MEAN stack. Unlike previous chapters, we will not be using Bootstrap in this chapter, preferring to use Angular Material instead.

The following topics will be covered in this chapter:

- The components of the MEAN stack
- Creating our application
- Using Angular Material to create the UI
- Using Material to add our navigation
- Creating a file upload component
- Using services to read the file in
- Introducing Express support into our application
- Providing Express routing support
- Introducing MongoDB
- Displaying images
- Using RxJS to watch for images
- Transferring data using `HttpClient`

Technical requirements

The finished project can be downloaded from `https://github.com/PacktPublishing/`
`Advanced-TypeScript-3-Programming-Projects/tree/master/Chapter04`.

After downloading the project, you will have to install the package requirements using `npm`
`install`.

The MEAN stack

When we use the term the MEAN stack, we are talking about a set of separate JavaScript
technologies that go together to create web applications that span both the client and server
side. MEAN is an acronym of the core technologies used:

- **MongoDB**: This is something called a document database, which is used to store
data in JSON form. Document databases are different from relational databases,
so if you have come from a technology such as SQL Server or Oracle, it can take a
little bit of time to adjust to the way that document databases work.
- **Express**: This is a backend web application framework that sits on top of Node.js.
The idea behind having Express in the stack is that it simplifies things that
Node.js provides on the server side. While Node.js can do everything that
Express does, the complexity of writing code to do things such as adding cookies
or routing web requests means that Express's simplification aids us by cutting
development time.
- **Angular**: Angular is a client-side framework that runs the client side of an
application. Typically, Angular is used to create **Single-Page Applications**
(**SPAs**), whereby small sections of the client are updated rather than having to
reload the whole page when a navigation event happens.
- **Node.js**: Node.js is the server-side runtime environment for an application. We
can think of this as the web server.

The following diagram shows where the components of the MEAN stack exist in terms of our application architecture. The part of the application that our user sees, sometimes known as the frontend, is the client in this diagram. The rest of our application is commonly referred to as the backend and is the web server and database in the diagram:

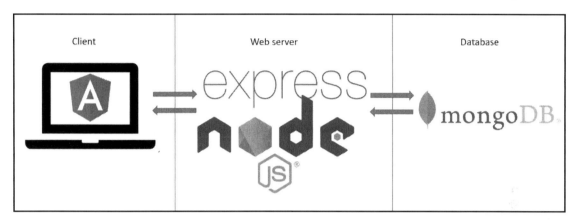

 There is an equivalent for using React in place of Angular. It's known as the MERN stack.

Project overview

The project we are going to build in this chapter will introduce us to writing server-side applications as well as introduce us to the popular Angular framework. We will build a picture gallery application where our users can upload pictures and save them in a server-side database that allows them to view them again later.

As long as you work alongside the code in the GitHub repository, this chapter should take about three hours to complete. The finished application will look like this:

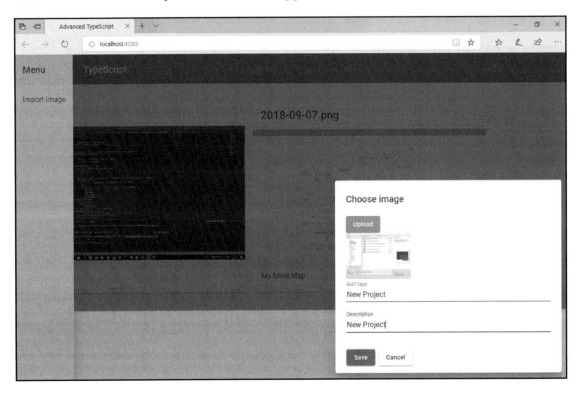

This chapter is not intended to be a comprehensive tutorial on all aspects of the MEAN stack. By the end of the chapter, we will only have begun to scratch the surface of what the different parts provide. As we are introducing many topics here, we will focus more on those topics than on advanced features of TypeScript because this could lead to information overload, but we will still be covering features such as generic constraints and fluent code, even though we aren't going to refer to them explicitly. At this point, we should be familiar enough with them to recognize them when we encounter them.

Getting started

Just as in the previous chapter, this chapter will use Node.js, which is available at `https://nodejs.org`. We will also be using the following components:

- The Angular **Command-Line Interface** (**CLI**) (I'm using version 7.2.2)
- `cors` (version 2.8.5 or greater)
- `body-parser` (version 1.18.3 or greater)
- `express` (version 4.16.4 or greater)
- `mongoose` (version 5.4.8 or greater)
- `@types/cors` (version 2.8.4 or greater)
- `@types/body-parser` (version 1.17.0 or greater)
- `@types/express` (version 4.16.0 or greater)
- `@types/mongodb` (version 3.1.19 or greater)
- `@types/mongoose` (version 5.3.11 or greater)

We will also be using MongoDB. The Community Edition is available at `https://www.mongodb.com/download-center/community`.

MongoDB also comes with a GUI that makes it easier to view, query, and edit your MongoDB databases. MongoDB Community Edition can be downloaded from `https://www.mongodb.com/download-center/compass`.

Creating an Angular photo gallery with the MEAN stack

As we did in previous chapters, we are going to start out by defining the requirements of our application:

- The user must be able to select a picture to transfer to the server
- The user will be able to supply additional metadata for the pictures, such as descriptions
- Uploaded pictures will be saved in a database with the metadata
- The user will be able to automatically view the uploaded pictures

Understanding Angular

Angular was created as a platform for creating client-side applications using a combination of HTML and TypeScript. Originally, Angular was written in JavaScript (it was known as Angular.js back then), but it underwent a complete rewrite using TypeScript and was rebranded to just Angular. The architecture of Angular itself revolves around a series of modules that we can bring into our application or write ourselves, which can contain services and components that we can use to build up our client-side code.

Originally, one of the key drivers behind Angular was the idea that fully reloading web pages is a wasteful practice. So many websites were serving the same navigation, headers, footers, sidebars, and more that it was a waste of time reloading those items every time the user navigated to a new page because they hadn't actually changed. Angular helped to popularize an architecture known as the SPAs, where only small parts of the page that need to change actually do so. This reduces the amount of traffic that a web page has to deal with so that, when done properly, the responsiveness of a client application is increased.

The following screenshot shows a typical SPA format. The vast majority of the page is static in nature so it doesn't have to be re-sent, but the **Junk Email** section in the center will be dynamic—only that part needs to be updated. This is the beauty of SPAs:

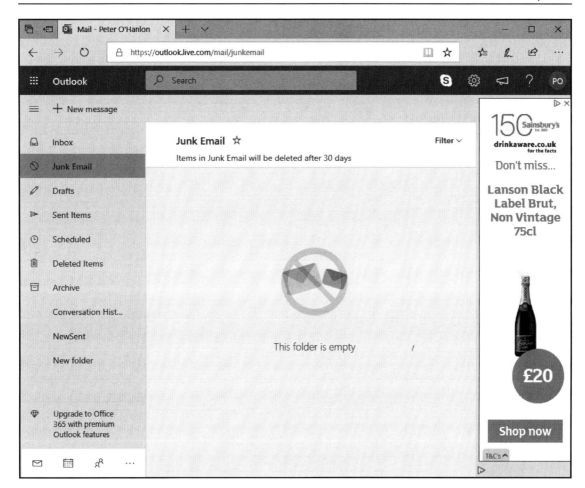

This does not mean that we can't create multi-page applications in Angular. It just means that unless we have a real need to create a multi-page application, then Angular SPA applications are the way we should write our Angular applications.

Now that we have an idea of what Angular is about, we can move on to using Angular to write our client.

Creating our application

Unless you have recently installed Angular, you need to install it using npm. The part that we are going to install is the Angular CLI. This gives us everything we need to run from Command Prompt to generate our application, add components, scaffold the application, and more:

```
npm install -g @angular/cli
```

As we are going to develop both client and server code, it will be helpful to keep our code together to do this; therefore, we are going to create Client and Server folders under a common directory. Any Angular commands will be run in the Client folder. It is relatively common to share code between the client and server side, so this arrangement is a simple way to keep the application together and simplify sharing.

Creating an application with Angular is easily accomplished using the ng new command, which was added to our system when we added the Angular CLI. We are going to specify command-line arguments to choose SCSS to generate our CSS, as well as choosing the prefix we want to give to any components that we create:

```
ng new Chapter04 --style scss --prefix atp
```

The naming convention I have chosen to follow reflects the name of the book, so we use atp to reflect *Advanced TypeScript Projects*. While we aren't going to make heavy use of CSS in this chapter, I tend to use SCSS as my CSS pre-processor more than I use raw CSS because it has a rich syntax for using things such as style mixins, which means that this is the style engine I tend to go to by default. The reason that we are choosing to use the atp prefix is to make our component selectors unique. Suppose that we had a component that we wanted to call label; obviously, this would clash with the built-in HTML label. To avoid the clash, our component selector would be the atp label. As HTML controls never use hyphens, we guarantee that we aren't going to *collide* with existing control selectors.

We are going to accept the installation defaults, so just press *Enter* when prompted about whether or not to add Angular routing support. When the installation completes, we are going to start our Angular server, which also watches to see whether files change and rebuilds the application on the fly. Normally, I would install all of the required components before I did this part, but it is useful to see exactly what Angular gives us as a starting point and the ability to view live changes is highly useful:

```
ng serve --open
```

Unlike React, the default web address for opening our application is `http://localhost:4200`. When the browser opens, it displays the default Angular sample page. Obviously, we are going to remove lots from this, but in the short term, we are going to keep this page as it is while we start adding some of the infrastructure we need.

Angular creates a lot of files for us, so it's worth identifying which ones are the ones that we are going to work with the most and what purpose they serve.

App.Module.ts

During the process of developing large Angular applications, especially if we are just one of a number of teams developing different parts of the same overall application, it's common to break them down into modules. We can view this file as our entry point into saying how a module is grouped together. For our purposes, we are interested in two sections in the module definition covered by `@NgModule`.

The first section is the `declarations` section, which tells Angular what components we have developed. For our application, we will develop three components that belong in here—`AppComponent` (which is added by default), `FileuploadComponent`, and `PageBodyComponent`. Fortunately for us, when we use the Angular CLI to generate components, their declarations are automatically added into this section.

The other section we are interested in is the `imports` section. This tells us what external modules need to be imported into our application. We cannot just reference a feature from an external module in our application; we actually have to tell Angular that we are going to use the module that the feature comes from. This means that Angular is very good at minifying the dependencies that we have when we deploy the application because it will only deploy modules that we have said that we are using.

As we go through this chapter, we will add items into this section in order to enable features such as Angular Material support.

Using Angular Material for our UI

The frontend of our application is going to use something called Angular Material instead of relying on Bootstrap. We are going to look at Material because it's widely used with Angular applications; therefore, if you are going to develop with Angular commercially, there's a good chance that you will use it in your career at some point.

Angular Material was built by the Angular team to bring Material Design components to Angular. The idea behind them is that they integrate seamlessly into the Angular development process so that they feel no different to using standard HTML components. These design components go well beyond what we can do with single standard controls, so we can easily build complex navigation layouts with them, for instance.

Material components bring behaviors and visual appearance together so that, out of the box, we can use them to create professional-looking applications with minimal effort on our part. To a certain extent, Material can be thought of as a similar experience to using Bootstrap. In this chapter, we are going to concentrate on using Material instead of Bootstrap.

A couple of paragraphs ago, we rather glibly mentioned that Angular Material brings Material Design components to Angular. This is a largely circular statement until we understand what Material Design is. If we search Google for the term, we get lots of articles telling us that Material Design is Google's design language.

Certainly, if we do Android development, the term comes up frequently because Android and Material are fundamentally linked. The idea behind Material is that it is in the best interests of our users if we can present interface elements in a way that is consistent. So, if we adopt Material, our applications will look familiar to users who are used to applications such as Gmail.

The term *design language* is too vague, though. What does it actually mean to us? Why does it have its own fancy term? In the same way that our own language is broken down and structured into words and punctuation, we can break visual elements down into structures such as color and depth. As an example, the language tells us what colors mean, so if we see a button with one color on one screen in our application, it should have the same underlying usage across other screens in our application; we wouldn't use a green button to signify **OK** on one dialog and then **Cancel** on another.

Installing Angular Material is a simple process. We run the following command to add support for Angular Material, the **Component Design Toolkit** (**CDK**), flexible layout support, and animation support:

```
ng add @angular/material @angular/cdk @angular/animation @angular/flex-
layout
```

During the installation of the libraries, we will be prompted to choose what theme we want to use. The most visible aspect of the theme is the color scheme that is applied.

We can choose from the following themes (examples of the themes are also supplied):

- Indigo/Pink (https://material.angular.io?theme=indigo-pink)
- Deep Purple/Amber (https://material.angular.io?theme=deeppurple-amber)
- Pink/Blue Grey (https://material.angular.io?theme=pink-bluegrey)
- Purple/Green (https://material.angular.io?theme=purple-green)
- Custom

For our application, we are going to use the Indigo/Pink theme.

We are also prompted about whether or not we want to add HammerJS support. This library provides gesture recognition so our applications can respond to things such as panning or rotating using touch or the mouse. Finally, we have to choose whether or not we want to set up browser animations for Angular Material.

 The CDK is an abstraction that says how common Material features work, but it does not say what they will look like. Without installing the CDK, many features of the Material library just won't work, so it's important to ensure that it is installed alongside @angular/material.

Using Material to add navigation

We will see, over and over again, that so much of what we need to do to add features to our application requires us to start with changes in app.module.ts. Material is no different, so we start by adding the following import lines:

```
import { LayoutModule } from '@angular/cdk/layout';
import { MatToolbarModule, MatButtonModule, MatSidenavModule,
MatIconModule, MatListModule } from '@angular/material';
```

Now that the modules are available to us, we need to reference them in the `import` section of `NgModule`. Any module listed in this section will have its capabilities available in the templates that are in our application. When we add side-navigation support, for instance, we are relying on the fact that we have made `MatSidenavModule` available in this section:

```
imports: [
    ...
    LayoutModule,
    MatToolbarModule,
    MatButtonModule,
    MatSidenavModule,
    MatIconModule,
    MatListModule,
]
```

We are going to set our application to use side navigation (the navigation strip that appears down the side of the screen). Structurally, we need to add three elements to enable side navigation:

- `mat-sidenav-container` to host side navigation
- `mat-sidenav` to display side navigation
- `mat-sidenav-content` to add the content that we are going to display

To start, we are going to add the following content to our `app.component.html` page:

```
<mat-sidenav-container class="sidenav-container">
  <mat-sidenav #drawer class="sidenav" fixedInViewport="true"
[opened]="false">
  </mat-sidenav>
  <mat-sidenav-content>
  </mat-sidenav-content>
</mat-sidenav-container>
```

The `mat-sidenav` line sets up a couple of the behaviors that we will exploit. We want the navigation to be fixed in the viewport and we give it the ID of drawer through the use of `#drawer`. We will use this ID shortly, when we trigger toggling whether the drawer is open or not.

Possibly the most interesting part of this line is `[opened]="false"`. This is the first point at which we encounter binding in our application. The use of `[]` here tells us that we want to bind to a particular property, `opened` in this case, and set it to `false`. As we will see as we go through this chapter, Angular has a rich binding syntax.

Now that we have the container to hold our navigation, we are going to add side-navigation content. We are going to add a toolbar to hold the Menu text and a navigation list that allows the user to import an image:

```
<mat-toolbar>Menu</mat-toolbar>
<mat-nav-list>
  <a mat-list-item>Import Image</a>
</mat-nav-list>
```

Using mat-list-item in a standard anchor tag simply tells the Material engine that we want to lay the anchors in a list. Effectively, this section is an unordered list of anchors that are styled using Material styles.

Now, we want to add the ability to toggle our navigation. The way that we do this is by adding a toolbar to our navigation content area. This toolbar will host a button that triggers the opening of the side-navigation drawer. In the mat-sidenav-content section, add the following:

```
<mat-toolbar color="primary">
  <button type="button" aria-label="Toggle sidenav" mat-icon-button
(click)="drawer.toggle()">
    <mat-icon aria-label="Side nav toggle icon">menu</mat-icon>
  </button>
</mat-toolbar>
```

The button uses another example of binding here—in this case, reacting to the click event—to trigger the toggle operation on the mat-sidenav item with the drawer ID. Rather than using [eventName] to bind to commands, we use (eventName) instead. Inside the button, we host mat-icon to represent the image used to toggle the navigation. In keeping with the philosophy that Material design represents a common way to show applications, Angular Material provides us with a number of standard icons, such as menu.

The Material fonts that we are using represent certain words, such as home and menu, as particular images via something called **ligatures**. This is a standard typography term that just means that there are well-known combinations of letters, numbers, and symbols that can be represented as an image. For instance, if we had mat-icon with the text home, this would be represented as a home icon.

Creating our first component – the FileUpload component

The `Import Image` link on our navigation has to actually do something, so we are going to write a component that will be displayed inside a dialog. As we are going to upload a file, we are going to call this `FileUpload`, and creating it is as simple as running the following Angular CLI command:

```
ng generate component components/fileupload
```

We can shorten these standard Angular commands if we want, so we can use `ng g c` instead of `ng generate component`.

This command creates four files for us:

- `fileupload.component.html`: The HTML template for our component.
- `fileupload.component.scss`: Anything that we need to convert into CSS for our component.
- `fileupload.component.spec.ts`: Now, `spec.ts` files are used when we want to run unit tests against our Angular applications. Properly testing web applications is outside the scope of this book as it's a book in its own right.
- `fileupload.component.ts`: The logic for the component.

Running the `ng` command to generate the component also results in it being added into the `declarations` section in `app.module.ts`.

When we open up `fileupload.component.ts`, the structure roughly looks like this (ignoring the imports at the top):

```
@Component({
  selector: 'atp-fileupload',
  templateUrl: './fileupload.component.html',
  styleUrls: ['./fileupload.component.scss']
})
export class FileuploadComponent implements OnInit {
  ngOnInit() {
  }
}
```

Here, we can see that Angular is making full use of TypeScript features that we have already looked at. In this case, `FileuploadComponent` has a `Component` decorator that tells Angular that we use `atp-fileupload` when we want to use a `FileuploadComponent` instance in our HTML. As we are using a separate HTML template and style, the other parts of the `@Component` decorator identify where those elements are. We could define styles and templates directly in this class, but in general, it's better to separate them out into their own files.

 We can see our naming convention here, having specified `atp` when we created our application. It's a good idea to use something meaningful. When working in a team, you should find out what the standard is that your team follows and, if there is no standard, you should take the time to agree on how you want this to be named up front.

One of the features of the dialog is that it will show us a preview of the image that the user selects. We are going to separate the logic for reading the image from the component to keep a nice and clean separation of concerns going on.

Previewing files using a service

One of the challenges of developing UI applications is that there is a tendency for logic to creep into views that does not belong there. It becomes convenient to put a piece of logic in our `ts` views file because we know that the view is going to call out to it, but it does something that does not have any visible impact on the client.

We might, for instance, want to write some values from the UI back to the server. The only part of this that is relevant to the view is the data part; the actual writing to the server is a completely different responsibility. It would be useful to us if we had a simple way to create external classes that we could inject wherever we needed so that we would not need to worry about how to instantiate them. They would just be available to us to use whenever we needed them. Fortunately for us, the authors of Angular saw that there would be a need for this and provided us with services.

A service is simply a class that uses the `@Injectable` decorator and has an entry in the `declarations` section of the module. Apart from those requirements, there's nothing else that is needed, so we could easily handcraft the class if we needed to. While we could do this, there's no real reason to, because Angular helps us to generate the service using the following command:

```
ng generate service <<servicename>>
```

When we create the `service`, we don't actually have to add `service` at the end of the name as this command automatically does that for us. To see how this works, we are going to create a `service` that takes a file that has been chosen using the file selector and then reads it in so that it can be displayed back in the image upload dialog and on the main screen, or transferred over to be saved in the database. We start with the following command:

```
ng generate service Services/FilePreviewService.
```

 I like to generate my services in a `Services` sub-folder. Putting this in the filename creates it in the `Services` folder.

The `ng generate service` command gives us the following basic outline:

```
import { Injectable } from '@angular/core';
@Injectable({
 providedIn: 'root'
})
export class FilePreviewService {
}
```

Reading a file can be a time-consuming process, so we know that we want this operation to happen asynchronously. As we discussed in earlier chapters, we could do this with a callback, but a much better method is to use a promise. We add the following method call to the service:

```
public async Preview(files: any): Promise<IPictureModel> {
}
```

As this is the point at which we are going to read the file in, this is when we are going to create the model that we are going to use to pass the data around our application. The model that we are going to use looks like this:

```
export interface IPictureModel {
  Image: string;
  Name: string;
  Description: string;
  Tags: string;
}
export class PictureModel implements IPictureModel {
  Image: string;
  Name: string;
  Description: string;
  Tags: string;
}
```

`Image` holds the actual image that we are going to read in, and `Name` is the name of the file. This is why we populate this model at this point; we are working with the file itself so this is the point at which we have the filename available to us. The `Description` and `Tags` strings will be added by the image upload component. While we could create an intersection type at that point, for a simple model like this, it is enough to have a single model hold them.

The fact that we have said that we are using `Promise` means that we need to `return` an appropriate `Promise` from our `Preview` method:

```
return await new Promise((resolve, reject) => {});
```

Inside the `Promise`, we are going to create an instance of our model. As it is good practice, we are going to add some defensive code to ensure that we have an image file. If the file is not an image file, we are going to reject it, which can be handled gracefully by the calling code:

```
if (files.length === 0) {
  return;
}
const file = files[0];
if (file.type.match(/image\/*/) === null) {
  reject(`The file is not an image file.`);
  return;
}
const imageModel: IPictureModel = new PictureModel();
```

When we reach this point, we know that we have a valid file, so we are going to set the name in the model using the filename, as well as using `FileReader` to read the image using `readAsDataURL`. When the read finishes, the `onload` event is raised, allowing us to add the image data to our model. At this point, we can resolve our promise:

```
const reader = new FileReader();
reader.onload = (evt) => {
  imageModel.Image = reader.result;
  resolve(imageModel);
};
reader.readAsDataURL(file);
```

Using the service in the dialog

Now that we have a working `preview` service, we can use it in our dialog. In order to use it, we are going to pass it into our constructor. As the service is injectable, we can let Angular take care of injecting it for us as long as we add an appropriate reference in our constructor. At the same time, we are going to add in a reference to the dialog itself, as well as a set of declarations that will be used in the corresponding HTML template:

```
protected imageSource: IPictureModel | null;
protected message: any;
protected description: string;
protected tags: string;

constructor(
  private dialog: MatDialogRef<FileuploadComponent>,
  private preview: FilePreviewService) { }
```

 The technique that allows Angular to automatically build up constructors with dependencies, without us having to explicitly instantiate them with `new`, is known as dependency injection. This fancy term simply means that we tell Angular what our class needs and leave the building of the objects for that class to Angular. In effect, we tell Angular *what* we need without worrying about *how* it will be built. The act of building the classes can lead to very complex internal hierarchies, as the dependency injection engine may have to build up classes that our code relies on as well.

With this reference in place, we are going to create a method to accept the file selection from the file upload component and call our `Preview` method. `catch` is in place to cater for our defensive coding in the service, as well as to cater for situations where the user tries to upload a non-image file. If the file is invalid, the dialog will show a message informing the user of this:

```
public OnImageSelected(files: any): void {
  this.preview.Preview(files).then(r => {
    this.imageSource = r;
  }).catch(r => {
    this.message = r;
  });
}
```

The last thing we need to do with the code side of the dialog is to allow the user to close the dialog and pass the selected values back to the calling code. We update the image source description and tags with the relevant local values. The `close` method closes the current dialog and returns `imageSource` back to the calling code:

```
public Save(): void {
  this.imageSource.Description = this.description;
  this.imageSource.Tags = this.tags;
  this.dialog.close(this.imageSource);
}
```

The file upload component template

The final bit of work on our component is the actual HTML template in `fileupload.component.html`. As this is going to be a Material dialog, we are going to use a number of Material tags here. The simplest of these tags is used to add the dialog title, which is a standard header tag with the `mat-dialog-title` attribute. The reason that this attribute is used is to anchor the title to the top of the dialog so that if there was any scrolling, the title would stay fixed in place:

```
<h2 mat-dialog-title>Choose image</h2>
```

With the title anchored to the top, we are ready to add our content and action buttons. First, we are going to add our content using the `mat-dialog-content` tag:

```
<mat-dialog-content>
  ...
</mat-dialog-content>
```

The first element inside our content is the message that will be displayed if the message in the code for the component is set. The test to show whether or not the message is displayed uses another Angular binding, `*ngIf`. Here, the Angular binding engine evaluates the expression and renders out the value if the expression is true. In this case, it's checking to see whether a message is present. It's probably not going to come as a surprise to learn that the funny-looking `{{}}` code is also a binding. This one is used to write out the text of the item being bound to, in this case the message:

```
<h3 *ngIf="message">{{message}}</h3>
```

The next part of the change is one of my favorite parts of the application. There is no Material version of the standard HTML file component, so if we want to display a modern-looking equivalent, we have to show the file input as a hidden component and trick it into thinking it has been activated when the user presses a **Material** button. The file upload input is given the `fileUpload` ID and triggered when the button is clicked using `(click)="fileUpload.click()"`. When the user chooses something, the change event triggers the `OnImageSelected` code we wrote a couple of minutes ago:

```
<button class="mat-raised-button mat-accent" md-button
(click)="fileUpload.click()">Upload</button>
  <input hidden #fileUpload type="file" accept="image/*"
(change)="OnImageSelected(fileUpload.files)" />
```

Adding an image preview is as simple as adding an `img` tag that is bound to the preview image created when we successfully read in the image:

```
<div>
  <img src="{{imageSource.Image}}" height="100" *ngIf="imageSource" />
</div>
```

Finally, we need to add in fields for reading in the tags and description. We lay these out inside the `mat-form-field` sections. `matInput` tells the template engine what styling should be put in place for text input. The most interesting part is the use of the `[(ngModel)]="..."` part. This applies model binding for us, telling the binding engine what field to use from our underlying TypeScript component code:

```
<mat-form-field>
  <input type="text" matInput placeholder="Add tags" [(ngModel)]="tags" />
</mat-form-field>
<mat-form-field>
  <input matInput placeholder="Description" [(ngModel)]="description" />
</mat-form-field>
```

If you have previously used an earlier version of Angular (prior to version 6), you have probably come across `formControlName` as a means of binding to values. In Angular 6+, trying to combine `formControlName` and `ngModel` no longer works. See `https://next.angular.io/api/forms/FormControlName#use-with-ngmodel` for more information.

There is a touch of styling that needs to be associated with `mat-form-field`. In the `fileupload.component.scss` file, we add `.mat-form-field { display: block; }` to style the field so that it appears on a new line. If we miss this out, the input fields appear side by side.

It's no good having a dialog that we cannot close, or that cannot return values back to the calling code. The convention that we should follow for such operations is to put our **Save** and **Cancel** buttons inside a `mat-dialog-actions` section. The **Cancel** button is marked with `mat-dialog-close` so that it closes the dialog for us without us having to take any actions. The **Save** button follows the pattern that we should be familiar with by now, and calls the `Save` method in our component code when the button click is detected:

```
<mat-dialog-actions>
  <button class="mat-raised-button mat-primary"
(click)="Save()">Save</button>
  <button class="mat-raised-button" mat-dialog-close>Cancel</button>
</mat-dialog-actions>
```

We have reached the point where we need to consider where we are going to store the images when they have been selected by the user, and where they are going to be retrieved from. In the previous chapter, we used a client-side database to store our data. From now on, we are going to work with server-side code as well. Our data is going to be stored in a MongoDB database, so we now need to look at how to use Node.js and Express to connect to the MongoDB database.

Introducing Express support into our application

When we develop client/server applications with Node.js, it makes our lives a lot easier if we can use a framework that allows us to develop the server-side part, especially if it comes with a rich ecosystem of *add-in* functionality to cover features such as connecting to databases and working with the local filesystem. This is where Express comes into play; it's a middleware framework that fits neatly alongside Node.js.

As we are going to create our server-side code completely from scratch, we should start off by creating the base `tsconfig.json` and `package.json` files. To do this, run the following commands in the `Server` folder, which will also add Express support by importing the Express and TypeScript Express definitions:

```
tsc --init
npm init -y
npm install express @types/express parser @types/body-parser --save
```

There are a number of unnecessary options in our `tsconfig.json` file. We only need the bare minimum of options, so we set our configuration to look like this:

```
{
  "compilerOptions": {
    "target": "es2015",
    "module": "commonjs",
    "outDir": "./dist",
    "strict": true,
    "allowSyntheticDefaultImports": true,
    "esModuleInterop": true
  },
}
```

Our server-side code is going to start with a class called `Server`. This class is going to `import express`:

```
import express from "express";
```

In order to create an instance of the Express application, we are going to create a private instance called `app` and set it to `express()` in the constructor. This has the effect of initializing the Express framework for us.

The constructor also accepts a port number, which we will use when we tell our application to listen in our `Start` method. Obviously, we need to respond to web requests, so when our app receives a `get` request from `/`, we are going to respond by using `send` to send a message back to the web page. In our example, if we navigate to `http://localhost:3000/`, the web page URL that this method receives is the root and the function that is called returns `Hello from the server` back to the client. If we browse to anything other than `/`, our server will respond with `404`:

```
export class Server {
  constructor(private port : number = 3000, private app : any = express())
  {
  }

  public Start() : void {
```

```
    this.OnStart();
    this.app.listen(this.port, () => console.log(`Express server running on
port ${this.port}`));
  }

  protected OnStart() : void {
    this.app.get(`/`, (request : any, response : any) => res.send(`Hello
from the server`));
  }
}
```

To start our server, we must give it the port that we want to serve the content from and call `Start`:

```
new Server(3000).Start();
```

 The reason that we have started off with a `Server` class, rather than following the approach of most Node.js/Express tutorials we see on the internet, is that we are looking to build the foundations of something that we will be able to re-use in future chapters. This chapter represents a starting point for this class, as future chapters will take what we have done here and grow the capabilities of the server.

In its current state, the server will not be able to handle any incoming requests from Angular. It's time to start enhancing the server so that it can cope with requests that come across from the client. When the client sends its data, it will come across as a JSON-formatted request. This means that we need to tell the server to take the request and expose it in the body of any request we see.

When we cover routing, shortly, we will see an example of us taking in the `request.Body` in its entirety. Something that we have to be aware of is that we will receive large requests from Angular; photographs can take up a lot of space. By default, the body parser has a limit of 100 KB, which won't be large enough. We are going to raise the limit for the size of requests to 100 MB, which should be more than enough for any image we care to throw at our picture gallery:

```
public Start(): void {
  this.app.use(bodyParser.json({ limit: `100mb` }));
  this.app.use(bodyParser.urlencoded({ limit: `100mb`, extended: true }));
  this.OnStart();
  this.app.listen(this.port, () => console.log(`Express server running on
port ${this.port}`));
}
```

Now that we are talking about the data that is going to come across from Angular, we need to think about whether or not our application will accept the requests. Before we get into the topic of how our server will know which operation to perform based on which request, we need to address the issue of something called **Cross-Origin Request Sharing** (**CORS**).

With CORS, we let known outside locations have access to restricted operations on our site. As Angular is running from a different site to our web server (`localhost:4200` as opposed to `localhost:3000`), we need to enable CORS support to post; otherwise, we will not return anything when we make requests from Angular. The first thing we have to do is add the `cors` middleware to our Node.js server:

```
npm install cors @types/cors --save
```

Adding CORS support is as simple as telling the application to use CORS:

```
public WithCorsSupport(): Server {
    this.app.use(cors());
    return this;
}
```

 CORS support provides a lot of fine-tuning that we don't need to take advantage of. For instance, it allows us to set the types of request methods that we are allowing, using `Access-Control-Allow-Methods`.

Now that we can accept requests from Angular, we need to put the mechanism in place to route requests to appropriate request handlers.

Providing routing support

Whenever a request comes into our web server, we have to determine what response we want to send back. What we are building is going to respond to post and receive requests, which is similar to the way we build REST APIs. The ability to route incoming requests to responses is known as routing. Our application is going to handle three types of request:

- A `POST` request with `add` as the URL (in other words, when we see `http://localhost:3000/add/`). This will add an image and the associated details to the database.

- A GET request with `get` in the URL (as in `http://localhost:3000/get/`). This gets the IDs of all the saved pictures and returns an array of these IDs back to the caller.
- A GET request with `/id/` in the URL. This uses an additional parameter in the URL to get the ID of the individual picture to send back to the client.

 The reason that we are returning an array of IDs is that an individual image can be large. If we were to attempt to return all the images in one go, we would slow down the displaying of the images at the client side as they can be displayed as each one is being loaded. We could also breach the limits of how big the response we are passing back can be. In the case of large chunks of data, it's always worth looking to see how we can minimize what we are transmitting with each request.

The destination of each request corresponds to a unique action that we want to take. This gives us a hint that we should be able to split each route into a single class that does nothing but service that action. To enforce the single action, we define the interface that we want our routing classes to use:

```
export interface IRouter {
   AddRoute(route: any): void;
}
```

We are going to add a helper class that will be responsible for instantiating each router instance. The class starts off simply enough, creating an IRouter array that the route instances will be added into:

```
export class RoutingEngine {
   constructor(private routing: IRouter[] = new Array<IRouter>()) {
   }
}
```

Things get interesting with the method that we use to add the instances in. What we are going to do is accept a generic type as a parameter and instantiate the type. To do this, we must take advantage of a TypeScript feature that allows us to accept a generic type and specify that when new is called on it, it returns an instance of the type.

As we have specified a generic constraint on our type, we will only accept `IRouter` implementations:

```
public Add<T1 extends IRouter>(routing: (new () => T1), route: any) {
  const routed = new routing();
  routed.AddRoute(route);
  this.routing.push(routed);
}
```

 The route that is passed into the method comes from Express. It's the router instance that we tell our application to use.

Now that we have our routing support in place, we need to write the classes that correspond with the route requests we identified previously. The first one that we are going to look at is the class that accepts the add post:

```
export class AddPictureRouter implements IRouter {
  public AddRoute(route: any): void {
    route.post('/add/', (request: Request, response: Response) => {

    }
  }
}
```

This method works by stating that when we receive an `/add/` post, we will take the request, process it, and send a response back. What we do with the request is up to us, but whenever the routing determines that we have a match here, we will execute this method. In this method, we are going to create a server-side representation of the picture and save it to the database.

For the purposes of this application, we have only introduced Express routing. Angular has its own routing engine, but for the purposes of what we wanted to put in place in our code, we have no need for it. In Chapter 5, *Angular ToDo App with GraphQL and Apollo*, we introduce Angular routing.

Introducing MongoDB

Working with MongoDB requires us to use something such as the popular Mongoose package. Installing Mongoose requires us to add both the `mongoose` and `@types/mongoose` packages:

```
npm install mongoose @types/mongoose --save-dev
```

Before we do anything with our database, we need to create a schema to represent the object that we want to save to the database. Unfortunately, this is where things can become a little bit tedious when we are developing applications using MEAN. While the schema superficially represents the model that we created on the Angular side, it is not the same model, so we have to type it in again.

More importantly, this means that if we change our Angular model, we have to regenerate our MongoDB schema to go hand in hand with the changes:

```
export const PictureSchema = new Schema({
  Image: String,
  Name: String,
  Description: String,
  Tags: String,
});
```

For the purposes of our application, we are going to keep the image in the database—in the `Image` field—because this simplifies the infrastructure we have to put in place. In commercial-grade applications, we would choose to store the actual image separate to the database and the `Image` field would point to the physical location of the image. The location of the image would have to be accessible to our web application, and there would be policies in place to ensure that the images were safely backed up and could be easily restored.

With the schema in place, we want to create a model that represents it. A good way to think about the interaction between the model and the schema is that the schema tells us *what* we want our data to look like. The model tells us *how* we want to manipulate it with the database:

```
export const Picture = mongoose.model('picture', PictureSchema);
```

Now that we have the model ready, we need something to establish a connection to the database. The connection string for the MongoDB database has its own protocol, so it starts with the `mongodb://` pattern. For the purposes of our application, we are going to have MongoDB running on the same server as our server-side code; for larger applications, we really would want to separate these out, but for now, we are going to use `localhost:27017` in the connection string as MongoDB is listening on port `27017`.

As we want to be able to host many databases in MongoDB, the mechanism to tell the engine what database to use will supply a database name as part of the connection string. If the database doesn't exist, it will be created. For our application, our database is going to be called `packt_atp_chapter_04`:

```
export class Mongo {
  constructor(private url : string =
"mongodb://localhost:27017/packt_atp_chapter_04") {
  }

  public Connect(): void {
    mongoose.connect(this.url, (e:any) => {
      if (e) {
        console.log(`Unable to connect ` + e);
      } else {
        console.log(`Connected to the database`);
      }
    });
  }
}
```

As long as `Connect` is called before we attempt to do anything inside the database, our database should be available for us to use. Internally, `Connect` calls `mongoose.connect` using our connection string.

Back to our routing

With the `Picture` model available to us, we can populate it directly from inside our `add` route. The request body contains the same parameters as our schema, so the mapping is invisible to us. When it has been populated, we call the `save` method. If there's an error, we will send this back to the client; otherwise, we are going to send the picture back to the client:

```
const picture = new Picture(request.body);
picture.save((err, picture) => {
  if (err) {
    response.send(err);
  }
  response.json(picture);
});
```

In production applications, we wouldn't really want to send the error back to the client as that exposes the inner workings of our application. With a small application, intended for our own use only, it is less of an issue and it is a useful way to determine what has gone wrong with our application because we can simply view the error in the browser console window. Professionally, I would recommend sanitizing the error and sending one of the standard HTTP responses back instead.

The handler for `get` requests is no more complicated. It starts off in a similar fashion to the add router:

```
export class GetPicturesRouter implements IRouter {
  public AddRoute(route: any): void {
    route.get('/get/', (request: Request, response: Response) => {

    });
  }
}
```

The `Request` and `Response` types in our routes come from Express, so they should be added as `imports` in the class.

What we are trying to do with this call is get the unique list of pictures the user has uploaded. Internally, each schema adds an `_id` field, so we are going to use the `Picture.distinct` method to get the full list of these IDs, which we are then going to send back to the client code:

```
Picture.distinct("_id", (err, picture) => {
  if (err) {
    response.send(err);
  }
  response.send(pic);
});
```

The last router that we need to put in place takes an individual ID request and retrieves the related item from the database. What makes this class slightly more complicated than the preceding ones is that we need to manipulate the schema slightly to exclude the `_id` field before we transmit the data back to the client.

If we didn't remove this field, the data our client would receive wouldn't match the type that it was expecting, so it wouldn't be able to automatically populate an instance. This would result in our client not displaying this data even though it received it back unless we manually populated it at the client side:

```
export class FindByIdRouter implements IRouter {
  public AddRoute(route: any): void {
    route.get('/id/:id', (request: Request, response: Response) => {
    });
  }
}
```

 The syntax with `:id` tells us that we are going to receive a parameter called `id` here. The request exposes a `params` object, which will expose this parameter as `id`.

We know that the `id` parameter we have received is unique so we can use the `Picture.findOne` method to retrieve the matching entry from the database. In order to exclude the `_id` field from the result we are going to send back to the client, we must use `-_id` in the parameters to remove this:

```
Picture.findOne({ _id: request.params.id }, '-_id', (err, picture) => {
  if (err) {
    response.send(err);
  }
  response.json(picture);
});
```

The `Server` class needs a little bit of extra attention at this point. We have created the `RoutingEngine` and `Mongo` classes, but there is nothing in the `Server` class to hook them up. This is easily sorted by extending the constructor to add instances of them. We also need to add a call to `Start` to `connect` to the database. If we changed our `Server` class to an abstract class and added an `AddRouting` method, we would stop anyone from directly instantiating the server.

Our applications will need to derive from this class and add their own routing implementations using the `RoutingEngine` class. This is the first step to breaking the server into smaller discrete units that separate out the responsibilities. One of the big changes in the `Start` method is that, once we have added our routing, we tell the application to use the same `express.Router()` that our routing engine is using, so any requests are then automatically hooked up:

```
constructor(private port: number = 3000, private app: any = express(),
  private mongo: Mongo = new Mongo(), private routingEngine: RoutingEngine =
```

```
new RoutingEngine()) {}

protected abstract AddRouting(routingEngine: RoutingEngine, router: any):
void;

public Start() : void {
   ...
  this.mongo.connect();
  this.router = express.Router();
  this.AddRouting(this.routingEngine, this.router);
  this.app.use(this.router);
  this.OnStart();
  this.app.listen(this.port, () => console.log(`Express server running on
port ${this.port}`));
}
```

With this in place, we can now create a concrete class that extends our `Server` class and adds the routers that we have created. This is the class that we will start when we run our application:

```
export class AdvancedTypeScriptProjectsChapter4 extends Server {
  protected AddRouting(routingEngine: RoutingEngine, router: any): void {
    routingEngine.Add(AddPictureRouter, router);
    routingEngine.Add(GetPicturesRouter, router);
    routingEngine.Add(FindByIdRouter, router);
  }
}

new AdvancedTypeScriptProjectsChapter4(3000).WithCorsSupport().Start();
```

 Don't forget to remove the original call to start the `new Server(3000).Start();` server.

Our server-side code is finished. We aren't going to add any more features to it, so we can get back to the client-side code.

Displaying images

After all our hard work writing the server-side code and letting the user choose what image they want to upload, we need something to actually show the images. We are going to create a `PageBody` component, which we will display and add as an element inside our main navigation. Again, we're going to let Angular do the hard work and create the infrastructure for us:

```
ng g c components/PageBody
```

With this component created, we're going to update `app.component.html` with the `PageBody` component as follows:

```
...
      <span>Advanced TypeScript</span>
    </mat-toolbar>
    <atp-page-body></atp-page-body>
  </mat-sidenav-content>
</mat-sidenav-container>
```

When we installed Material support, one of the features we added was Flex Layout, which provides flexible layout support for Angular. We are going to take advantage of this in our application by setting the cards to lay out, initially in rows of three, wrapping to the next line when we need to. Internally, the layout engine uses **Flexbox** (a **flexible box**) to perform the layout.

The idea is that the engine can adjust widths and heights as it sees fit, in order to take advantage of screen real estate. This behavior should be familiar to you, from the way we set up Bootstrap, which adopted Flexbox. As Flexbox defaults to trying to lay items out on one line, we're going to start by creating a `div` tag that alters the behavior to wrap along rows with a 1% space gap:

```
<div fxLayout="row wrap" fxLayout.xs="column" fxLayoutWrap fxLayoutGap="1%"
fxLayoutAlign="left">
</div>
```

With the layout container in place, we now need to set up the cards to hold the images and relevant details. As we could have a dynamic number of cards, we really hope that Angular has a means that allows us to define a card effectively as a template and add the individual elements inside. A card is added using `mat-card`, and with a little bit of Angular magic (okay, another bit of Angular binding), we can iterate over the pictures:

```
<mat-card class="picture-card-layout" *ngFor="let picture of Pictures">
</mat-card>
```

What this section is doing is setting up our card using `ngFor`, which is an Angular directive that iterates over an underlying array, `Pictures` in this case, and is effective for creating a variable that we can use in the body of our card. With this, we are going to add a card title that binds to `picture.Name`, and an image that binds the source to `picture.Image`. Finally, we are going to display `picture.Description` below the image inside a paragraph:

```
<mat-card-title fxLayout.gt-xs="row" fxLayout.xs="column">
  <span fxFlex="80%">{{picture.Name}}</span>
</mat-card-title>
<img mat-card-image [src]="picture.Image" />
<p>{{picture.Description}}</p>
```

For completeness, we have added a bit of styling to our `picture-card-layout`:

```
.picture-card-layout {
  width: 25%;
  margin-top: 2%;
  margin-bottom: 2%;
}
```

It would be good to see what our card styling looks like in action:

That's the HTML in place for our page body, but we need to put the code in the TypeScript behind this to actually start serving some of the data that our cards are going to bind to. In particular, we have to provide the `Pictures` array that we are going to populate:

```
export class PageBodyComponent implements OnInit {
  Pictures: Array<IPictureModel>;
  constructor(private addImage: AddImageService, private loadImage:
LoadImageService,
    private transfer: TransferDataService) {
    this.Pictures = new Array<IPictureModel>();
  }

  ngOnInit() {
  }
}
```

We have a number of services here that we haven't encountered yet. We are going to start by looking at how our application knows when instances of `IPictureModel` have become available.

Using RxJS to watch for images

It's no good having our application be capable of choosing images through the dialog, or fetching them from the server during the load process, if we can't display them in the page body. As our application has features that are loosely related to each other, we don't want to introduce events as the mechanism for controlling when these happen, since this introduces tight coupling between things such as our page body component and the loading service.

What we need are services that sit between the code that handles the interaction (such as loading the data) and the page body, and passes notifications from one side to the other when something interesting has happened. The mechanism that Angular provides to do this is called **Reactive Extensions for JavaScript (RxJS)**.

Reactive extensions are an implementation of something called the observer pattern (there's that word pattern again). This is a simple pattern to understand and you will have been using it for a while now, possibly without even recognizing it. The idea with the observer pattern is that we have a class that has something called a `Subject` type. Internally, this `Subject` type maintains a list of dependencies and, when it needs to do so, notifies those dependencies that they need to react, potentially passing the state over that they need to react to.

This might ring a vague bell that this is precisely what events do, so why should we concern ourselves with this pattern? You would be correct in your understanding—events are just a very specialist form of the observer pattern, but they have some weaknesses that things such as RxJS are designed to overcome. Suppose we had a real-time stock trading application where we had tens of thousands of stock ticks coming to our client every second. Obviously, we wouldn't want our client to handle all of those ticks, so we would have to write code inside our event handlers to start filtering out notifications. That's a lot of code that we would have to write, which would potentially be duplicated across different events. There also has to be a tight relationship between classes when we use events, so one class has to know about another in order to hook up to an event.

As our applications get bigger and more complex, there could be a lot of *distance* between the class that brings in the stock tick and the one that displays it. Therefore, we would end up building a complex hierarchy of events, where `class A` listens to an event on `class B` and when `class B` raises that event, it has to re-raise it so that `class C` can react to it. The more distributed our code becomes internally, the less we want to encourage this tight coupling.

With libraries such as RxJS, we solve these issues (and many more) by decoupling away from events. With RxJS, we can make sophisticated subscription mechanisms, where we can do things such as throttling the number of notifications we react to or choosing only to subscribe to data and changes where certain conditions are met. As new components are added at runtime, they can query the observable class to see what values are already available, in order to prepopulate the screen with data that has already been received. These features are more than we need in this application, but as we will use them in future chapters, it makes sense for us to be aware that they are available to us.

Our application has two things we need to react to:

- When the page is loaded, the images will be loaded from the server, so we need to react to each image being loaded in
- When the user chooses an image from the dialog, after the dialog has closed because the user chose **Save**, we need to trigger a save to the database, and also display the image on the page

It's probably not going to come as a surprise to learn that we are going to create services to satisfy these two requirements. As they both internally do the same thing, the only difference is what the subscriber needs to do once it reacts. We start off by creating a simple base class that these services will derive from:

```
export class ContextServiceBase {
}
```

Our starting point in this class is to define the `Subject` that our observable will use. As we noted, there are different `Subject` specializations in RxJS. As we only want our `Subject` to notify other classes of the latest value, we are going to use `BehaviorSubject` and set the current value to `null`:

```
private source = new BehaviorSubject(null);
```

We aren't going to expose the `Subject` to external classes; instead, we are going to create a new observable with this subject as the source. We do this so that, if we wanted to, we could customize the subscription logic—the throttling issue being an example of why we might want to do this:

```
context: this.source.asObservable();
```

 We call this property the `context` property because it will carry the context of the change.

With this in place, external classes now have access to the observable source, so whenever we notify them that they need to react, they can. As the operation that we want to perform is based either on the user adding `IPictureModel`, or the data loading adding one, we are going to call the method that triggers the observable `add` chain. Our `add` method will receive the instance of the model that we want to send to our subscribing code:

```
public add(image: IPictureModel) : void {
  this.source.next(image);
}
```

We identified that we needed two services to handle the different ways `IPictureModel` was received. The first service is called `AddImageService` and, as we would expect, can be generated for us by using Angular:

```
ng generate service services/AddImage
```

As we have already written the logic for our observable, our service simply looks like this:

```
export class AddImageService extends ContextServiceBase {
}
```

Our second service is called `LoadImageService`:

```
ng generate service services/LoadImage
```

Again, this class is going to extend `ContextServiceBase`:

```
export class LoadImageService extends ContextServiceBase {
}
```

 At this point, you might be wondering why we have two services that appear to do the same thing. Theoretically, we could have had both do exactly the same thing. The reason that I chose to implement two versions comes back to understanding that one of the things that we want to do is display the image and trigger a save whenever we raise a notification through `AddImageService`. Suppose we also used `AddImageService` when the page was loaded. If we did this, then whenever the page was loaded, it would also trigger the save so we would end up duplicating images. Now, we could introduce filtering to prevent duplicates from happening, but I chose to keep things simple by using two separate classes for this first visit to RxJS. In the coming chapters, we will see how to make more complex subscriptions.

Transferring the data

We have covered one side of the client/server interaction. It's now time for us to address the other side—the code that actually calls the routes that our server exposes. Not surprisingly, we add a service that takes care of this communication. We start with the code to create the service:

```
ng g service services/TransferData
```

Our service is going to make use of three things. The first thing that it will rely on is an `HttpClient` instance to manage the `get` and `post` operations. We also bring in the `AddImageService` and `LoadImageService` classes that we have just created:

```
export class TransferDataService {
  constructor(private client: HttpClient, private addImage:
AddImageService,
    private loadImage: LoadImageService) {
  }
}
```

The first point of contact between our server and client is the piece of code we are going to use when the user has chosen the image from the dialog. Once they have clicked **Save**, we are going to set off a chain of actions that results in the data being saved in the server. We are going to set up our HTTP header to set the content type to JSON:

```
private SubscribeToAddImageContextChanges() {
  const httpOptions = {
    headers: new HttpHeaders({
      'Content-Type': 'application/json',
    })
  };
}
```

Thinking back to our RxJS classes, we know that we have two separate subscriptions available to us. The one that we want to use here reacts when `AddImageService` is pushed out, so we are going to add this subscription to `SubscribeToAddImageContextChanges`:

```
this.addImage.context.subscribe(message => {
});
```

When we receive a message in this subscription, we are going to post it to the server, which will end up saving the data to the database:

```
if (message === null) {
  return;
}
this.client.post<IPictureModel>('http://localhost:3000/add/', message,
httpOptions)
  .subscribe(callback => { });
```

The format of the post is to pass the endpoint address, which ties nicely back to the server-side code that we wrote earlier, along with the message and any HTTP options. Because our message content is semantically the same as the model that is received at the server side, it will automatically be decoded at that side. As we can receive content back from the server, we have a subscription that we can use to decode the messages coming back from our Express code base. When we put this code together, we end up with this:

```
private SubscribeToAddImageContextChanges() {
  const httpOptions = {
    headers: new HttpHeaders({
      'Content-Type': 'application/json',
    })
  };
  this.addImage.context.subscribe(message => {
    if (message === null) {
      return;
    }
```

```
    this.client.post<IPictureModel>('http://localhost:3000/add/', message,
httpOptions)
        .subscribe(callback => {
      });
    });
}
```

The other side of our transfer service is responsible for getting the images back from the server. As you may remember from our Express code, we are going to receive the data in two stages. The first stage is that we will receive an array of IDs that match all the pictures available to us. To fetch this array, we call `get` on `HttpClient`, telling it that we are going to get an array of strings, by pointing to the `/get/` endpoint:

```
private LoadImagesWithSubscription() {
  const httpOptions = {
    headers: new HttpHeaders({
      'Content-Type': 'application/text',
    })
  };
  this.client.get<string[]>('http://localhost:3000/get/',
httpOptions).subscribe(pic => {
  });
}
```

Now that we have the array of strings, we need to iterate over each element and call `get` again, this time adding `/id/...` to tell the server which one we are interested in. When the data comes back, we call the `add` method on `LoadImageService`, passing in `IPictureModel`. This ties back to our page body, as we will see shortly:

```
pic.forEach(img => {
  this.client.get<IPictureModel>('http://localhost:3000/id/' +
img).subscribe(pic1 => {
    if (pic1 !== null) {
      this.loadImage.add(pic1);
    }
  });
});
```

Finally, we are going to add an `Initialize` method, which we will use to initialize the service:

```
public Initialize(): void {
  this.SubscribeToAddImageContextChanges();
  this.LoadImagesWithSubscription();
}
```

Back to the page body component

Now that we have `LoadImageService`, `AddImageService`, and `TransferDataService` written, we can use them in the `PageBodyComponent` initialization code in `ngOnInit`, which is called when the component is initializing. The first thing we need to do is affect is to call the `Initialize` function in `TransferDataService`:

```
ngOnInit() {
  this.transfer.Initialize();

}
```

To finish off this component, and to actually populate the `Pictures` array, we need to hook up to the context for both of our RxJS services:

```
this.addImage.context.subscribe(message => {
  if (!message) {
    return;
  }
  this.Pictures.push(message);
});
this.loadImage.context.subscribe(message => {
  if (!message) {
    return;
  }
  this.Pictures.push(message);
});
```

Wrapping up by displaying the dialog

By now, you have probably noticed that we haven't actually put any code in place to display the dialog or trigger `AddImageService` when the user closes the dialog. To do this, we are going to add the code in `app.component.ts` and make a minor adjustment to the related HTML.

Add a constructor that accepts a Material dialog and `AddImageService`:

```
constructor(private dialog: MatDialog, private addImage: AddImageService) {
}
```

We need to add a public method that our HTML template will bind to. We are going to call this ImportImage:

```
public ImportImage(): void {
}
```

The related change to our HTML template is to add the call to ImportImage to respond to the click event, via the (click) event binding, on our menu list item in app.component.html. Once again, we see Angular binding coming into play:

```
<a mat-list-item (click)="ImportImage()">Import image</a>
```

We are going to configure our dialog to behave in a certain way. We don't want the user to be able to automatically close it by pressing the *Esc* key. We want it to be automatically focused and to be 500 pixels wide:

```
const config = new MatDialogConfig();
config.disableClose = true;
config.autoFocus = true;
config.width = '500px';
```

Now, we can show our dialog using this configuration:

```
this.dialogRef = this.dialog.open(FileuploadComponent, config);
```

We want to be able to identify when the dialog is closed and automatically call our add image service—our add method—which will notify the transfer data service that the data must be sent to the client, and will also notify the page body that there is a new image to display:

```
this.dialogRef.afterClosed().subscribe(r => {
  if (r) {
    this.addImage.add(r);
  }
});
```

That's the last piece of code that we put in place. Our client code now has neatly segregated services and components that work in co-operation with our Material dialog. Our dialog looks like this when in use:

We have finished wiring our dialog into our Angular code. We have a fully working application that we can use to save images into our database.

Summary

In this chapter, using the MEAN stack, we have developed an application that allows the user to load images from their disk, add information about the images, and transfer data from the client to the server. We wrote code that created a server that could respond to incoming requests, as well as being able to save data to and retrieve data from a database. We discovered how to use Material Design and laid out our screen using Angular Material, along with navigation elements.

In the next chapter, we are going to expand our Angular knowledge and create a ToDo application that uses GraphQL to visualize its data.

Questions

1. When we say that we are developing an application using the MEAN stack, what are the major components of the stack?
2. Why did we supply a prefix when we created our Angular client?
3. How do we start an Angular application?
4. When we state that Material is a design language, what do we mean?
5. How do we tell Angular to create a service?
6. What is Express routing?
7. Which pattern does RxJS implement?
8. What is CORS and why do we need it?

Further reading

- To learn more about the full MEAN stack, Packt has the following book available: *MongoDB, Express, Angular, and Node.js Fundamentals* by Paul Oluyege (https://www.packtpub.com/web-development/mongodb-express-angular-and-nodejs-fundamentals)
- For more information about learning reactive coding with JavaScript, Packt also has the following book available: *Mastering Reactive JavaScript* by Erich de Souza Oliveira (https://www.packtpub.com/in/web-development/mastering-reactive-javascript)

5
Angular ToDo App with GraphQL and Apollo

There are many different ways to communicate data backward and forward from the client to the server. In this chapter, we are going to look at how we can use GraphQL to pick data from a server, and then send and mutate data back from an Angular client. We will also look at how we can leverage calculated values from GraphQL. Building on the content of the previous chapter, we will once again be using Angular Material for our user interface to see how we can work with Angular routing to serve up different content.

The following topics will be covered in this chapter:

- Understanding the GraphQL-to-REST relationship
- Creating a reusable database class
- Prefilling data and using singletons
- Creating a GraphQL schema
- Setting up GraphQL types using `type-graphql`
- Creating a GraphQL resolver with queries and mutations
- Using Apollo Server as our application server
- Creating a GraphQL Angular client application
- Adding Apollo support to the client
- Using routing in Angular
- Controlling input with Angular validation
- Sending GraphQL mutations from the client to the server
- Sending GraphQL queries from the client to the server
- Switching between read-only and editable templates

Technical requirements

The finished project can be downloaded from `https://github.com/PacktPublishing/` `Advanced-TypeScript-3-Programming-Projects/tree/master/Chapter05`.

After downloading the project, you will have to install the package requirements using the `npm install` command.

Understanding the GraphQL-to-REST relationship

One of the great things about web-based technologies is the number of ways you can solve common problems that crop up. With REST, we used a simple, but powerful, way to communicate from the client to the server; however, that's not the only way that we can do this. REST solved a set of problems, but also introduced new problems that newer techniques have come to the fore to fix. The three problems that need to be solved are as follows:

- In order to build up complex information, we may end up having to make multiple REST calls to the REST server. For a shopping application, for instance, we may use one REST call to pick up a person's name and another REST call to pick up their address, with a third call being needed to get their shopping basket details.
- Over time, we may go through multiple versions of our REST API. Having our clients keep track of the versioning can be restrictive, which means that, right at the start of our API, we also have to define what our versioning experience is going to be like. Unless our APIs follow the same versioning standards, this can lead to confusing code.
- These REST calls could end up bringing far more information than we actually need. So, while we are making these detailed calls, we only actually need three or four items of information out of maybe 20 or 30 fields.

One of the things to understand about REST is that it isn't actually a technology. A good way to think about REST is that it's more of an agreed architectural standard that can use pretty much any transport mechanism as a means of communication. Okay, to clarify, while I said it was a standard, in practical terms, very few people actually follow the original concept of REST, which means that we also need to understand the intent of the developers. For instance, when we issue an update over REST, are we using the `PUT HTTP` verb or the `POST` verb? Knowing this level of detail is vital if we want to consume a third-party API.

Originally developed by Facebook, but now maintained by the GraphQL foundation (`https://foundation.graphql.org/`), GraphQL is a great mechanism to use to address issues like these. Unlike pure REST, GraphQL is simply a query language with tooling support. GraphQL revolves around the idea that our code will interact with fields, and as long as there is a definition of how to get these fields, we can write arbitrarily complex queries to retrieve data from multiple locations in one hit, or mutate the data to update it. A properly designed GraphQL system takes care of versioning requirements as well as fields, which can be added and deprecated on demand.

With GraphQL, we can only retrieve the information that we need with a query. This saves us from oversubscribing for information at the client level. Similarly, our query can patch the result together from multiple locations for us so that we don't have to perform multiple round trips. We send our query from our client and let our GraphQL server retrieve the relevant data items. We also don't have to worry about REST endpoints in our client code. We simply communicate with our GraphQL server, letting the query take care of the data.

In this chapter, we are going to look at how we can use the Apollo GraphQL engine (`https://www.apollographql.com/`) and the incredibly useful `TypeGraphQL` library (`https://typegraphql.ml/`), which provides a convenient way to target GraphQL from TypeScript. With Apollo, we have a complete front-to-back infrastructure to completely manage our GraphQL behaviors. As well as providing client-side libraries, we can use Apollo on our servers, as well as for iOS and Android applications.

> Note that GraphQL is not intended to completely replace RESTful services. There are many cases where we would want REST and GraphQL to work together, side by side. It could be that we have a REST service that communicates with our GraphQL implementation and caches information for us, for example. For the purposes of this chapter, however, we are going to be concentrating purely on creating a GraphQL implementation.

Project overview

In this chapter, our project is going to introduce us to writing GraphQL applications, both on the server side and the client side. We are also going to start investigating features that were introduced in TypeScript 3 to create a ToDo application. We will be expanding on the Angular concepts from the previous chapter to introduce client-side routing, which will allow us to show different content and effectively navigate between pages. We will also introduce Angular validation.

Working alongside the GitHub code, the task in this chapter should take about four hours to complete.

When completed, the application should look like this:

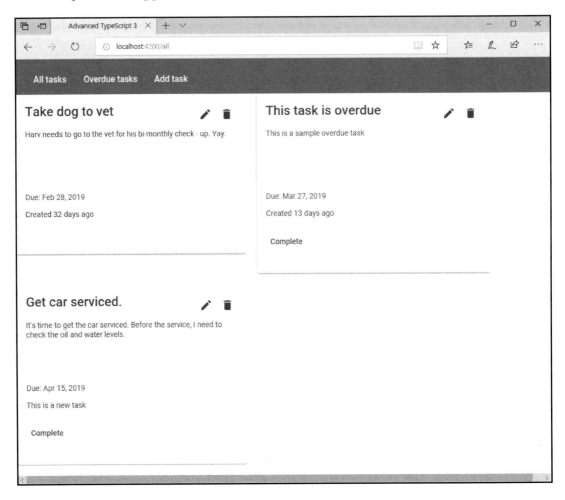

Getting started with the project

Just like in the previous chapter, this chapter will use Node.js (available from `https://nodejs.org`). We will also be using the following components:

- The Angular CLI (I'm using version 7.2.2)
- `express` (version 4.16.4 or greater)
- `mongoose` (version 5.4.8 or greater)
- `@types/cors` (version 2.8.4 or greater)
- `@types/body-parser` (version 1.17.0 or greater)
- `@types/express` (version 4.16.0 or greater)
- `@types/mongodb` (version 3.1.19 or greater)
- `@types/mongoose` (version 5.3.11 or greater)
- `type-graphql` (version 0.16.0 or greater)
- `@types/graphql` (version 14.0.7 or greater)
- `apollo-server` (version 2.4.0 or greater)
- `apollo-server-express` (version 2.4.0 or greater)
- `guid-typescript` (version 1.0.9 or greater)
- `reflect-metadata` (version 0.1.13 or greater)
- `graphql` (version 14.1.1 or greater)
- `apollo-angular` (version 1.5.0 or greater)
- `apollo-angular-link-http` (version 1.5.0 or greater)
- `apollo-cache-inmemory` (version 1.4.3 or greater)
- `apollo-client` (version 2.4.13 or greater)
- `graphql` (version 14.1.1 or greater)
- `graphql-tag` (version 2.10.1 or greater)

As well as using MongoDB, we will be using Apollo to serve up our GraphQL data.

Creating a ToDo application with GraphQL and Angular

As is our custom now, we are going to start off by defining the requirements:

- A user must be able to add a ToDo task consisting of a title, a description, and the date the task is due
- Validation will ensure that these items are always set and that the due date cannot be before today
- The user will be able to see a list of all tasks
- The user will be able to delete a task
- The user will be able to see overdue tasks (where an overdue task is one that has not been completed and the due date has passed)
- The user will be able to edit a task
- Data is transferred to the server, or from the server, using GraphQL
- Transferred data will be saved to a MongoDB database

Creating our application

For our ToDo application, we are going to start off with the server implementation. As in the previous chapter, we are going to create a separate client and server folder structure, with the Node.js code being added to the server code.

We're going to start our journey into creating a GraphQL server with the database code. All the data for our client is going to come from the database, so it makes sense for us to put everything we need in place. As in the previous chapter, we are going to install the `mongoose` packages that we need to work with MongoDB:

```
npm install mongoose @types/mongoose --save-dev
```

Something to bear in mind when choosing which command to use to install packages relates to the use of `--save` versus `--save-dev`. These are both used to install packages, but there is a practical difference between them and how we would expect the application to be deployed based on them. When we use `--save`, we are stating that this package must be downloaded for the application to run, even if we install the application on another computer. This can be wasteful if we intend to deploy our application to a machine that already has the correct version of the package installed globally. The alternative case is to use `--save-dev` to download and install the package as something called a development dependency. In other words, the package is installed locally for the developer.

With this in place, we are going to start writing a variation of the `Mongo` class we introduced in the previous chapter. The reason that we aren't going to reuse that implementation is because we are going to start introducing TypeScript 3-specific features before we move on to adding a generic database framework.

The big change to our class is that we are going to change the signature to our `mongoose.connect` method. One of the changes tells Mongoose to use a new format URL parser, but the other change ties into the signature of the event that we use as a callback:

```
public Connect(): void {
  mongoose.connect(this.url, {useNewUrlParser: true}, (e:unknown) => {
    if (e) {
      console.log(`Unable to connect ` + e);
    } else {
      console.log(`Connected to the database`);
    }
  });
}
```

From the previous chapter, we should remember that our callback had a signature of `e:any`. Now, we are changing it to use `e:unknown` instead. This is a new type—introduced to TypeScript 3—that allows us to add an extra level of type safety. To a large extent, we can think of the `unknown` type as being similar to `any` in that we can assign any type to it. What we can't do, however, is assign it to another type without a type assertion. We are going to start moving `any` types to `unknown` throughout our code.

So far, we have been using a lot of interfaces to provide the shapes of types. We can apply the same technique to Mongo schemas as well so that we can describe the shape of our ToDo schema as a standard TypeScript interface, and then map it to a schema. Our interface is going to be straightforward:

```
export interface ITodoSchema extends mongoose.Document {
   Id: string,
   Title: string,
   Description: string,
   DueDate: Date,
   CreationDate: Date,
   Completed: boolean,
}
```

We are going to create a `mongoose` schema that will be mapped into the database. A schema simply states what information will be stored using types that MongoDB expects. For instance, our `ITodoSchema` exposes `Id` as `string`, but this is not the type that MongoDB would expect; instead, it expects to see `String`. Knowing this, it's simple enough to create a mapping from `ITodoSchema` to `TodoSchema`, as follows:

```
export const TodoSchema = new Schema({
   Id: String,
   Title: String,
   Description: String,
   DueDate: Date,
   CreationDate: Date,
   Completed: Boolean,
});
```

We now have a schema model that we can use to query, update, and more. Of course, Mongo doesn't limit us to just one schema. If we wanted to use more, there would be nothing stopping us from doing so.

A note about what our schema is going to contain—the `Title` and `Description` fields are fairly straightforward in that they contain details about what our todo item is about. `DueDate` simply tells us when our item is due and `CreationDate` tells us when we created this record. We have a `Completed` flag that the user will trigger to say when they have completed the task.

The interesting field is the `Id` field. This field differs from the Mongo `Id` field, which will still be internally generated. The schema `Id` field is assigned something called a **Globally Unique IDentifier (GUID)**, which is a unique string identifier. The reason that we want the UI to add this field is because we are going to use it as a known field in our database queries, and we want the client to know the value of the `Id` before it needs to perform any round trips. When we cover the Angular side, we will see how this field gets populated.

We need to create a database model that maps the `mongoose.Document` instance of our `ITodoSchema` to our `TodoSchema`. This is a straightforward task when using `mongoose.model`:

```
export const TodoModel = mongoose.model<ITodoSchema>('todo', TodoSchema,
'todoitems', false);
```

 Case is very important when we create our `mongoose.model`. As well as `mongoose.model`, we also have `mongoose.Model` available, which we would have to instantiate with a `new` statement.

We are now in a position to write a relatively generic database class. We do, however, have a constraint—we are expecting our schema to have an `Id` field. This constraint is purely a convenience to let us concentrate on the logic for our demonstration application.

The first thing we are going to do is create a generic base class that accepts `mongoose.Document` as the type. It will probably not come as a surprise to realize that the type we will ultimately use against this is `ITodoSchema`. The constructor is going to accept a model that we can use for our various database operations. Again, we have already created the model that we are going to use as `TodoModel`:

```
export abstract class DataAccessBase<T extends mongoose.Document> {
  private model: Model;
  constructor(model: Model) {
    this.model = model;
  }
}
```

Our concrete implementation of this class is very straightforward:

```
export class TodoDataAccess extends DataAccessBase<ITodoSchema> {
  constructor() {
    super(TodoModel);
  }
}
```

We are now going to start adding features to `DataAccessBase`. We will start off with a method to get all the records that match our schema. We should be happy enough with promises at this stage, so it should be natural for us to return a `Promise` type. In this case, the `Promise` type will be an array of `T`, which we know maps onto `ITodoSchema`.

Internally, we call the `find` method on our model to retrieve all records and once the find completes, we call back the result:

```
GetAll(): Promise<T[]> {
  return new Promise<T[]>((callback, error) => {
    this.model.find((err: unknown, result: T[]) => {
      if (err) {
        error(err);
      }
      if (result) {
        callback(result);
      }
    });
  });
}
```

Adding a record is just as simple. The only real differences are that we call the `model.create` method and return a `boolean` value to indicate that we succeeded:

```
Add(item: T): Promise<boolean> {
  return new Promise<boolean>((callback, error) => {
    this.model.create(item, (err: unknown, result: T) => {
      if (err) {
        error(err);
      }
      callback(!result);
    });
  });
}
```

As well as retrieving all records, we could choose to retrieve a single one. The big change between this and the `GetAll` method is that the `find` method is using search criteria:

```
Get(id: string): Promise<T> {
  return new Promise<T>((callback, error) =>{
    this.model.find({'Id': id}, (err: unknown, result: T) => {
      if (err) {
        error(err);
      }
      callback(result);
    });
  });
}
```

Finally, we have the ability to remove or update records. These are very similar in the way we write them:

```
Remove(id: string): Promise<void> {
  return new Promise<void>((callback, error) => {
    this.model.deleteOne({'Id': id}, (err: unknown) => {
      if (err) {
        error(err);
      }
      callback();
    });
  });
}
Update(id: string, item: T): Promise<boolean> {
  return new Promise<boolean>((callback, error) => {
    this.model.updateOne({'Id': id}, item, (err: unknown)=>{
      if (err) {
        error(err);
      }
      callback(true);
    });
  })
}
```

With the actual database code in place, we can now turn our attention to accessing the database. Something that we are going to consider is that we may end up having a significant number of todo items building up over time and, if we attempt to read them from the database every time we need them, we are going to slow the system down as we add more and more todos. To this end, we are going to create a basic caching mechanism that will be populated as soon as the database finishes loading during the server startup process.

Since the cache is going to be pre-populated, we want to use the same instance of our class from GraphQL and from our server, so we are going to create something called a **singleton**. A singleton is just another way of saying that we will have only one instance of a class present in memory and each class will use the same instance. To prevent other classes from being able to create their own instances, we will make use of a couple of tricks.

The first thing we are going to do is create our class with a private constructor. A private constructor means that the only place we can instantiate our class from is inside the class itself:

```
export class Prefill {
  private constructor() {}
}
```

It might seem counter-intuitive that we can only create the class from itself. After all, if we cannot instantiate the class, how can we access any members? The trick to this is to add a field to hold a reference to the class instance, and then offer a public static property to access that instance. The public property will take care to instantiate the class if it's not already available, so we will always be able to access an instance of the class:

```
private static prefill: Prefill;
public static get Instance(): Prefill {
  return this.prefill || (this.prefill = new this());
}
```

We now have a way to access the methods we are going to write, so let's start off by creating a method to populate a list of the available items. Since this could be a long-running operation, we are going to make it asynchronous:

```
private items: TodoItems[] = new Array<TodoItem>();
public async Populate(): Promise<void> {
  try
  {
    const schema = await this.dataAccess.GetAll();
    this.items = new Array<TodoItem>();
    schema.forEach(item => {
      const todoItem: TodoItem = new TodoItem();
      todoItem.Id = item.Id;
      todoItem.Completed = item.Completed;
      todoItem.CreationDate = item.CreationDate;
      todoItem.DueDate = item.DueDate;
      todoItem.Description = item.Description;
      todoItem.Title = item.Title;
      this.items.push(todoItem);
    });
  } catch(error) {
    console.log(`Unfortunately, we couldn't retrieve all records
${error}`);
  }
}
```

This method works by calling `GetAll` to retrieve all the records from our MongoDB database. Once we have the records, we are going to iterate over them and create copies of them to push into our array.

 The `TodoItem` class is a special class that we are going to use to map types to GraphQL. We will look at this class shortly when we start writing our GraphQL server functionality.

It's all very well populating the array of items, but if there is no way to access the items elsewhere in the code, this class would not be much help. Fortunately, accessing the elements is as simple as adding an `Items` property:

```
get Items(): TodoItem[] {
  return this.items;
}
```

Creating our GraphQL schema

With our database code in place, we are now ready to turn our attention to writing our GraphQL server. One of the earliest decisions I took when writing the sample code for this chapter was that we would simplify the process of writing our code as much as possible. If we look at a reference sample that Facebook posted, we will find that the code can be tediously long-winded:

```
import {
  graphql,
  GraphQLSchema,
  GraphQLObjectType,
  GraphQLString
} from 'graphql';

var schema = new GraphQLSchema({
  query: new GraphQLObjectType({
    name: 'RootQueryType',
    fields: {
      hello: {
        type: GraphQLString,
        resolve() {
          return 'world';
        }
      }
    }
  })
});
```

This example is from `https://github.com/graphql/graphql-js`. We can see that we have a lot of reliance on special types that don't map one to one onto TypeScript types.

Since we want to make our code that bit more TypeScript-friendly, we are going to use `type-graphql`. We will install it via `npm`, along with the `graphql` type definitions and `reflect-metadata`:

```
npm install type-graphql @types/graphql reflect-metadata --save
```

At this stage, we should also set our `tsconfig` file up to look like this:

```
{
  "compileOnSave": false,
  "compilerOptions": {
    "target": "es2016",
    "module": "commonjs",
    "lib": ["es2016", "esnext.asynciterable", "dom"],
    "outDir": "./dist",
    "noImplicitAny": true,
    "esModuleInterop": true,
    "experimentalDecorators": true,
    "emitDecoratorMetadata": true,
  }
}
```

 The main thing worth mentioning in this `tsconfig` file relates to the fact that `type-graphql` uses features that are only found in ES7, so we need to use ES2016 in the lib (ES7 maps onto ES2016).

Setting up our GraphQL types

As we just saw, GraphQL types can be a little bit complicated to set up. With the aid of `type-graphql` and some handy decorators, we are going to create a schema to represent a single item.

We don't need to worry about creating a type to represent multiple items just yet. Our item will consist of the following fields:

- `Id` (defaulted to an empty string)
- `Title`
- `Description` (we are going to set this up as a nullable value for the moment. When we create the UI, we are going to add validation to make sure that we always supply a description.)
- The date the task is due (again, this is nullable)
- When the task was created
- The number of days since the task was created (this will be automatically calculated when we query the data)
- Whether or not the task has been completed

If we pay attention, we will see that the fields here map very closely to the ones we defined in our MongoDB schema. This is because we will be populating our GraphQL type from the database, as well as updating the database directly from these types.

As we are used to doing now, we are going to start off with a simple class:

```
export class TodoItem {
}
```

I mentioned that we are going to use decorators with this class. We are going to decorate the class definition with `@ObjectType`, which gives us the ability to create complex types. Being good developers, we will also supply a description so that consumers of our type have documentation about what it represents. Right now, our class definition looks like this:

```
@ObjectType({description: "A single to do"})
export class TodoItem {
}
```

We are going to add the fields to our type, one step at a time. First, we are going to add the `Id` field, which matches the `Id` field in the database:

```
@Field(type=>ID)
Id: string="";
```

Again, we have supplied a decorator to this field, which will tell `type-graphql` how to transform our class into a GraphQL type. By applying `type=>ID`, we are using the special GraphQL `ID` type. This type is a string that maps to a unique value. It is an identity field, after all, and convention states that identity fields must be unique.

We are going to add three nullable fields next—the `Description`, `DueDate`, and `CreationDate` fields. We aren't really going to be allowing null values in these, as we will see when we start adding Angular validation later on in this chapter, but it's important for us to see how we can add nullable types for any future GraphQL types that we create:

```
@Field({ nullable: true, description: "The description of the item." })
Description?: string;
@Field({ nullable: true, description: "The due date for the item" })
DueDate?: Date;
@Field({ nullable: true, description: "The date the item was created" })
CreationDate: Date;
```

We do have some more simple fields that we are going to make available:

```
@Field()
Title: string;
@Field(type => Int)
DaysCreated: number;
@Field()
Completed: boolean;
```

Our `TodoItem`, which represents the schema that makes up the entirety of our query type, now looks like this:

```
@ObjectType({ description: "A single to do" })
export class TodoItem {
  constructor() {
    this.Completed = false;
  }
  @Field(type=>ID)
  Id: string = "";
  @Field()
  Title: string;
  @Field({ nullable: true, description: "The description of the item." })
  Description?: string;
  @Field({ nullable: true, description: "The due date for the item" })
  DueDate?: Date;
  @Field({ nullable: true, description: "The date the item was created" })
  CreationDate: Date;
  @Field(type => Int)
  DaysCreated: number;
  @Field()
  Completed: boolean;
}
```

As well as having a class for the query, we also need one to represent the data that we are going to use to mutate the state for subsequent queries, as well as for updating the database.

When we mutate state, we are changing it. We want those changes to be persisted across server restarts so they will update both the database and the state we are going to cache at runtime.

The class we are going to use for the mutation looks very similar to our `TodoItem` class. The key differences are that we use `@InputType` in place of `@ObjectType` and the class implements a generic `Partial` type of `TodoItem`. The other difference is that this class does not have the `DaysCreated` field because that is going to be calculated by our query, so we don't have to add any values to hold it:

```
@InputType()
export class TodoItemInput implements Partial<TodoItem> {
  @Field()
  Id: string;
  @Field({description: "The item title"})
  Title: string = "";
  @Field({ nullable: true, description: "The item description" })
  Description?: string = "";
  @Field({ nullable: true, description: "The item due date" })
  DueDate?: Date;
  @Field()
  CreationDate: Date;
  @Field()
  Completed: boolean = false;
}
```

If you don't know what `Partial` does, it simply makes all the properties of `TodoItem` optional. This lets us tie our new mutation class back to our old class without having to supply every property.

Creating our GraphQL resolver

The `TodoItem` and `TodoItemInput` classes were aimed at giving us schemas that describe the fields, types, and arguments. While they are an important part of our GraphQL jigsaw, we have a missing piece—the ability to execute functions against our GraphQL server.

We need a way to resolve the fields of our types. With GraphQL, a resolver is something that represents a single field. It fetches the data that we need, effectively giving the GraphQL server detailed instructions on how to convert queries into data items (we can think of this as one of the reasons why we have separate schemas for mutating data over querying data—we cannot mutate fields using the same logic as querying fields). From this, we can work out that there is a one-to-one mapping between fields and resolvers.

With `type-graphql`, we can create complex resolver relationships and operations with ease. We are going to start off by defining our class.

The `@Resolver` decorator tells us that this class behaves in the same way that a controller class would in a REST type:

```
@Resolver(()=>TodoItem)
export class TodoItemResolver implements ResolverInterface<TodoItem>{
}
```

Strictly speaking, `ResolverInterface` is not necessary for our class, but we will be using it as a safety net when we add a field resolver to our `DaysCreated` field. This field is going to return the difference between today's date and the day the task was created. Since we are creating a field resolver, `ResolverInterface` checks that our field has the `@Root` decorator of the object type as a parameter and that the return type is the correct type.

Our `DaysCreated` field resolver is decorated with `@FieldResolver` and looks like this:

```
private readonly milliSecondsPerDay = 1000 * 60 * 60 * 24;
@FieldResolver()
DaysCreated(@Root() TodoItem: TodoItem): number {
  const value = this.GetDateDifference(...[new Date(),
TodoItem.CreationDate]);
  if (value === 0) {
    return 0;
  }
  return Math.round(value / this.milliSecondsPerDay);
}
private GetDateDifference(...args: [Date, Date]): number {
  return Math.round(args[0].valueOf() - args[1].valueOf());
}
```

While these methods look complicated, they are actually very simple. Our `DaysCreated` method receives the current `TodoItem` and works out the difference between today and the `CreationDate` value using `GetDateDifference`.

Our `type-graphql` resolver can also define the queries and mutations that we want to perform. What would be useful for us to define is a means to retrieve all the todo items. We will create a method decorated with `@Query` to identify that this will be a query operation. Since our query has the potential to return multiple items, we tell the resolver that the return type is an array of `TodoItem` types. Just like we did the hard work of creating our `Prefill` class earlier on, our method is as simple as this:

```
@Query(() => [TodoItem], { description: "Get all the TodoItems" })
async TodoItems(): Promise<TodoItem[]> {
  return await Prefill.Instance.Items;
}
```

One of the operations that we want to allow our users to do is only query the records that are overdue. We can leverage largely similar logic to the last query, but we are going to filter on those uncompleted records that have gone past their due date:

```
@Query(() => [TodoItem], { description: "Get items past their due date" })
async OverdueTodoItems(): Promise<TodoItem[]> {
  const localCollection = new Array<TodoItem>();
  const testDate = new Date();
  await Prefill.Instance.Items.forEach(x => {
    if (x.DueDate < testDate && !x.Completed) {
      localCollection.push(x);
    }
  });
  return localCollection;
}
```

Strictly speaking, for an operation that was shaping data like this, I would normally delegate the filtering logic to the data layer so that it only returned appropriate records. In this case, I decided to filter in the resolver so that we could see that the same source of data could be shaped in whatever way we needed. After all, we might have retrieved this data from a source that wouldn't let us shape it in a suitable way.

 One thing I must emphasize is that we must import reflect-metadata before we attempt to execute any queries or mutations. This has to happen because of the reliance of reflection when working with the decorators. Without reflect-metadata, we will not be able to use the decorators since they use reflection internally.

It's all very well having the ability to query data, but resolvers should also be able to perform mutations on the data. To this end, we are going to add resolvers to add, update, and remove new todo items, as well as set the Completed flag when the user decides that the task is complete. We're going to start off with the Add method.

Since this is a mutation, type-graphql provides the @Mutation decorator. Our method will accept a TodoItemInput parameter. This is passed in with a matching @Arg decorator. The reason that we need to supply this explicit @Arg is because GraphQL expects mutations to have parameters as arguments. By using @Arg, we provide them with the needed context. While supplying the mutation, we have an expectation that we will also be supplying a return type, so it is important to get the mapping between the mutation and the actual return type of the method correct:

```
@Mutation(() => TodoItem)
async Add(@Arg("TodoItem") todoItemInput: TodoItemInput): Promise<TodoItem>
{
}
```

One of the features of our mutation methods is that, as well as updating the `Prefill` items, we are also going to be updating the database, meaning that we have to convert the input in our method into our `ITodoSchema` type.

To help us, we are going to use the following simple method:

```
private CreateTodoSchema<T extends TodoItem | TodoItemInput>(todoItem: T):
ITodoSchema {
  return <ITodoSchema>{
    Id: todoItem.Id,
    CreationDate: todoItem.CreationDate,
    DueDate: todoItem.DueDate,
    Description: todoItem.Description,
    Title: todoItem.Title,
    Completed: false
  };
}
```

 We accept both `TodoItem` and `TodoItemInput` because we are going to use the same method to create a record that will be acceptable to our database layer. Since the source of that record could come from either finding a particular record from the `Prefill` items, or having been passed over from our UI, we need to make sure that we can handle both cases.

The first part of our `Add` method involves creating a `TodoItem` item that will be stored in our `Prefill` collection. Once we have added the item to the collection, we are going to add the record to the database. Our full `Add` method looks like this:

```
@Mutation(() => TodoItem)
async Add(@Arg("TodoItem") todoItemInput: TodoItemInput): Promise<TodoItem>
{
  const todoItem = <TodoItem> {
    Id : todoItemInput.Id,
    CreationDate : todoItemInput.CreationDate,
    DueDate : todoItemInput.DueDate,
    Description : todoItemInput.Description,
    Title : todoItemInput.Title,
    Completed : todoItemInput.Completed
  };
  todoItem.Completed = false;
  await Prefill.Instance.Items.push(todoItem);
  await this.dataAccess.Add(this.CreateTodoSchema(todoItem));
  return todoItem;
}
```

Now that we know how to add a record, we can turn our attention to using a mutation to update the record. We already have most of the code infrastructure in place, so the update becomes a lot more straightforward to code. The `Update` method starts off by retrieving the entry that is already cached by searching for the item with the matching `Id` we have amended. If we find this record, we update it with the related `Title`, `Description`, and `DueDate` before we update the matching database record:

```
@Mutation(() => Boolean!)
async Update(@Arg("TodoItem") todoItemInput: TodoItemInput):
Promise<boolean> {
  const item: TodoItem = await Prefill.Instance.Items.find(x => x.Id ===
todoItemInput.Id);
  if (!item) return false;
  item.Title = todoItemInput.Title;
  item.Description = todoItemInput.Description; '
  item.DueDate = todoItemInput.DueDate;
  this.dataAccess.Update(item.Id, this.CreateTodoSchema(item));
  return true;
}
```

Removing a record is no more complicated than the `Update` method. In order to remove the record, we only need to supply the `Id` value so our method signature moves from having a complex type as an input to having a simple type—in this case, a string. We search through the cached entries to find the index of the record that matches the `Id` and, when found, we remove the cached entry by using the splice method. When we use splice on an array, we are really saying remove the entry that starts at the relevant index and remove the number of entries we choose. So, to remove 1 record, we supply 1 as the second parameter to this method. We need to make sure that our database is consistent, so we remove the database entry as well:

```
@Mutation(() => Boolean!)
async Remove(@Arg("Id") id: string): Promise<boolean> {
  const index = Prefill.Instance.Items.findIndex(x => x.Id === id);
  if (index < 0) {
    return false;
  }
  Prefill.Instance.Items.splice(index, 1);
  await this.dataAccess.Remove(id);
  return true;
}
```

The final mutation that we are interested in is the one that sets the Completed flag to true. This method is largely a combination of the Remove and Update methods in that it follows the same logic to identify a record and update it. However, like the Remove method, it only needs the Id as the input argument. As we only intend to update the Completed field, that is the only field that we are going to touch on in this method:

```
@Mutation(() => Boolean!)
async Complete(@Arg("Id") id: string) : Promise<boolean> {
  const item: TodoItem = await Prefill.Instance.Items.find(x => x.Id ===
id);
  if (!item) return false;
  item.Completed = true;
  await this.dataAccess.Update(item.Id, this.CreateTodoSchema(item));
  return true;
}
```

We could have chosen to reuse the Update method and set Completed to true from our client code, but that would have used a more complex call to achieve a much simpler end. By using a separate method, we are ensuring that we have code that does one thing and one thing only. This keeps us to the principle of single responsibility that we are interested in.

With our resolver and schemas in place, we can now turn our attention to adding the code to actually serve up our GraphQL server.

Using Apollo Server as our server

We are going to create a new server implementation for this project, rather than reusing any of the server infrastructure from the previous chapter. Apollo provides its own server implementation (called Apollo Server), which we are going to use in place of Express. As usual, we are going to start off by bringing in the necessary types, and then we will create our class with the class definition. In the constructor, we are going to bring in a reference to our Mongo database class.

Apollo Server is part of the overall Apollo GraphQL strategy for providing out-of-the-box GraphQL support. The server can either stand on its own or work with server frameworks such as Express for serving up self-documenting GraphQL data. The reason we are going to use Apollo Server is because it has built-in support for working with GraphQL schemas. If we were to try and add this support ourselves, we would end up redoing what we get for free from Apollo Server.

First, we are going to import our types:

```
npm install apollo-server apollo-server-express --save
```

Then, we are going to write our `server` class:

```
export class MyApp {
  constructor(private mongo: Mongo = new Mongo()) { }
}
```

Our server is going to expose a `Start` method that will be responsible for connecting to the database and starting our Apollo Server:

```
public async Start(): Promise<void> {
  this.mongo.Connect();
  await Prefill.Instance.Populate();
  const server = new ApolloServer({ schema, playground: true });
  await server.listen(3000);
}
```

When we create our Apollo Server instance, we indicate that we want to use `GraphQLSchema`, but we don't define anything about that schema. We use the `buildSchema` function, which takes a series of options and uses them to bring in the schema that Apollo Server will use. `resolvers` takes an array of GraphQL resolvers, so we are going to supply `TodoItemResolver` as the resolver we want to use. The implication here, of course, is that we can use multiple resolvers.

The `validate` flag states whether or not we want to validate objects that are passed into resolver parameters. Since we are using simple objects and types, we are going to set this to `false`.

Something I like to do to validate the GQL I am creating is to emit the schema using `emitSchemaFile`. This uses the path operation to build up a fully qualified path name. In this case, we will be resolving to the `dist` folder, where we will output the `apolloschema.gql` file:

```
const schema: GraphQLSchema = await buildSchema({
  resolvers: [TodoItemResolver],
  validate: false,
  emitSchemaFile: path.resolve(__dirname, 'apolloschema.gql')
});
```

Now that we have finished coding the server side up, we can add `new MyApp().Start();` to start and run our application. When we build and run our server side, it will start an instance of our Apollo-enabled GraphQL server on `http://localhost:3000`. We do have one little surprise left and it's to do with the last parameter that we supply to the Apollo Server options, namely `playground: true`. The playground is a visual editor area that lets us run `graphql` queries and see what results they bring.

> I would recommend switching the playground off in production code. For testing purposes, however, it is an invaluable aid for trying out queries.

In order to check that we have everything wired up correctly, try entering a GraphQL query into the query window. While entering the query, remember that just because there is a superficial resemblance to a JavaScript object, there is no need to use separate entries. Here's a sample query to get started with. This query exercises the `TodoItems` query we created in `TodoItemResolver`:

```
query {
  TodoItems {
    Id
    Title
    Description
    Completed
    DaysCreated
  }
}
```

The GraphQL Angular client

Just like we did in the previous chapter, we are going to create an Angular client that uses Angular Material as its UI. Again, we are going to use the `ng new` command to create a new application, and we will set the prefix to `atp`. Since we want to add support for routing to our application, we are going to add an extra `--routing` parameter to our command line. We are doing this because it adds the necessary `AppRoutingModule` entries to `app.module.ts` and creates the `app-routing.module.ts` routing file for us:

```
ng new Chapter05 --style scss --prefix atp --routing true
```

In the previous chapter, even though we used Material, we didn't take advantage of routing with it. We are going to use Material one last time before we get back to using Bootstrap for the rest of this book, so we need to add support for Material to our application (don't forget to accept adding support for browser animations when prompted):

```
ng add @angular/material @angular/cdk @angular/animation @angular/flex-
layout
```

At this stage, our `app.module.ts` file should look like this:

```
import { BrowserModule } from '@angular/platform-browser';
import { NgModule } from '@angular/core';
import { AppRoutingModule } from './app-routing.module';
import { AppComponent } from './app.component';
import { BrowserAnimationsModule } from '@angular/platform-
browser/animations';
@NgModule({
  declarations: [
    AppComponent
  ],
  imports: [
    BrowserModule,
    AppRoutingModule,
    BrowserAnimationsModule
  ],
  providers: [],
  bootstrap: [AppComponent]
})
export class AppModule { }
```

We need to add the Material module imports to our `imports` array:

```
HttpClientModule,
HttpLinkModule,
BrowserAnimationsModule,
MatToolbarModule,
MatButtonModule,
MatSidenavModule,
MatIconModule,
MatListModule,
FlexLayoutModule,
HttpClientModule,
MatInputModule,
MatCardModule,
MatNativeDateModule,
MatDatepickerModule,
```

We add `MatNativeDateModule` alongside `MatDatepickerModule` because of the way that the Material date-picker was built. It does not provide any hard assumptions about the way that dates will be implemented, so we need to import an appropriate date representation. While we could write our own date handling module implementation, we are going to have real success by bringing in `MatNativeDateModule`. If we failed to do this, we would end up with a runtime error telling us `No provider found for DateAdapter`.

Adding client-side Apollo support

Before we get around to creating our user interface, we are going to set up the client side of our Apollo integration. While we could install all the individual parts of Apollo using `npm`, we are going to use the power of `ng` again:

```
ng add apollo-client
```

Going back to `AppModule`, we are going to set up Apollo to interact with the server. The `AppModule` constructor is the perfect place for us to inject Apollo to create the connection to our server. Our constructor starts off looking like this:

```
constructor(httpLink: HttpLink, apollo: Apollo) {
}
```

The way that we create the connection to the server is through the `apollo.create` command. This accepts a number of options, but we're just going to concentrate on three of them. We need a link, which establishes the link to our server; a cache, if we want to cache the results of our interactions; and an override of the default Apollo options where we set up the watch query to always fetch from the network. If we don't fetch from the network, we can encounter issues where cached data becomes stale until a refresh:

```
apollo.create({
  link: httpLink.create({ uri: 'http://localhost:3000' }),
  cache: new InMemoryCache(),
  defaultOptions: {
    watchQuery: {
      // To get the data on each get, set the fetchPolicy
      fetchPolicy: 'network-only'
    }
  }
});
```

Don't forget that injecting components requires us to add the relevant modules to the `imports` section of the `@NgModule` module. In this case, we need to add `HttpLinkModule` and `ApolloModule` if we want to be able to automatically use these elsewhere.

That is all the code that we need to put in place to have our client side communicate with a working Apollo Server. Of course, in a production system, we would pick up the address of the server elsewhere and use that instead of the hardcoded localhost. But for our example, this is all we need. We can now get on with the task of adding the screens and the ability to navigate to them using routing.

Adding routing support

The requirements that we have set for our application are such that we will have three main screens. Our main screen will show all todo tasks, including whether they have been completed or not. The second will show overdue tasks, and the last will let our users add new tasks. Each of these will be created as separate components. For now, we are going to add dummy implementations of them, which will allow us to set up our routing:

```
ng g c components/AddTask
ng g c components/Alltasks
ng g c components/OverdueTasks
```

Our routing is configured and controlled from the `app-routing.module.ts` file. Here, we are going to define a set of rules that we expect Angular to follow.

Before we start adding routes, we should actually work out what the term routing means here. The simple way to think of routing is to think of the URL. The route corresponds to the URL, or rather, to the part of the URL other than the base address. Since our page will be running on `localhost:4000`, our full URL is `http://localhost:4000/`. Now, if we wanted our `AllTasks` component to map onto `http://localhost:4000/all`, we would consider the route to be `all`.

Now that we know what a route is, we need to map these three components to their own routes. We start off by defining an array of routes:

```
const routes: Routes = [
];
```

We associate our routes with our routing module by supplying them in the module definition, as follows:

```
@NgModule({
  imports: [RouterModule.forRoot(routes)],
```

```
    exports: [RouterModule]
})
export class AppRoutingModule { }
```

We want to map the `AllTasks` component to `all`, so we add this as an array element inside our routes:

```
{
  path: 'all',
  component: AlltasksComponent
},
```

At this point, when we start our Angular application, we can show the `all` tasks page if we type in `http://localhost:4000/all`. While this is reasonably impressive, it's going to annoy users if we don't have the concept of a default landing page for our site. Our users are generally going to expect that they can enter the site without having to know details about any of our page names, and they should be able to navigate from there because we will direct them to an appropriate page. Fortunately, we can accomplish this really easily. We are going to add another route that contains an empty path. When we encounter the empty path, we are going to redirect the user to the `all` page:

```
{
  path: '',
  redirectTo: 'all',
  pathMatch: 'full'
},
```

Now, when the user navigates to `http://localhost:4000/`, they are redirected to see all of our outstanding tasks.

We have two more components that we want the user to be able to navigate to: our `AddTask` page and our `OverdueTasks` page. Again, we will add support to navigate to these pages through new routes. Once we add these routes in, we can close this file since we have added all the core routing support that we need:

```
{
  path: 'add',
  component: AddTaskComponent
},
{
  path: 'overdue',
  component: OverduetasksComponent
}
```

The routing user interface

The final part of adding routing support to our application is to set up the contents of app-component.html. In here, we are going to add a toolbar that will contain links to our pages and a place to show the page components themselves. The toolbar simply contains three navigation list items. The interesting part of each link is routerLink, which ties our link back to the addresses we previously added in. Effectively, what this part is doing is telling the code that, when we link in that route, we want the content to be rendered into the special router-outlet tag, which is just a placeholder for the actual component content:

```
<mat-toolbar color="primary">
  <mat-nav-list><a mat-list-item routerLink="all">All tasks</a></mat-nav-list>
  <mat-nav-list><a mat-list-item routerLink="overdue">Overdue tasks</a></mat-nav-list>
  <mat-nav-list><a mat-list-item routerLink="add">Add task</a></mat-nav-list>
</mat-toolbar>
<div>
  <router-outlet></router-outlet>
</div>
```

Now, when we run our application, clicking the different links will show the appropriate page, albeit with very little actual content in them.

Adding content to our page components

Now that we have our routing all sorted, we are ready to start adding some functionality to our pages. As well as adding content, we are going to start adding some polish to our application by making use of Angular validation to provide instant feedback to our users. The component that we are going to start with is the AddTask component. Without the ability to add tasks, we aren't going to be able to display any, so let's give ourselves the opportunity to start adding some todo tasks.

Before I start adding in user interface elements, I like to make sure that I have as much of the logic in place behind the component as possible. Once this is in place, actually adding the user interface becomes straightforward. In some cases, this will mean that I have decided on UI constraints before I have even considered how the particular piece of display should be shown, or what control to use to show it. With this in mind, we know that one of the things that makes up our todo item is `DueDate`. If we think about this for a moment, we realize that it makes no sense for us to create a task that has a due date that has already passed. To that end, we are going to set the earliest date that a task can end as being today's date. This will be used as a constraint against whatever control we use to choose the date:

```
EarliestDate: Date;
ngOnInit() {
  this.EarliestDate = new Date();
}
```

We have three things that we are going to be capturing from the user in order to create our todo task. We need to capture the title, the description, and the date the task is due. This tells us that we are going to need three items to act as our model:

```
Title: string;
Description?: string;
DueDate: Date;
```

This is all we need on the model side of our add task component, but we are missing the ability to actually save anything over to our GraphQL server. Before we can start talking to our server, we need to bring support for Apollo into our component. This is as simple as adding a reference to it in our constructor:

```
constructor(private apollo: Apollo) { }
```

The operation we are going to perform must match with what our resolver is expecting. This means that types must match exactly and our GraphQL must be well-formed. Since the task we are going to perform is an add operation, we are going to call the method that we use to add the data, `Add`:

```
Add(): void {
}
```

The add operation is going to trigger the `Add` mutation on the resolver we created on the server. We know that this accepts a `TodoItemInput` instance, so we need to transform our client-side model into a `TodoItemInput` instance, as follows:

```
const todo: ITodoItemInput = new TodoItemInput();
todo.Completed = false;
todo.Id = Guid.create.toString();
```

```
todo.CreationDate = new Date();
todo.Title = this.Title;
todo.Description = this.Description;
todo.DueDate = this.DueDate;
```

There is a bit in the preceding snippet that is unfamiliar to us, namely
the `Guid.create.toString()` call. This command is responsible for creating a unique
identifier known as a **Globally Unique Identifier** (**GUID**). A GUID is a 128-bit number that
is externally represented in string and number format, which generally looks something
like this—**a14abe8b-3d9b-4b14-9a66-62ad595d4582**. Since GUIDs are mathematically based
to guarantee uniqueness, rather than having to call out to a central repository to get a
unique value, they are quick to generate. Through the use of a GUID, we have given our
todo item a unique value. We could have done this at the server if we needed to, but I chose
to generate the entirety of the message on the client.

In order to use a GUID, we will use the `guid-typescript` component:

```
npm install --save guid-typescript
```

We can now put the code in place to transfer the data over to the GraphQL server. As I
mentioned previously, we are going to be using the `Add` mutation, which tells us that we
are going to be calling `mutate` on our `apollo` client:

```
this.apollo.mutate({
  ... logic goes here
})
```

The mutation is a specialist form of string that is covered by `gql`. If we can see what the
entirety of this code looks like, we will be able to break it down immediately after:

```
this.apollo.mutate({
  mutation: gql`
    mutation Add($input: TodoItemInput!) {
      Add(TodoItem: $input) {
        Title
      }
    }
  `, variables: {
    input: todo
  }
}).subscribe();
```

We already knew that we were going to call a mutation, so our `mutate` method accepts a
mutation as `MutationOption`.

One of the parameters we can supply to `MutationOption` is `FetchPolicy`, which we could use to override the default options we set up when we created our Apollo link earlier.

The mutation uses `gql` to create the specially formatted query. Our query is broken down into two parts: the string text that tells us what the query is and any variables that we need to apply. The variables section creates an input variable that maps onto `TodoItemInput`, which we created previously. This is represented by `$` inside our `gql` string, so any variable name must have a matching `$variable` in the query. When the mutation has completed, we tell it that we want the title back. We don't actually have to bring any values back, but when I was debugging earlier on, I found it useful to use the title to check whether we were getting a response from the server.

We are using the ` backtick because this lets us spread our input over multiple lines.

The `mutate` method is triggered from the call to `subscribe`. If we fail to supply this, our mutation will not run. As a convenience, I also added a `Reset` method so that we can clear values away from the UI when the user finishes. I did this so that the user would be able to immediately enter new values:

```
private Reset(): void {
  this.Title = ``;
  this.Description = ``;
  this.DueDate = null;
}
```

That is the logic inside our component taken care of. What we need to do now is add the HTML that will be displayed in the component. Before we add any elements to our component, we want to display the card that will contain our display. This will be centered vertically and horizontally in the display. This is not something that comes naturally to Material, so we have to supply our own local styling. We have a couple of other styles that we are going to set as well, to fix the size of the text area and the width of the card, and to set how we display form fields to make sure each one appears on its own line.

Initially, we will set up a style to center the card. The card will be displayed inside a `div` tag, so we will apply the styling to the `div` tag, which will center the card inside it:

```
.centerDiv{
  height: 100vh;
  display: flex;
```

```
  justify-content: center;
  align-items: center;
}
```

Now, we can style the Material card and form fields:

```
.mat-card {
  width: 400px;
}
.mat-form-field {
  display: block;
}
```

Finally, we are going to set the height of the textarea tag that the user will use to enter their description to 100 pixels:

```
textarea {
  height: 100px;
  resize: vertical;
}
```

Getting back to our display, we are going to set up the container for our card so that it is centered:

```
<div class="centerDiv" layout-fill layout="column" layout-align="center none">
  .... content here
</div>
```

We have reached a point where we want to start leveraging the power of Angular to control the validation of the user input. In order to start treating user input as though it's all related, we are going to put the input parts of our display inside an HTML form:

```
<form name="form" (ngSubmit)="f.form.valid && Add()" #f="ngForm">
  .... the form content goes here.
</form>
```

We need to break this form statement down a bit. We will start by working out what #f="ngForm" actually does. This statement assigns the ngForm component to a variable called f. When we use ngForm, we are referring to the component inside FormsModule (make sure that it's registered inside the app.module imports section). The reason that we do this is because this assignment means that we have access to properties of the component itself. The use of ngForm means that we are working with the top-level form group so that we can do things such as track whether or not the form is valid.

We can see this inside `ngSubmit`, where we are subscribing to the event that tells us that the user has triggered the form submission, which results in the validation being checked; when the data is valid, this results in triggering the `Add` method. With this in place, we don't have to directly call `Add` when the **Save** button is clicked because the submit event will take care of this for us.

There is a short-circuit logic in play with `ngSubmit`. In other words, if the form is not valid, then we won't call the `Add` method.

We are now ready to add the card itself. This lives entirely inside our form. The title section is placed inside a `mat-card-title` section and our buttons are situated inside the `mat-card-actions` section, which aligns the buttons at the bottom of the card. As we just covered, we aren't supplying a click event handler to our **Save** button because the form submission will take care of this:

```
<div layout="row" layout-align="center none">
  <mat-card>
    <mat-card-title>
      <span class="mat-headline">Add ToDo</span>
    </mat-card-title>
  <mat-card-content>
  .... content here.
  <mat-card-content>
    <mat-card-actions>
      <button mat-button class="btn btn-primary">Save</button>
    </mat-card-actions>
  </mat-card>
</div>
```

We are ready to start adding the fields so that we can tie them back to the fields in our underlying model. We will start with the title as the description field largely follows this format as well. We will add the field and its related validation display in first, and then we will break down what is happening:

```
<mat-form-field>
  <input type="text" matInput placeholder="Title" [(ngModel)]="Title"
name="title" #title="ngModel" required />
</mat-form-field>
<div *ngIf="title.invalid && (title.dirty || title.touched)" class="alert
alert-danger">
  <div *ngIf="title.errors.required">
    You must add a title.
  </div>
</div>
```

The first part of our input element is largely self-explanatory. We created it as a text field and used `matInput` to hook the standard input so that it can be used inside `mat-form-field`. With this, we can set the placeholder text to something appropriate.

I opted to use `[(ngModel)]` instead of `[ngModel]` because of the way binding works. With `[ngModel]`, we get one-way binding so that it changes flow from the underlying property through to the UI element that displays it. Since we are going to be allowing the input to change the values, we need a form of binding that allows us to send information back from the template to the component. In this case, we are sending the value back to the `Title` property in the element.

The `name` property must be set. If it is not set, Angular throws internal warnings and our binding will not work properly. What we do here is set the name and then use # with the value set in the name to tie it to `ngModel`. So, if we had `name="wibbly"`, we would have `#wibbly="ngModel"` as well.

Since this field is required, we simply need to supply the `required` attribute, and our form validation will start working here.

Now that we have the input element hooked up to validation, we need some way of displaying any errors. This is where the next `div` statement comes in. The opening `div` statement basically reads as *if the title is invalid (because it is required and has not been set, for instance), and it has either had a value changed in it or we have touched the field by setting focus to it at some point, then we need to display internal content using the alert and alert-danger attributes.*

As our validation failure might just be one of several different failures, we need to tell the user what the problem actually was. The inner `div` statement displays the appropriate text because it is scoped to a particular error. So, when we see `title.errors.required`, our template will display the **You must add a title.** text when no value has been entered.

 We aren't going to look at the description field because it largely follows the same format. I would recommend looking at the Git code to see how that is formatted.

We still have to add the `DueDate` field to our component. We are going to use the Angular date picker module to add this. Effectively, the date picker is made up of three parts.

We have an input field that the user can type directly into. This input field is going to have a `min` property set on it that binds the earliest date the user can select to the `EarliestDate` field we created in the code behind the component. Just like we did in the title field, we will set this field to required so that it will be validated by Angular, and we will apply `#datepicker="ngModel"` so that we can associate the `ngModel` component with this input field by setting the name with it:

```
<input matInput [min]="EarliestDate" [matDatepicker]="picker"
name="datepicker" placeholder="Due date"
 #datepicker="ngModel" required [(ngModel)]="DueDate">
```

The way that we associate the input field is by using `[matDatepicker]="picker"`. As part of our form field, we have added a `mat-datepicker` component. We use `#picker` to name this component `picker`, which ties back to the `matDatepicker` binding in our input field:

```
<mat-datepicker #picker></mat-datepicker>
```

The final part that we need to add is the toggle that the user can press to show the calendar part on the page. This is added using `mat-datepicker-toggle`. We tell it what date picker we are applying the calendar to by using `[for]="picker"`:

```
<mat-datepicker-toggle matSuffix [for]="picker"></mat-datepicker-toggle>
```

Right now, our form field looks like this:

```
<mat-form-field>
  <input matInput [min]="EarliestDate" [matDatepicker]="picker"
name="datepicker" placeholder="Due date"
    #datepicker="ngModel" required [(ngModel)]="DueDate">
  <mat-datepicker-toggle matSuffix [for]="picker"></mat-datepicker-toggle>
  <mat-datepicker #picker></mat-datepicker>
</mat-form-field>
```

All that we are missing now is the validation. Since we have already defined that the earliest date we can choose is today, we don't need to add any validation to that. We have no maximum date to worry about, so all we need to do is check that the user has chosen a date:

```
<div *ngIf="datepicker.invalid && (datepicker.dirty || datepicker.touched)"
class="alert alert-danger">
  <div *ngIf="datepicker.errors.required">
    You must select a due date.
  </div>
</div>
```

So, we have reached the point where we can add tasks to our todo list and they will be saved to the database, but that isn't much use to us if we can't actually view them. We are now going to turn our attention to the `AllTasksComponent` and `OverdueTasksComponent` components.

Our `AllTasksComponent` and `OverdueTasksComponent` components are going to display the same information. All that differs between the two is the GQL call that is made. Because they have the same display, we are going to add a new component that will display the todo information. `AllTasksComponent` and `OverdueTasksComponent` will both use this component:

```
ng g c components/Todo-Card
```

Just like in our add task component, `TodoCardComponent` is going to start off with an `EarliestDate` field and the Apollo client being imported:

```
EarliestDate: Date;
constructor(private apollo: Apollo) {
  this.EarliestDate = new Date();
}
```

We have reached the point where we need to consider what this component is actually going to be doing. It will receive a single `ITodoItem` as input from either `AllTasksComponent` or `OverdueTasksComponent`, so we will need a means for the containing component to be able to pass this information in. We will also need a means to notify the containing component of when the todo item has been deleted so that it can be removed from the tasks being displayed (we will just do this on the client side rather than triggering a requery via GraphQL). Our UI will add a **Save** button when the user is editing the record, so we are going to need some way to track that the user is in the edit section.

With those requirements for the component, we can add in the necessary code to support this. First, we are going to address the ability to pass in a value to our component as an input parameter. In other words, we are going to add a field that can be seen and has values set on it by using data binding by the containers. Fortunately, Angular makes this a very simple task. By marking a field with `@Input`, we expose it for data binding:

```
@Input() Todo: ITodoItem;
```

That takes care of the input, but how do we let the container know when something has happened? When we delete a task, we want to raise an event as output from our component. Again, Angular makes this simple by using `@Output` to expose something; in this case, we are going to expose `EventEmitter`. When we expose this to our containers, they can subscribe to the event and react when we emit the event. When we create `EventEmitter`, we are going to create it to pass the `Id` of our task back, so we need `EventEmitter` to be a string event:

```
@Output() deleted: EventEmitter<string> = new EventEmitter<string>();
```

With this code in place, we can update our `AllTasksComponent` and `OverdueTasksComponent` templates that will hook up to our component:

```
<div fxLayout="row wrap" fxLayout.xs="column" fxLayoutWrap
fxLayoutGap="20px grid" fxLayoutAlign="left">
  <atp-todo-card
    *ngFor="let todo of todos"
    [Todo]="todo"
    (deleted)="resubscribe($event)"></atp-todo-card>
</div>
```

Before we finish adding the logic to `TodoCardComponent`, let's get back to `AllTasksComponent` and `OverdueTasksComponent`. Internally, these are both very similar, so we will concentrate on the logic in `OverdueTasksComponent`.

It shouldn't come as a shock now that these components will accept an Apollo client in the constructor. As we saw from `ngFor` previously, our component will also expose an array of `ITodoItem` called `todos`, which will be populated by our query:

```
todos: ITodoItem[] = new Array<ITodoItem>();
constructor(private apollo: Apollo) { }
```

You may notice, from looking at the code in the repository, that we have not added this code into our component. Instead, we are using a base class called `SubscriptionBase` that provides us with a `Subscribe` method and a resubscribe event.

Our `Subscribe` method is generic accepts either `OverdueTodoItemQuery` or `TodoItemQuery` as the type, along with a `gql` query, and returns an observable that we can subscribe to in order to pull out the underlying data. The reason we have added the base class goes back to the fact that `AllTasksComponent` and `OverdueTasksComponent` are just about identical, so it makes sense to reuse as much code as possible. The name that is sometimes given to this philosophy is **Don't Repeat Yourself (DRY)**:

```
protected Subscribe<T extends OverdueTodoItemQuery |
TodoItemQuery>(gqlQuery: unknown): Observable<ApolloQueryResult<T>> {
}
```

All this method does is create a query using `gql` and set `fetch-policy` to `no-cache` to force the query to read from the network rather than relying on the cache set in `app-module`. This is just another way of controlling whether or not we read from the in-memory cache:

```
return this.apollo.query<T>({
  query: gqlQuery,
  fetch-policy: 'no-cache'
});
```

We extend from a choice of two interfaces because they both expose the same items but with different names. So, `OverdueTodoItemQuery` exposes `OverdueTodoItems` and `TodoItemQuery` exposes `TodoItems`. The reason that we have to do this, rather than using just one interface, is because the field must match the name of the query. This is because Apollo client uses this to automatically map results back.

The `resubscribe` method is called after the user clicks the delete button in the interface (we will get to building up the UI template shortly). We saw that our `resubscribe` method was wired up to the event and that it would receive the event as a string, which would contain the `Id` of the task we want to delete. Again, all we are going to do to delete the record is find the one with the matching `Id`, and then splice the todos list to remove it:

```
resubscribe = (event: string) => {
  const index = this.todos.findIndex(x => x.Id === event);
  this.todos.splice(index, 1);
}
```

Going back to `OverdueTasksComponent`, all we need to do is call `subscribe`, passing in our `gql` query and subscribing to the return data. When the data comes back, we are going to populate our todos array, which will be displayed in the UI:

```
ngOnInit() {
  this.Subscribe<OverdueTodoItemQuery>(gql`query ItemsQuery {
    OverdueTodoItems {
      Id,
      Title,
      Description,
      DaysCreated,
      DueDate,
      Completed
    }
  }`).subscribe(todo => {
    this.todos = new Array<ITodoItem>();
    todo.data.OverdueTodoItems.forEach(x => {
      this.todos.push(x);
    });
  });
}
```

 A note on our subscription—as we are creating a new list of items to display, we need to clear `this.todos` before we start pushing the whole list back into it.

With `AllTasksComponent` and `OverdueTasksComponent` complete, we can turn our attention back to `TodoCardComponent`. Before we finish off adding the component logic, we really need to take a look at the way the template is created. A large part of the logic is similar to the add task UI logic, so we aren't going to worry about how to hook up to a form or add a validation. The things I want to concentrate on here relate to the fact that the task component will display differently when the user is in edit mode, as opposed to a read-only or label-based version. Let's start by looking at the title. When the task is in read-only mode, we are just going to display the title in span, like this:

```
<span>{{Todo.Title}}</span>
```

When we are editing the task, we want to show input elements and validation, as follows:

```
<mat-form-field>
  <input type="text" name="Title" matInput placeholder="Title"
[(ngModel)]="Todo.Title" #title="ngModel"
    required />
</mat-form-field>
<div *ngIf="title.invalid && (title.dirty || title.touched)" class="alert
```

```
alert-danger">
  <div *ngIf="title.errors.required">
    You must add a title.
  </div>
</div>
```

We do this by using a neat trick of Angular. Behind the scenes, we are maintaining an InEdit flag. When that is false, we want to display the span. If it is true, we want to display a template in its place that contains our input logic. To do this, we start off by wrapping our span inside a div tag. This has an ngIf statement that is bound to InEdit. The ngIf statement contains an else clause that picks up the template with the matching name and displays this in its place:

```
<div *ngIf="!InEdit;else editTitle">
  <span>{{Todo.Title}}</span>
</div>
<ng-template #editTitle>
  <mat-form-field>
    <input type="text" name="Title" matInput placeholder="Title"
[(ngModel)]="Todo.Title" #title="ngModel"
      required />
  </mat-form-field>
  <div *ngIf="title.invalid && (title.dirty || title.touched)" class="alert
alert-danger">
    <div *ngIf="title.errors.required">
      You must add a title.
    </div>
  </div>
</ng-template>
```

Other fields are displayed in a similar way. There is one more point of interest in the way we display the read-only fields. DueDate needs to be formatted in order to be displayed as a meaningful date rather than as the raw date/time that is saved in the database. We use | to pipe DueDate into a special date formatter that controls how the date is displayed. For instance, March 21, 2018 would be displayed as Due: Mar 21st, 2019 using the following date pipe:

```
<p>Due: {{Todo.DueDate | date}}</p>
```

Please take the time to review the rest of todo-card.component.html. Swapping templates is heavily done, so it is a good way to review how to make the same UI serve two purposes.

In the component itself, we have three operations left to look at. The first one that we will cover is the `Delete` method, which is triggered when the user presses the delete button on the component. This is a simple method that calls the `Remove` mutation, passing the `Id` across to be removed. When the item has been removed from the server, we call `emit` on our `deleted` event. This event passes the `Id` back to the containing component, which results in this item being removed from the UI:

```
Delete() {
  this.apollo.mutate({
    mutation: gql`
    mutation Remove($Id: String!) {
      Remove(Id: $Id)
    }
    `, variables: {
      Id: this.Todo.Id
    }
  }).subscribe();
  this.deleted.emit(this.Todo.Id);
}
```

The `Complete` method is just as simple. When the user clicks the `Complete` link, we call the `Complete` query, which passes across the current `Id` as the matching variable. As we could be in edit mode at this point, we call `this.Edit(false)` to switch back to read-only mode:

```
Complete() {
  this.apollo.mutate({
    mutation: gql`
    mutation Complete($input: String!) {
      Complete(Id: $input)
    }
    `, variables: {
      input: this.Todo.Id
    }
  }).subscribe();
  this.Edit(false);
  this.Todo.Completed = true;
}
```

The `Save` method is very similar to the `Add` method in the add task component. Again, we need to switch back from edit mode when this mutation finishes:

```
Save() {
  const todo: ITodoItemInput = new TodoItemInput();
  todo.Completed = false;
  todo.CreationDate = new Date();
```

```
    todo.Title = this.Todo.Title;
    todo.Description = this.Todo.Description;
    todo.DueDate = this.Todo.DueDate;
    todo.Id = this.Todo.Id;
    this.apollo.mutate({
      mutation: gql`
        mutation Update($input: TodoItemInput!) {
          Update(TodoItem: $input)
        }
      `, variables: {
        input: todo
      }
    }).subscribe();

    this.Edit(false);
  }
```

At this point, we have a fully functioning client- and server-based GraphQL system.

Summary

In this chapter, we have investigated the benefits that GraphQL can bring to us by viewing it as an alternative to REST services for retrieving and updating data. We investigated setting up Apollo as a server-side GraphQL engine and added Apollo to an Angular client to interact with the server, as well as look at the specialist GQL query language. In order to leverage the full power of TypeScript, we brought in the `type-graphql` package to simplify the creation of GraphQL schemas and resolvers.

Building on our experiences from the previous chapter, we saw how we could begin to build a reusable MongoDB data access layer; while there is some way to go with this, we have made a good start with it, leaving room to remove application constraints such as needing to use an `Id` to find records.

This chapter also introduced us to Angular routing to serve up different views, depending on the route the user chooses. We kept using Material so that we could see how we could apply this logic to the navigation content we covered in `Chapter 4`, *The MEAN Stack – Building a Photo Gallery*. We also looked at how to prevent the user from making mistakes with their input by looking at what Angular provides in terms of validation, and how we can use it alongside inline templates to provide consistent feedback to the user about any problems.

In the next chapter, we are going to look at another way of communicating with a server by using Socket.IO to maintain an open connection between the client and server. We will build an Angular chat application that will automatically forward conversations to all open connections to the application. As an added bonus, we will see how we can integrate Bootstrap into Angular in place of Material and still use features such as routing. We will also introduce a feature that most professional applications rely on: user authentication.

Questions

1. Does GraphQL intend to fully replace REST clients?
2. What purpose do mutations serve in GraphQL? What type of operations would we expect to see with them?
3. How do we pass a parameter into a subcomponent in Angular?
4. What is the difference between a schema and a resolver?
5. How do we create a singleton?

The complete function does not remove a completed task from the overdue items page. Enhance the code to remove the item from the page after the user clicks complete.

Further reading

- In order to delve further into the mysteries of GraphQL, I would recommend Brian Kimokoti's excellent *Beginning GraphQL* (https://www.packtpub.com/in/application-development/beginning-graphql).
- To see GraphQL in use in React, Sebastian Grebe has written *Hands-on Full-Stack Web Development with GraphQL and React* (https://www.packtpub.com/in/web-development/hands-full-stack-web-development-graphql-and-react).

6
Building a Chat Room Application Using Socket.IO

In this chapter, we are going to cover how to build an Angular chat room application using Socket.IO in order to delve into the ability to send messages back and forth between the client and server without having to establish REST APIs or through the use of GraphQL queries. The technology we are going to use involves the establishment of a long-running connection from the client to the server, making communication as simple as passing a message.

In this chapter, we are going to cover the following topics:

- Long-running client/server communications using Socket.IO
- Creating a Socket.IO server
- Creating an Angular client and adding Socket.IO support
- Using decorators to add client-side logging
- Using Bootstrap in our client
- Adding Bootstrap navigation
- Signing up to Auth0 to authenticate our client
- Adding Auth0 support to our client
- Adding secure Angular routing
- Hooking up to Socket.IO messages at our client and server
- Using Socket.IO namespaces to segregate messages
- Adding room support
- Receiving and sending messages

Technical requirements

The finished project can be downloaded from `https://github.com/PacktPublishing/ Advanced-TypeScript-3-Programming-Projects/tree/master/Chapter06`.

After downloading the project, you will have to install the package requirements using the `npm install` command.

Long-running client/server communications using Socket.IO

So far, we have covered a variety of ways of communicating back and forth between a client and a server, but they have all had one thing in common—they were reacting to some form of interaction to trigger the transfer of data. Irrespective of whether we clicked a link or pushed a button, there was some user input that triggered that back and forth between the two sides.

There are some situations, however, where we would like to keep the lines of communication between the client and the server open permanently so that data can be pushed as soon as it's available. If we were playing an online game, for instance, we wouldn't want to have to push a button just to get other players' statuses updated on our screen. What we need is a technology that maintains the connection for us and allows us to pass messages without issues.

Over the years, there have been a number of technologies that have evolved with a view of addressing precisely this problem. Some of these technologies, such as flash sockets, have fallen out of favor because they rely on proprietary systems. Collectively, these are known as **push technologies**, and a standard called **WebSocket** has emerged and become commonplace, with all the major browsers supporting it. What is worth knowing is that WebSocket sits alongside HTTP as a cooperative protocol.

Here is a piece of WebSocket trivia for you. While HTTP uses HTTP or HTTPS to identify the protocol, the specification for WebSockets defines **WS** or **WSS** (short for **WebSocket Secure**) as the protocol identifier.

In the node world, Socket.IO has become the *de facto* standard for enabling WebSocket communication. We are going to use it to build a chat room application that keeps the chat open for all connected users.

Project overview

The *classic* socket-based application is creating a chat room. It's almost the *Hello World* of socket applications. The reason that a chat room is so useful for this is because it allows us to explore techniques such as sending messages to other users, reacting to messages from other users, and using rooms to separate where chats are sent.

Material design played a large part in its development over the past couple of chapters, so now is a suitable time for us to return to Bootstrap 4 and see how we can use it to lay out the interface in an Angular application. We will also work with Socket.IO at the client and the server to enable bi-directional communication. Something that has been lacking in previous chapters has been the ability to authenticate the user. In this chapter, we are going to bring in authentication support by signing up to use Auth0 (`https://auth0.com/`).

Working alongside the GitHub code, this chapter should take about two hours to complete. When completed, the application should appear as follows:

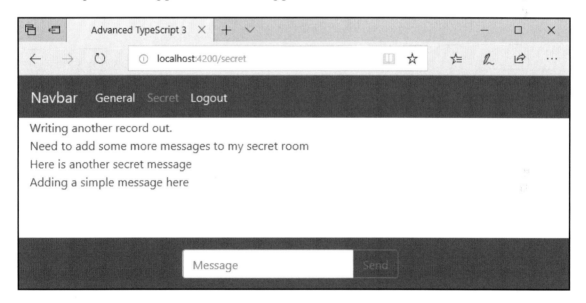

Now that we know what type of application we want to build, and what we want it to look like, we are ready to start building our application. In the next section, we are going to look at how to add external authentication to our application using Auth0.

Getting started with Socket.IO and Angular

Most of the requirements, such as Node.js and Mongoose, are the same as in earlier chapters, so we are no longer going to list the additional components. As we go through this chapter, we will call out any new components that we need. As always, the canonical place for finding out what we are using is the code in GitHub.

As part of this chapter, we are going to use Auth0 (`https://auth0.com`) to authenticate our users. Auth0 is one of the most popular choices available for authentication as it takes care of all of the infrastructure. All we need to provide is a secure login and information storage mechanism. The idea behind us using Auth0 is that we will take advantage of their APIs to verify the identity of someone who is using our application through the use of the **open authentication (OAuth)** framework, which allows us to automatically show or hide access to parts of our application based on this authentication. With OAuth, and its successor OAuth 2, we are using a standard authorization protocol that allows authenticated users access to features of our application without having to sign up to our site and provide login information.

Initially, this chapter was going to use a passport to provide authentication support but, given recent high-profile security issues from companies such as Facebook, I decided that we would look at Auth0 to take care of and manage our authentication. With authentication, I find that it's best to make sure I'm using the best of breed when it comes to security.

Before we write any code at all, we are going to sign up to Auth0 and create the infrastructure we need for a single page web application. Begin by clicking the **Sign Up** button, which will redirect you to the following URL: `https://auth0.com/signup?signUpData=%7B%22category%22%3A%22button%22%7D`. I chose to sign up with my GitHub account, but you can choose any of the options available.

Auth0 provides us with a variety of premium paid-for services as well as the free version. We only require the basic features, so the free version is perfect for our needs.

Once you have signed up, you need to press the **Create Application** button, which will bring up the **Create Application** dialog. Give it a name and choose **Single Page Web App** before clicking the **CREATE** button to create the Auth0 application:

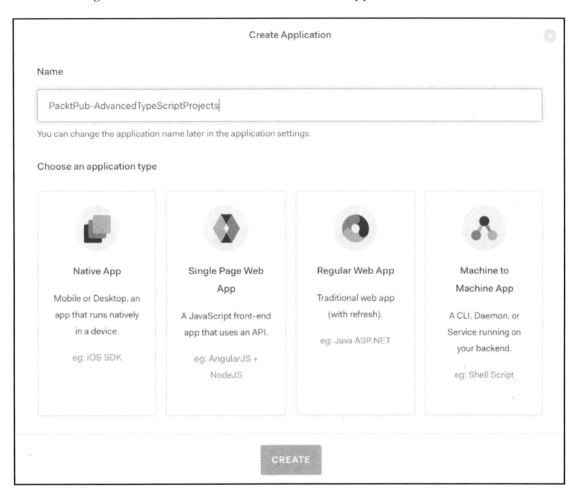

If you click the **Settings** tab, you should have something that looks like the following:

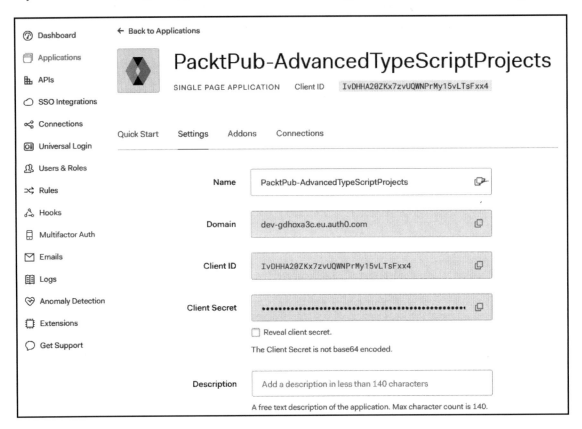

There are options available for callback URLs, allowed web origins, logout URLs, CORS, and so on.

The full scope of Auth0 is outside the scope of this book, but I would recommend reading the documentation provided and setting these settings as appropriate for any applications you create.

Security note: Where I am providing details about client IDs or similar unique identifiers in this book, these are purely for the purpose of illustrating the code. Any live IDs will be deactivated as a matter of security. I would advise you to adopt similar good practices and not commit live identifiers or passwords in a public location such as GitHub.

Creating a chat room application using Socket.IO, Angular, and Auth0

Before we start with our development, we should figure out what we want to build. Since a chat room is a common enough application, it is easy for us to come up with a standard set of requirements that will help us exercise the different aspects of Socket.IO. The requirements for the application we are going to build are as follows:

- A user will be able to send a message to be seen by all users in a general chat page
- The user will be able to log in to the application, at which point a secure page will be available
- Logged-in users will be able to send messages that are visible only to other logged-in users
- Old messages will be retrieved and displayed to the user when they connect

Creating our application

By now, creating a node application should be second nature, so we aren't going to cover how to do that anymore. The `tsconfig` file that we are going to use is as follows:

```
{
  "compileOnSave": true,
  "compilerOptions": {
    "incremental": true,
    "target": "es5",
    "module": "commonjs",
    "outDir": "./dist",
    "removeComments": true,
    "strict": true,
    "esModuleInterop": true,
    "inlineSourceMap": true,
    "experimentalDecorators": true,
  }
}
```

The incremental flag in the settings is a new feature introduced in TypeScript 3.4 that allows us to perform incremental builds. What this feature does is build something called a project graph when the code is compiled. The next time the code is built, the project graph is used to identify code that hasn't changed, meaning that it doesn't need to be rebuilt. In bigger applications, this can save a lot of time in terms of compiling.

We are going to save messages to a database, so it's going to come as no surprise that we are going to start off with the database connection code. What we are going to do on this occasion is move our database connection to a class decorator that accepts the name of the database as the parameter to the decorator factory:

```
export function Mongo(connection: string) {
  return function (constructor: Function) {
    mongoose.connect(connection, { useNewUrlParser: true}, (e:unknown) => {
      if (e) {
        console.log(`Unable to connect ${e}`);
      } else {
        console.log(`Connected to the database`);
      }
    });
  }
}
```

Don't forget to install `mongoose` and `@types/mongoose` before creating this.

With this in place, when we create our `server` class, we simply need to decorate it, like this:

```
@Mongo('mongodb://localhost:27017/packt_atp_chapter_06')
export class SocketServer {
}
```

That's it. When `SocketServer` is instantiated, the database will be connected automatically. I have to admit that I really like the simplicity of this approach. It's an elegant technique that can be carried over into other applications.

In the previous chapter, we built a `DataAccessBase` class to simplify the way we worked with data. We are going to take that class and remove some of the methods we aren't going to use in this application. At the same time, we are going to see how we can remove the hard model constraints. Let's start with the class definition:

```
export abstract class DataAccessBase<T extends mongoose.Document>{
  private model: Model;
  protected constructor(model: Model) {
    this.model = model;
  }
}
```

The `Add` method should also look familiar from the previous chapter:

```
Add(item: T): Promise<boolean> {
  return new Promise<boolean>((callback, error) => {
    this.model.create(item, (err: unknown, result: T) => {
      if (err) {
        error(err);
      }
      callback(!result);
    });
  });
}
```

In the previous chapter, we had a constraint that finding a record needed to have a field called `Id` on it. While that was an acceptable limitation there, we really don't want to force applications to have `Id` as a field. We are going to provide a more open implementation that will allow us to specify any criteria we need for retrieving records and the ability to select what fields to return:

```
GetAll(conditions: unknown, fields: unknown): Promise<unknown[]> {
  return new Promise<T[]>((callback, error) => {
    this.model.find(conditions, fields, (err: unknown, result: T[]) => {
      if (err) {
        error(err);
      }
      if (result) {
        callback(result);
      }
    });
  });
}
```

Just like in the previous chapter, we are going to create a `mongoose.Document`-based interface and a `Schema` type. This will form the message contract and will store details about the room, the message text, and the date when we received the message. These will then be combined to create the physical model that we need to use as our database. Let's see how:

1. First, we define the `mongoose.Document` implementation:

```
export interface IMessageSchema extends mongoose.Document{
  room: string;
  messageText: string;
  received: Date;
}
```

2. The `Schema` type that corresponds to this looks like this:

```
export const MessageSchema = new Schema({
  room: String,
  messageText: String,
  received: Date
});
```

3. Finally, we create a `MessageModel` instance, which we will use to create the data access class that we will use to save and retrieve data:

```
export const MessageModel =
mongoose.model<IMessageSchema>('message', MessageSchema,
'messages', false);
export class MessageDataAccess extends
DataAccessBase<IMessageSchema> {
  constructor() {
    super(MessageModel);
  }
}
```

Adding Socket.IO support to our server

We have now reached the point where we are ready to bring Socket.IO into our server and create a running server implementation. Run the following command to incorporate Socket.IO and the related `DefinitelyTyped` definitions:

```
npm install --save socket.io @types/socket.io
```

With these definitions available to us, we are going to bring Socket.IO support into our server and begin running it, ready to receive and transmit messages:

```
export class SocketServer {
  public Start() {
    const appSocket = socket(3000);
    this.OnConnect(appSocket);
  }
  private OnConnect(io: socket.Server) {
  }
}
new SocketServer.Start();
```

The parameter that our `OnConnect` method receives is the starting point for receiving and reacting to messages in Socket.IO. We use this to *listen* for a connection message that will indicate that a client has connected. When the client connects, it opens up what amounts to a socket for us on which to start receiving and sending messages. When we want to send messages directly to a particular client, we will use methods available from the `socket` that's returned in the following code snippet:

```
io.on('connection', (socket:any) => {
});
```

At this point, we need to understand that even though the name of the technology is Socket.IO, this is not a WebSocket implementation. While it can use web sockets, there is no guarantee that it actually will; for instance, corporate policies might prohibit the use of sockets. So, how does Socket.IO actually work? Well, Socket.IO is made up of a number of different cooperating technologies, one of which is called Engine.IO, and this provides the underlying transport mechanism. The first type of connection it takes, when connecting, is an HTTP long poll, which is a fast and efficient transport mechanism to open. During idle periods, Socket.IO attempts to determine whether the transport can be changed over to a socket and, if it can use a socket, it seamlessly and invisibly upgrades the transport to use sockets. As far as the client is concerned, they connect quickly, and messages are reliable since the Engine.IO part establishes connections even if firewalls and load balancers are present.

One of the things we want to provide for our clients is a history of the conversations that have gone on beforehand. This means that we want to read and save our messages to the database. Inside our connection, we are going to read all of the messages for the room the user is currently in and return them to the user. If a user has not logged in, they will only be able to see messages where the room has not been set:

```
this.messageDataAccess.GetAll({room: room}, {messageText: 1, _id:
0}).then((msgs: string[]) =>{
  socket.emit('allMessages', msgs);
});
```

The syntax looks slightly strange, so we will break it down step by step. The call to `GetAll` is calling the general-purpose `GetAll` method from our `DataAccessBase` class. When we created that implementation, we discussed the need to make it more general purpose, and to allow the calling code to specify what fields to filter on as well as what fields to return. When we say `{room: room}`, we are telling Mongo that we want to filter our results based on the room. We can think of the equivalent SQL clause as being `WHERE room = roomVariable`. We also want to indicate what results we want back; in this case, we only want `messageText` without the `_id` field, so we use the `{messageText: 1, _id: 0}` syntax. When the results come back, we need to send the array of messages over to the client using `socket.emit`. This command sends these messages to the client that opened the connection, using `allMessages` as the key. If the client has code to receive `allMessages`, it will be able to react to these messages.

 The event name that we choose as the message leads us on to one of the limitations of Socket.IO. There are certain event names that we cannot use as a message because they have been restricted due to them having a special meaning to Socket.IO. These are `error`, `connect`, `disconnect`, `disconnecting`, `newListener`, `removeListener`, `ping`, and `pong`.

There isn't much point creating the server and sending messages if we haven't got anything at the client end to receive them. Even though we don't have all of our messages in place yet, we have sufficient infrastructure in place to start writing our client.

Creating our chat room client

Again, we are going to create our Angular application using the `ng new` command. We are going to be providing routing support, but when we get around to doing the routing part, we will see how we can ensure that users cannot bypass our authentication:

```
ng new Client --style scss --prefix atp --routing true
```

Since our Angular client will be making regular use of Socket.IO, we are going to bring support in for Socket.IO using an Angular-specific Socket.IO module:

```
npm install --save ngx-socket-io
```

In `app.module.ts`, we will create a connection to our Socket.IO server by creating a configuration that points to the server URL:

```
import { SocketIoModule, SocketIoConfig } from 'ngx-socket-io';
const config: SocketIoConfig = { url: 'http://localhost:3000', options: {}}
```

This configuration is passed into the static `SocketIoModule.forRoot` method when we import the module, which will configure the client-side socket for us. As soon as our client starts, it will establish a connection, triggering the connect message sequence we described in the server code:

```
imports: [
  BrowserModule,
  AppRoutingModule,
  SocketIoModule.forRoot(config),
```

Using decorators to add client-side logging

One of the features we want to use in our client code is to be able to log method calls, along with the parameters that are passed into them. We have encountered this type of feature before when we looked at creating decorators. In this case, we want to create a `Log` decorator:

```
export function Log() {
  return function(target: Object,
                  propertyName: string,
                  propertyDesciptor: PropertyDescriptor):
PropertyDescriptor {
    const method = propertyDesciptor.value;
    propertyDesciptor.value = function(...args: unknown[]) {
      const params = args.map(arg => JSON.stringify(arg)).join();
      const result = method.apply(this, args);
```

```
      if (args && args.length > 0) {
        console.log(`Calling ${propertyName} with ${params}`);
      } else {
        console.log(`Calling ${propertyName}. No parameters present.`)
      }
      return result;
    };
    return propertyDesciptor;
  }
}
```

The way that the `Log` decorator works is that it starts off by copying the method from `propertyDescriptor.value`. We then replace this method by creating a function that takes in any parameters that are passed into the method. Inside this inner function, we use `args.map` to create a stringified representation of the parameter and value, which then joins them together. After calling `method.apply` to run the method, we write out details pertaining to the method and parameters to the console. With the preceding code, we now have a simple mechanism to automatically log methods and parameters just by using `@Log`.

Setting up Bootstrap in Angular

Instead of using Material in Angular, we can choose to use Bootstrap to style our pages. Adding support is a simple enough task. We begin, as always, by installing the relevant packages. In this case, we are going to install Bootstrap:

```
npm install bootstrap --save
```

Once we have installed Bootstrap, we simply need to add a reference to our Bootstrap to our `styles` section in `angular.json`, as follows:

```
"styles": [
  "src/styles.scss",
  "node_modules/bootstrap/dist/css/bootstrap.min.css"
],
```

With this in place, we are going to create a `navigation` bar that will sit at the top of our page:

```
ng g c components/navigation
```

Before we add the `navigation` component body, we should replace the content of our `app.component.html` file so that it is serving up our navigation on every page:

```
<atp-navigation></atp-navigation>
<router-outlet></router-outlet>
```

Bootstrap navigation

Bootstrap provides the `nav` component to which we can add `navigation`. Inside this, we are going to create a series of links. Like in the previous chapter, we will use `routerLink` to say what Angular should route to:

```
<nav class="navbar navbar-expand-lg navbar-dark bg-dark">
  <a class="navbar-brand" href="#">Navbar</a>
  <div class="collapse navbar-collapse" id="navbarNavAltMarkup">
    <div class="navbar-nav">
      <a class="nav-item nav-link active" routerLink="/general">General</a>
      <a class="nav-item nav-link" routerLink="/secret"
*ngIf="auth.IsAuthenticated">Secret</a>
      <a class="nav-item nav-link active" (click)="auth.Login()"
routerLink="#" *ngIf="!auth.IsAuthenticated">Login</a>
      <a class="nav-item nav-link active" (click)="auth.Logout()"
routerLink="#" *ngIf="auth.IsAuthenticated">Logout</a>
    </div>
  </div>
</nav>
```

Where things get interesting with routing concerns the use of authentication to show and hide links. If the user is authenticated, we want them to be able to see the **Secret** and **Logout** links. If the user has not been authenticated, we want them to see the **Login** link.

In the navigation, we can see a number of auth references. Behind the scenes, these all map back to `OauthAuthorizationService`. We teased the use of this back when we signed up to Auth0 at the beginning of this chapter. Now, it's time for us to add the authorization service that will connect our users up to Auth0.

Authorizing and authenticating users using Auth0

Our authorization is going to consist of two parts—a service to perform the authorization, and a model to make working with the authorization simple. We will start off by creating our `Authorization` model, which contains the details we will receive back from a successful login. Note that the constructor brings in the `Socket` instance:

```
export class Authorization {
  constructor(private socket: Socket);
  public IdToken: string;
  public AccessToken: string;
  public Expired: number;
```

```
    public Email: string;
}
```

We can use this to create a series of useful helper methods. The first one we are going to create is a method to set the public properties if the user logs in. We are identifying a successful login as one where we receive an access token and an ID token as part of the result:

```
@Log()
public SetFromAuthorizationResult(authResult: any): void {
    if (authResult && authResult.accessToken && authResult.idToken) {
        this.IdToken = authResult.idToken;
        this.AccessToken = authResult.accessToken;
        this.Expired = (authResult.expiresIn * 1000) + Date.now();
        this.Email = authResult.idTokenPayload.email;
        this.socket.emit('loggedOn', this.Email);
    }
}
```

When the user logs on, we are going to send a `loggedOn` message back to the server, passing over the `Email` address. We will come back to this message shortly when we cover sending the messages to the server and handling the responses that come back. Note that we are logging the method and the properties.

When the user logs off, we want to clear the values and send the `loggedOff` message to the server:

```
@Log()
public Clear(): void {
    this.socket.emit('loggedOff', this.Email);
    this.IdToken = '';
    this.AccessToken = '';
    this.Expired = 0;
    this.Email = '';
}
```

The final helper tells us whether the user has been authenticated by checking whether the `AccessToken` field is present, and whether the date when the ticket is due to expire exceeds the time when we perform the check:

```
public get IsAuthenticated(): boolean {
    return this.AccessToken && this.Expired > Date.now();
}
```

Before we create our OauthAuthorizationService service, we need some means of communicating with Auth0, so we will bring in support for it:

```
npm install --save auth0-js
```

With this in place, we add a reference to auth0.js as a script tag:

```
<script type="text/javascript" src="node_modules/auth0-
js/build/auth0.js"></script>
```

We now have all the pieces in place to create our service:

```
ng g s services/OauthAuthorization
```

The start of our service is straightforward enough. When we construct the service, we instantiate the helper class we just created:

```
export class OauthAuthorizationService {
  private readonly authorization: Authorization;
  constructor(private router: Router, private socket: Socket) {
    this.authorization = new Authorization(socket);
  }
}
```

We are now ready to hook up to Auth0. You may recall that, when we signed up to Auth0, we were given a series of settings. From the settings, we require the client ID and domain. We are going to use these when we instantiate WebAuth from auth0-js, in order to uniquely identify our application. responseType tells us that we need the user's authentication token and ID token back following a successful login. scope tells the user what features we want access to when they log in. If we wanted the profile, for instance, we could set the scope to openid email profile. Finally, we supply redirectUri to tell Auth0 what page we want to come back to following a successful login:

```
auth0 = new auth0.WebAuth({
  clientID: 'IvDHHA20ZKx7zvUQWNPrMy15vLTsFxx4',
  domain: 'dev-gdhoxa3c.eu.auth0.com',
  responseType: 'token id_token',
  redirectUri: 'http://localhost:4200/callback',
  scope: 'openid email'
});
```

redirectUri must match precisely what is contained in the Auth0 settings section. I prefer to set it to a page that doesn't exist on the site and control the redirection manually, so callback is a useful one for me because I can apply conditional logic to determine the page the user is redirected to if needs be.

Now, we can add in our `Login` method. This uses the `authorize` method to load up the authentication page:

```
@Log()
public Login(): void {
  this.auth0.authorize();
}
```

Logging out is as simple as calling `logout` and then calling `Clear` on our helper class to reset the expiration point and clear the other properties:

```
@Log()
public Logout(): void {
  this.authorization.Clear();
  this.auth0.logout({
    return_to: window.location.origin
  });
}
```

Obviously, we are going to need a means to check the authentication. The following method retrieves the authentication in the URL hash and parses it using the `parseHash` method. If the authentication is unsuccessful, the user is redirected back to the general page, which does not require a login. On the other hand, if the user is authenticated successfully, the user is directed to a secret page that is only available to authenticated users. Note that we are calling the `SetFromAuthorizationResult` method we wrote earlier to set the access token, expiry time, and so on:

```
@Log()
public CheckAuthentication(): void {
  this.auth0.parseHash((err, authResult) => {
    if (!err) {
      this.authorization.SetFromAuthorizationResult(authResult);
      window.location.hash = '';
      this.router.navigate(['/secret']);
    } else {
      this.router.navigate(['/general']);
      console.log(err);
    }
  });
}
```

When the user comes back to the site, it's good practice to let them access it again without requiring them to reauthenticate themselves. The following `Renew` method checks their session and, if they were successful, resets their authenticated status:

```
@Log()
public Renew(): void {
  this.auth0.checkSession({}, (err, authResult) => {
    if (authResult && authResult.accessToken && authResult.idToken) {
      this.authorization.SetFromAuthorizationResult(authResult);
    } else if (err) {
      this.Logout();
    }
  });
}
```

This code is all well and good, but where do we use it? In `app.component.ts`, we bring in our authorization service and check the user authentication:

```
constructor(private auth: OauthAuthorizationService) {
  this.auth.CheckAuthentication();
}

ngOnInit() {
  if (this.auth.IsAuthenticated) {
    this.auth.Renew();
  }
}
```

Don't forget to add a reference to `NavigationComponent` to hook up `OauthAuthorizationService`:

```
constructor(private auth: OauthAuthorizationService) {
}
```

Using secure routing

With our authentication in place, we want to ensure that users cannot bypass it just by typing in the URL of the page. We wouldn't have much security set up if users could easily bypass it, especially after we went to all the trouble of providing secure authorization. What we are going to do is put another service in place that the router will use to determine whether it can activate the route. First, we create the service, as follows:

```
ng g s services/Authorization
```

The service itself is going to implement the `CanActivate` interface, which the router will use to determine whether the route can be activated. The constructor for this service simply takes in the router and our `OauthAuthorizationService` service:

```
export class AuthorizationService implements CanActivate {
  constructor(private router: Router, private authorization:
OauthAuthorizationService) {}
}
```

The boilerplate code for the `canActivate` signature looks a lot more complicated than it needs to for our purposes. What we are really going to do here is check the authentication status and, if the user is not authenticated, we will reroute the user back to the general page. If the user is authenticated, we return `true` and the user continues on to the secured page:

```
canActivate(route: ActivatedRouteSnapshot, state: RouterStateSnapshot):
  Observable<boolean | UrlTree> | Promise<boolean | UrlTree> | boolean |
UrlTree {
  if (!this.authorization.IsAuthenticated) {
    this.router.navigate(['general']);
    return false;
  }
  return true;
}
```

We have two routes that we are going to follow here, as we saw in the navigation links. Before we add our routes, let's create the components that we are going to show:

```
ng g c components/GeneralChat
ng g c components/SecretChat
```

Finally, we have reached the point where we are going to hook up the routes. As we saw in the previous chapter, adding routes is straightforward. The secret sauce that we are going to add is `canActivate`. With that in our route, the user cannot bypass our authentication:

```
const routes: Routes = [{
  path: '',
  redirectTo: 'general',
  pathMatch: 'full'
}, {
  path: 'general',
  component: GeneralchatComponent
}, {
  path: 'secret',
  component: SecretchatComponent,
  canActivate: [AuthorizationService]
}];
```

Even though we have to supply a callback URL in our Auth0 configuration, we don't include it in our routes because we want to control the page—we do it to navigate to and from our authorization service.

At this point, we want to start writing messages from the client to the server and receive messages from it.

Adding client-side chat capabilities

When we wrote our authentication code, we relied heavily on putting services in place to take care of it. In a similar way, we are going to provide a chat service that provides the central point of the client-side socket messaging:

```
ng g s services/ChatMessages
```

Unsurprisingly, this service will also incorporate Socket in the constructor:

```
export class ChatMessagesService {
  constructor(private socket: Socket) { }
}
```

When we send a message from the client to the server, we use the emit method on the socket. The text that we want to send from the user will be sent over by means of the message key:

```
public SendMessage = (message: string) => {
  this.socket.emit('message', message);
};
```

Working in rooms

In Socket.IO, we use rooms to segregate messages as a means to send them only to certain users. When a client joins a room, any messages sent to that room will be available. A useful way to think of this is to imagine the rooms as being like rooms in a house with the doors shut. When someone wants to tell you something, they have to be in the same room as you to tell you.

Both our general and secret links will tie into rooms. The general page will use a blank room name that equates to the default Socket.IO room. The secret link will join a room called *secret* so that any messages sent to *secret* will automatically appear to any user on that page. To make our life easy, we will provide a helper method to `emit` the `joinRoom` method from the client to the server:

```
private JoinRoom = (room: string) => {
  this.socket.emit('joinRoom', room);
};
```

When we join a room, any messages that we send using `socket.emit` are automatically sent to the correct room. We don't have to do anything clever since Socket.IO takes care of this for us automatically.

Getting the messages

For both the general and the secret messages pages, we are going to be getting the same data. We are going to use RxJS to create an observable that wraps getting a single message back from the server as well as getting all currently sent messages back from the server.

Depending on the room string that's passed in, the `GetMessages` method joins either a secret room, just for logged in users, or the general room, available to all users. Having joined the room, we return an `Observable` instance where, on a particular event, we react. In the case of receiving the single message, we call the `Observable` instance's `next` method. This will be subscribed to by the client component, which will write this out. Similarly, we also subscribe on the socket to `allMessages` in order to receive all of the previously sent messages when we join the room. Again, we iterate over the messages and use `next` to write the message out.

My favorite part of this section is `fromEvent`. This is synonymous with the `socket.on` method of the `userLogOn` message and allows us to write out details about who logged in during the session:

```
public GetMessages = (room: string) => {
  this.JoinRoom(room);
  return Observable.create((ob) => {
this.socket.fromEvent<UserLogon>('userLogOn').subscribe((user:UserLogon) =>
{
      ob.next(`${user.user} logged on at ${user.time}`);
    });
    this.socket.on('message', (msg:string) => {
      ob.next(msg);
    });
```

```
    this.socket.on('allMessages', (msg:string[]) => {
      msg.forEach((text:any) => ob.next(text.messageText));
    });
  });
}
```

Thus far, I have been fairly loose when using the terms *messages* and *events* to help with the flow of reading this chapter. In this instance, they both refer to the same thing.

Finishing the server sockets

Before we add the actual component implementations, we are going to add in the rest of our server-side socket behavior. You may remember that we added the ability to read all the historical records and send them back to the newly connected client:

```
socket.on('joinRoom', (room: string) => {
  if (lastRoom !== '') {
    socket.leave(lastRoom);
  }
  if (room !== '') {
    socket.join(room);
  }
  this.messageDataAccess.GetAll({room: room}, {messageText: 1, _id:
0}).then((msgs: string[]) =>{
    socket.emit('allMessages', msgs);
  });
  lastRoom = room;
});
```

What we have here is the server reacting to `joinRoom` coming over from the client. When we receive this event, we leave the last room if it has been set and then join the room that's passed over from the client; again, only if it has been set. This allows us to get all the records and then `emit` them back on the current socket connection.

When the client sends the `message` event to the server, we are going to write the message to the database so that it can be retrieved later on:

```
socket.on('message', (msg: string) => {
  this.WriteMessage(io, msg, lastRoom);
});
```

This method starts off by saving the message to the database. If the room is set, we use `io.sockets.in` to `emit` the message to all of the clients who are actively in the room. If there is no room set, we want to send the message to all the clients in the general page by using `io.emit`:

```
private WriteMessage(io: socket.Server, message: string, room: string) {
  this.SaveToDatabase(message, room).then(() =>{
    if (room !== '') {
      io.sockets.in(room).emit('message', message);
      return;
    }
    io.emit('message', message);
  });
}
```

Here, we have seen the primary difference between `io.` and `socket.`. When we want to send the message to just the currently connected client, we use the `socket` part. When we need to send the message to a wider number of clients, we use the `io` part.

Saving the message is as simple as doing the following:

```
private async SaveToDatabase(message: string, room: string) {
  const model: IMessageSchema = <IMessageSchema>{
    messageText: message,
    received: new Date(),
    room: room
  };
  try{
    await this.messageDataAccess.Add(model);
  }catch (e) {
    console.log(`Unable to save ${message}`);
  }
}
```

 Something you might be asking yourself is why we allocate the date on the server rather than when we create the message at the client end. When we are running the client and the server on the same machine, it doesn't really matter which way we do it, but when we build distributed systems, we should always refer to a centralized time. Use of the centralized date and time means that events from all over the world will be coordinated as the same time zone.

On the client side, we reacted to a slightly more complex log-on event. We create the equivalent server-side event as follows when we receive the `loggedOn` event, transmitting it to anyone listening in the secret room:

```
socket.on('loggedOn', (msg: any) => {
  io.sockets.in('secret').emit('userLogOn', { user: msg, time: new Date()
});
});
```

We now have client infrastructure in place and the server has been completed. All we need to do now is add in the server-side components. Functionally speaking, since the `GeneralChat` and `SecretChat` components are almost identical (the only difference being the room they are listening to), we will concentrate on just one of them.

Namespaces in Socket.IO

Imagine that we are writing a server that can be used by any number of client applications, and those client applications could be using any number of other Socket.IO servers as well. We could be introducing bugs into the client application if we use the same message names as the messages coming from the other Socket.IO servers. To circumvent this issue, Socket.IO uses a concept called **namespaces** to allow us to segregate our messages so that they don't conflict with other applications.

A namespace is a convenient way to provide a unique endpoint to connect to, and we connect to it using code that looks as follows:

```
const socket = io.of('/customSocket');
socket.on('connection', function(socket) {
  ...
});
```

This code should look familiar because, apart from `io.of(...)`, it's the same code that we used previously to connect to a socket. What may come as a surprise is that our code has already been using namespaces, even though we didn't specify it ourselves. Unless we specify a namespace ourself, our sockets will connect to the default namespace, which is equivalent to `io.of('/')`.

When coming up with a name for your namespace, try to think of something that would be unique and meaningful. One standard I have seen adopted in the past utilizes the company name and the project to create the namespace. So, if your company was called `WonderCompany` and you were working on `Project Antelope`, you might use `/wonderCompany_antelope` as the namespace. Don't just assign random characters since they are hard for people to remember, and this would increase the possibility that they will make mistakes typing it in, meaning that the sockets would not connect.

Finishing off our application with the GeneralchatComponent

Let's start off by adding in the Bootstrap code for displaying the messages. We wrap the `row` message inside a Bootstrap container, or rather `container-fluid` in this case. In our component, we are going to be reading the messages from the array of messages we received over the socket:

```
<div class="container-fluid">
  <div class="row">
    <div *ngFor="let msg of messages" class="col-12">
      {{msg}}
    </div>
  </div>
</div>
```

We are also going to add a text box to the `navigation` bar at the bottom of our screen. This is bound to the `CurrentMessage` field in the component. We send the message using `SendMessage()`:

```
<nav class="navbar navbar-dark bg-dark mt-5 fixed-bottom">
  <div class="navbar-expand m-auto navbar-text">
    <div class="input-group mb-6">
      <input type="text" class="form-control" placeholder="Message" aria-label="Message"
        aria-describedby="basic-addon2" [(ngModel)]="CurrentMessage" />
      <div class="input-group-append">
        <button class="btn btn-outline-secondary" type="button"
(click)="SendMessage()">Send</button>
      </div>
    </div>
  </div>
</nav>
```

In the component behind this HTML, we need to hook up to the `ChatMessageService`. We are going to take a `Subscription` instance and use this to populate the `messages` array shortly:

```
export class GeneralchatComponent implements OnInit, OnDestroy {
    private subscription: Subscription;
    constructor(private chatService: ChatMessagesService) { }

    CurrentMessage: string;
    messages: string[] = [];
}
```

When the users type in a message and press the **Send** button, we are going to send it to the server using the chat service's `SendMessage` method. The groundwork we put in earlier really starts to pay off here:

```
SendMessage(): void {
    this.chatService.SendMessage(this.CurrentMessage);
    this.CurrentMessage = '';
}
```

Now, we only have two bits left to add. In our component initialization, we are going to retrieve the `Observable` instance from `GetMessages` and `subscribe` to it. When a message comes in on this subscription, we push it onto the messages where the magic of Angular binding really comes into play, and the interface is updated with the latest message:

```
ngOnInit() {
    this.subscription = this.chatService.GetMessages('').subscribe((msg:
string) =>{
        this.messages.push(msg);
    });
}
```

Note that the `GetMessages` method is the point where we link in the room. In `SecretchatComponent`, this will become `this.chatService.GetMessages('secret')`.

One of the things we did is take a reference to the subscription. When we destroy the current page, we are going to clear up the subscription so that we don't leak memory:

```
ngOnDestroy() {
    if (this.subscription) {
        this.subscription.unsubscribe();
    }
}
```

A final note on this implementation. When we started writing the code here, we had to make a conscious decision about how to populate the current screen with the message when the user pressed **Send**. Effectively, we had two choices. We could either choose to add the current message to the end of the messages array directly and not send it back from the server to the client, or we could send it to the server and then let the server send it back to us. We could choose either method, so why did I choose to send it to the server and then round trip it back to the client? The answer to this has to do with sequencing. In most chat applications I have used, the messages are seen by each user in exactly the same order. The easiest way to do this is to let the server coordinate the messages for us.

Summary

In this chapter, we discovered how to write code that established a permanent connection between the client and server, enabling us to pass messages back and forth in response to messages. We also saw how to sign up to Auth0 and use this as the authentication mechanism for our application. Then, we learned how to write client-side authentication. Having spent the last couple of chapters investigating Material in Angular, we moved back to using Bootstrap and saw how simple it is to use in Angular.

In the next chapter, we are going to learn how to apply Bing maps in order to create a custom map-based application that lets us select and save points of interest in a cloud-based database that also uses location-based searches to retrieve business information.

Questions

1. How would we send a message to all users?
2. How do we send a message to just the users in a certain room?
3. How do we send a message to all users except the user who sent the original message?
4. Why shouldn't we use a message called connect?
5. What is Engine.IO?

In our application, we only used a single room. Add other rooms that do not require the user to be authenticated prior to use and add rooms that do require the user to be authenticated. We also didn't store the details of who sent the messages. Enhance the application to store these details and transmit them both ways as part of the message.

Further reading

- If you want to find out how to use particular features of Socket.IO, I would recommend *Socket.IO Cookbook* by Tyson Cadenhead (`https://www.packtpub.com/web-development/socketio-cookbook`).

Angular Cloud-Based Mapping with Firebase

We have spent quite a few chapters writing our own backend systems for returning information to the client. In the last few years, there has been a trend toward using third-party cloud systems. Cloud systems can help lower the costs of writing applications, because other companies provide all of the infrastructure that we need to use and take care of testing, upgrades, and so on. In this chapter, we are going to look at using cloud infrastructure from the Bing mapping team and Firebase to provide data storage.

The following topics will be covered in this chapter:

- Signing up to Bing mapping
- The implications of billable cloud features
- Signing up to Firebase
- Adding a map component
- Using map search features
- Using `EventEmitter` to notify parent components of child component events
- Reacting to mapping events to add and remove your own points of interest
- Overlaying map search results on the map
- Tidying up event handlers
- Saving data to Cloud Firestore
- Configuring Cloud Firestore authentication

Technical requirements

The finished project can be downloaded from `https://github.com/PacktPublishing/` `Advanced-TypeScript-3-Programming-Projects/tree/master/Chapter07`.

After downloading the project, you will have to install the package requirements using the `npm install` command.

Modern applications and the move to cloud services

Throughout this book, we have been concentrating on writing applications where we control the infrastructure on which the application runs and where the data is physically stored. Over the last few years, the trend has been to move away from this type of application toward a model where other companies provide this infrastructure through something called **cloud-based services**. *Cloud services* has become a catch-all marketing term to describe the trend of using on-demand services from other companies, relying on them to provide application features, security, scaling, backup features, and so on. The idea behind this is that we can reduce capital costs by letting others take care of these features for us, freeing us to write applications that make use of these features in a mix-and-match fashion.

In this chapter, we are going to look at using cloud-based services from Microsoft and Google, so we will look at the process of signing up to these services, the implications of using them, and how to make use of them in our final Angular application.

Project overview

For our last Angular application, we are going to go to town and use Bing mapping services to display the types of maps we are used to using on a daily basis to search for locations. We will go even further and use Microsoft's Local Insights services to search for a particular business type in the currently visible map area. This is one of the two applications that excited me the most when I was putting together the plan for this book because I have a love for map-based systems.

As well as displaying maps, we are going to be able to select points of interest on the map by clicking directly on the map. These points will be represented by colored pins. We will save the location of these points, along with their name, in a cloud-based database from Google.

This application should take about an hour to complete, as long as you work alongside the code on GitHub.

Throughout this chapter, we will no longer provide details about how to add packages using npm, or how to create Angular applications, components, or the like, as you should be familiar with how to do this by this point.

When completed, the application should look like this (maybe not zoomed into Newcastle upon Tyne, though):

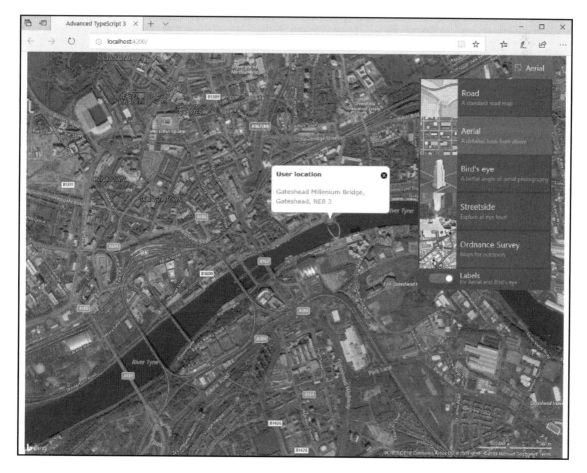

Getting started with Bing mapping in Angular

This is our last Angular application, so we will start off by creating it in the same way we created applications in previous chapters. Again, we are going to use Bootstrap, rather than Angular Material.

The packages we are going to concentrate on in this chapter are as follows:

- `bootstrap`
- `bingmaps`
- `firebase`
- `guid-typescript`

Since we are going to be hooking our code up to cloud-based services, we will have to sign up to them first. In this section, we will look at what we need to do to sign up.

Signing up to Bing mapping

If we want to use Bing Maps, we have to sign up to Bing Map Services. Navigate to `https://www.bingmapsportal.com` and click the **Sign in** button. This requires a Windows account, so if you don't have one, you will need to set one up. For now, we are going to assume that you have a Windows account available:

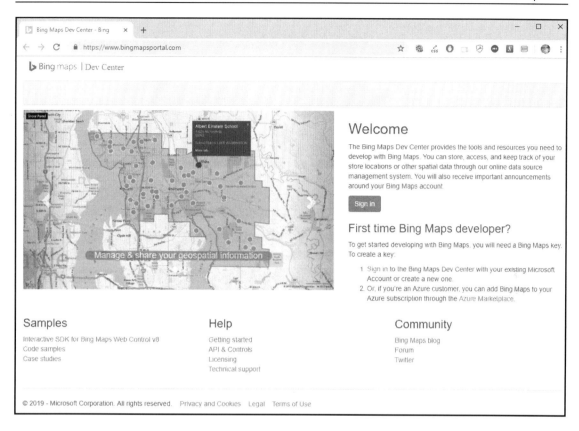

When we sign in, we need to create a key that our application will use to identify itself to the Bing Map Services so that they know who we are and can keep track of our map usage. From the **My account** option, select **My Keys**:

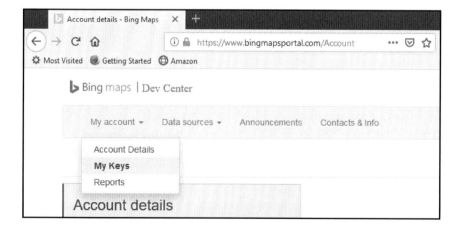

When the keys screen appears, you will see a link called **Click here to create a new key**. Clicking the link will show the following screen:

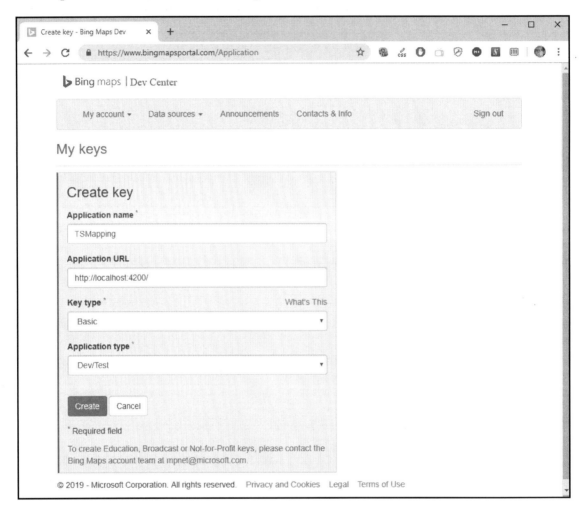

Most of the information on this screen is fairly self-explanatory. The application name is used if we have multiple keys and we need to search for them. The URL doesn't have to be set, but I like to do this if I am deploying to different web applications. It's a handy way to remember which key is associated with which application. Since we aren't going to be going for the paid-for enterprise service, the only key type that we have available is **Basic**.

The **Application type** is probably the most important field on here, from our point of view. There are a number of application types that we can choose from, each of which has limitations around the number of transactions that it can accept. We are going to stick with **Dev/Test**, which limits us to 125,000 billable transactions, cumulatively, over a year-long period.

 When we use the Local Insights code in this chapter, this will generate billable transactions. If you don't want to run the risk of incurring any costs, I would recommend that you disable the code that does this searching.

When we click **Create**, our map key is created, and is available by clicking the **Show key** or **Copy key** links in the table that appears. We have now set up everything that we need for the map key, so let's move on to signing up to the database.

Signing up to Firebase

Firebase requires a Google account. Assuming we have one available, we can access the features of Firebase at `https://console.firebase.google.com/`. When this screen appears, click the **Add project** button to start the process of adding Firebase support:

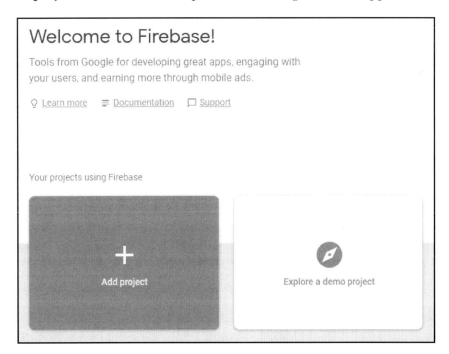

Choose a meaningful name for the project. Before we can create the project, we should read the terms and conditions for using Firebase and tick the checkbox if we agree with them. Note that if we choose to share usage statistics for Google Analytics, we should read the appropriate terms and conditions and check the **controller-controller terms** checkbox as well:

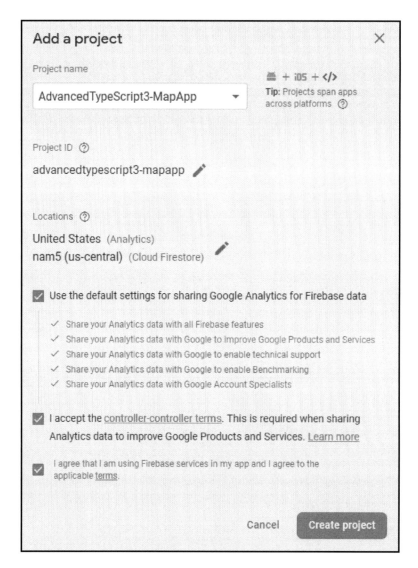

Having clicked **Create project**, we now have access to the Firebase project. While Firebase, as a cloud services provider, is more than just a database, offering storage, hosting, and so on, we are just going to use the **Database** option. When we click the **Database** link, we are presented with the **Cloud Firestore** screen, where we need to click **Create database** to start the process of creating the database:

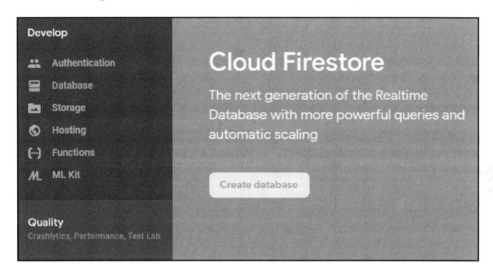

 Whenever I refer to Firebase in this chapter, I am using this as a shorthand way of saying that this is the Firestore feature of the Firebase cloud platform.

While we are creating the database, we will need to choose the level of security that we want to apply to our database. We have two options here. We can start with the database locked so that reading and writing is disabled. Access to the database will then have to be enabled by writing rules that the database will check to determine whether or not a write is allowed.

For our purposes, though, we are going to start in test mode, which allows unlimited reads and writes to the database:

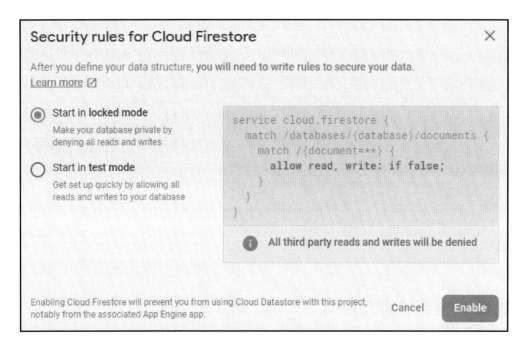

 Like Bing mapping, Firebase has usage limitations and cost implications. We are creating a Spark plan datastore, which is the free Firebase version. This version comes with hard limits, such as only being able to store 1 GB of data per month, with 50,000 reads a day and 20,000 writes a day. For details around pricing and limitations, please read `https://firebase.google.com/pricing/`.

Once we have clicked **Enable** and have a database available, we need to be able to get access to the key and project details that Firebase creates for us. To find this, click the **Project overview** link on the menu. The **</>** button pops up a screen that shows the details we will need to copy for our project:

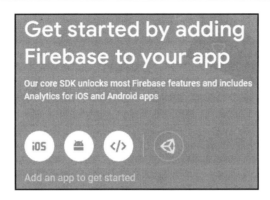

We now have our cloud infrastructure set up and have the keys and details we need available. We are now ready to write our application.

Creating a Bing Maps application using Angular and Firebase

One of the fastest-growing application types over the last few years has been the explosion of mapping applications, whether for your satnav system or running Google Maps on your phone. Underneath these applications lie mapping services that have been developed by companies such as Microsoft or Google. We are going to use the Bing Maps services to add mapping support to our application.

Our mapping application has the following requirements:

- Clicking on a location will add that location as a point of interest
- When a point of interest is added, an information box will be displayed, showing details about it
- Clicking on a point of interest again will delete it
- Points of interest will be saved to a database
- The user will be able to move the point of interest, updating details in the database
- Where available, business information will be automatically retrieved and displayed

Adding the map component

We are going to create two Angular components for this step—one called `MappingcontainerComponent`, and another called `MapViewComponent`.

I broke these up because I wanted to use `MappingcontainerComponent` to contain the bootstrap infrastructure, while `MapViewComponent` will just contain the map itself. If you want to, you can combine these together, but for the purposes of establishing a clear delineation to describe what is going on with each part, it was easier for me to create two components here. This does mean that we need to introduce some coordination between the two components, which will reinforce the `EventEmitter` behavior we covered in `Chapter 5`, *Angular ToDo App with GraphQL and Apollo*.

Before we add any body to these components, we have some models and services that we need to write to provide the infrastructure that our map and data access will need.

Points of interest

Each point of interest is represented by a pin, and can be represented as latitude and longitude coordinates, along with its name.

 Latitude and longitude are geographic terms that are used to identify exactly where something is on the planet. Latitude tells us how far north or south something is from the equator, with the equator being 0. This means that a positive number indicates we are north of the equator, and a negative number means we are going south from the equator. Longitude tells us how far east or west we are from the vertically centered line of the earth which, by convention, runs through Greenwich in London. Again, if we are moving east, the numbers are positive, while moving west from the line at Greenwich means the numbers will be negative.

The model that represents this looks as follows:

```
export class PinModel {
  id: string;
  lat: number;
  long: number;
  name: string;
}
```

We will be referring to both pins and points of interest throughout this section. They both represent the same thing, so we will be using them interchangeably.

When we create an instance of this, we are going to use a GUID to represent it. Since the GUID is unique, we use it as a convenient way to find the point of interest when we move or remove it. This isn't the exact representation of the way we are going to store our model in the database because this identifier is intended to make sense for tracking the pins on the map, not for tracking the pins in the database. To that end, we are going to add a separate model that we will use to store the model item in the database:

```
export interface PinModelData extends PinModel {
  storageId: string;
}
```

We create this as an interface because Firebase expects to receive data only, with no class infrastructure surrounding it. We could have created `PinModel` as an interface as well, but the syntax for instantiating it is slightly more cumbersome, which is why we chose to create it as a class.

With the models in place, we are now ready to hook up to Firebase. Rather than using the Firebase `npm` directly, we are going to use the official Angular Firebase library, called `AngularFire`. The `npm` reference for this is `@angular/fire`.

When we set up our Firebase datastore, we got the settings that we need to create a uniquely identified connection to it. We are going to copy these settings into our `environment.ts` and `environment.prod.ts` files. When we publish an application to production, Angular remaps `environment.prod.ts` to the environment file so that we can have separate dev and production settings:

```
firebase: {
  apiKey: "AIzaSyC0MzFxTtvt6cCvmTGE94xc5INFRYlXznw",
  authDomain: "advancedtypescript3-mapapp.firebaseapp.com",
  databaseURL: "https://advancedtypescript3-mapapp.firebaseio.com",
  projectId: "advancedtypescript3-mapapp",
  storageBucket: "advancedtypescript3-mapapp.appspot.com",
  messagingSenderId: "6102469443"
}
```

 It's generally bad practice to use the same endpoints for dev and production systems, so you could create a separate Firebase instance to hold the production mapping information and store that in `environment.prod.ts`.

In `app.module`, we are going to import the `AngularFire` modules and then reference them in the imports. When we reference `AngularFireModule`, we call the static `initializeApp` method that will use the `environment.firebase` setting to establish a connection to Firebase.

First, the `import` statements are as follows:

```
import { AngularFireModule } from '@angular/fire';
import { AngularFirestoreModule } from '@angular/fire/firestore';
import { AngularFireStorageModule } from '@angular/fire/storage';
```

Next, we set up the Angular `imports`:

```
imports: [
  BrowserModule,
  HttpClientModule,
  AngularFireModule.initializeApp(environment.firebase),
  AngularFireStorageModule,
  AngularFirestoreModule
],
```

For Firebase's functionality, it's helpful to have a service as a single point of implementation for interacting with the database itself. That's why we are going to create a `FirebaseMapPinsService`:

```
export class FirebaseMapPinsService {
}
```

Inside this class, we are going to use a feature from `AngularFire` called `AngularFirestoreCollection`. Firebase exposes the `Query` and `CollectionReference` types to perform CRUD operations on the underlying data from the database. `AngularFirestoreCollection` wraps this behavior into a handy stream for us. We set the generic type to `PinModelData` to say what data will be saved to the database:

```
private pins: AngularFirestoreCollection<PinModelData>;
```

Our service is going to provide a model that creates an observable of a `PinModelData` array that hooks into the `pins` property. The way that we hook this all together lies inside the constructor that receives the `AngularFirestore`. The `pins` collection is associated with the underlying collection by passing in the name of the collection that will be stored in the database (which saves the data as documents in JSON). Our `Observable` listens to `valueChanges` on the collection, as follows:

```
constructor(private readonly db: AngularFirestore) {
  this.pins = db.collection<PinModelData>('pins');
```

```
this.model = this.pins.valueChanges();
}
```

One of the decisions I took when designing this application was that removing a pin from the UI should result in removing the associated point of interest from the database. Since it isn't being referenced by anything else, we don't need to keep it as reference data. Deleting the data is as simple as using `doc` to get the underlying document record from the datastore using the `storageId`, and then deleting it:

```
Delete(item: PinModelData) {
  this.pins.doc(item.storageId).delete();
}
```

When the user adds a point of interest, we want to create a corresponding entry in the database, but when they move the pin, we want to update the record. Rather than using separate `Add` and `Update` methods, we can combine the logic into one method because we know that a record that has an empty `storageId` has not previously been saved to the database. Therefore, we give it a unique ID using the Firebase `createId` method. If `storageId` is present, then we want to update it:

```
Save(item: PinModelData) {
  if (item.storageId === '') {
    item.storageId = this.db.createId();
    this.pins.doc(item.storageId).set(item);
  }
  else {
    this.pins.doc(item.storageId).update(item);
  }
}
```

Representing the map pins

It's all very well us being able to save the pins to the database, but we also need a way to represent the pins on the map so that we can show them during the map session and move them as needed. This class will also act as the connection to the data service. The class that we are going to write will demonstrate a neat little trick introduced in TypeScript 3, called **rest tuples**, and starts off as follows:

```
export class PinsModel {
  private pins: PinModelData[] = [];
  constructor(private firebaseMapService: FirebaseMapService) { }
}
```

The first feature we are going to introduce deals with adding the data for a pin when the user clicks on the map. The signature for this method looks a little bit strange, so we'll take a minute or so to cover how it works. This is what the signature looks like:

```
public Add(...args: [string, string, ...number[]]);
```

When we see ...args as the last (or only) parameter, our immediate thought here is that we are going to be using a REST parameter. If we break the parameter list down from the start, we can think of this as starting off like this:

```
public Add(arg_1: string, arg_2: string, ...number[]);
```

That almost looks like it makes sense, but there's another REST parameter in there. This basically says that we can have any number of numbers at the end of the tuple. The reason that we have to apply ... to this, rather than just applying number[], is because we need to spread the elements out. If we just used the array format, we would have to push elements into this array in the calling code. With the REST parameter in the tuple, we can pull the data out, save it to the database, and add it to our pins array, like this:

```
public Add(...args: [string, string, ...number[]]) {
  const data: PinModelData = {
    id: args[0],
    name: args[1],
    lat: args[2],
    long: args[3],
    storageId: ''
  };
  this.firebaseMapService.Save(data);
  this.pins.push(data);
}
```

 The implication of using a tuple like this is that the calling code has to make sure that it is putting values into the correct location.

When we get to the code to call this, we can see that our method is called as follows:

```
this.pinsModel.Add(guid.toString(), geocode, e.location.latitude,
e.location.longitude);
```

When the user moves a pin on the map, we will use a similar trick to update its location. All we need to do is find the model in our array and update its values. We even have to update the name because the act of moving the pin will change the address of the pin. We call the same Save method on our data service just like we did in our Add method:

```
public Move(...args: [string,string, ...number[]]) {
  const pinModel: PinModelData = this.pins.find(x => x.id === args[0]);
  if (pinModel) {
    pinModel.name = args[1];
    pinModel.lat = args[2];
    pinModel.long = args[3];
  }
  this.firebaseMapService.Save(pinModel);
}
```

Other classes will need access to the data from the database too. We face two choices here—we could either have other classes also use the Firebase map service and potentially miss out calls to this class, or we could make this class the sole point of access to the map service. We are going to rely on this class to be the single point of contact with FirebaseMapPinsService, which means that we need to expose the model through a Load method:

```
public Load(): Observable<PinModelData[]>{
  return this.firebaseMapService.model;
}
```

Removing a point of interest uses a much simpler method signature than adding or moving one. All we need is the client-side id of the record, which we use to find the PinModelData item and call Delete to remove from Firebase. Once we have deleted the record, we find the local index of this record and remove it by splicing the array:

```
public Remove(id: string) {
  const pinModel: PinModelData = this.pins.find(x => x.id === id);
  this.firebaseMapService.Delete(pinModel);
  const index: number = this.pins.findIndex(x => x.id === id);
  if (index >= 0) {
    this.pins.splice(index,1);
  }
}
```

Trying interesting things with map searches

When it comes to getting the name of the location where the user has placed the pin, or moved it to, we want this to happen automatically. We really don't want the user to have to type in this value when mapping can pick this for us automatically. This means that we are going to have to use mapping features to get this information for us.

Bing mapping has a number of optional modules, which we can opt into using, that give us the ability to do things such as searches based on location. In order to do this, we are going to create a class called `MapGeocode` that will do the searching for us:

```
export class MapGeocode {
}
```

You may notice that, for some of our classes, we are creating them without creating services. This implies that we are going to have to take care of manually instantiating the class ourselves. That is fine since we can control the lifetime of our class manually. If you want to, when you are recreating the code, you could convert classes such as `MapGeocode` into a service and inject it.

Since search is an optional feature, we need to load it in. To do that, we are going to pass in our map and use `loadModule` to load the `Microsoft.Maps.Search` module, passing in a new instance of `SearchManager` as the option:

```
private searchManager: Microsoft.Maps.Search.SearchManager;
constructor(private map: Microsoft.Maps.Map) {
  Microsoft.Maps.loadModule('Microsoft.Maps.Search', () => {
    this.searchManager = new Microsoft.Maps.Search.SearchManager(this.map);
  });
}
```

All that remains for us to do is write a method to perform the lookup. Since this could be a lengthy operation, we need to make this a `Promise` type, returning the string that will be populated with the name. Inside this `Promise`, we create a request containing the location and a callback that, when executed by the `reverseGeocode` method, will update the callback in the `Promise` with the name of the location. With this in place, we call `searchManager.reverseGeocode` to perform the search:

```
public ReverseGeocode(location: Microsoft.Maps.Location): Promise<string> {
  return new Promise<string>((callback) => {
    const request = {
      location: location,
      callback: function (code) { callback(code.name); }
    };
    if (this.searchManager) {
```

```
        this.searchManager.reverseGeocode(request);
    }
  });
}
```

Names matter in coding. In mapping, when we geocode, we convert a physical address into a location. The act of converting a location into an address is called **reverse geocoding**. That is why our method has the rather cumbersome name of ReverseGeocode.

There is another type of search that we need to consider. We want a search that uses the visible map area (the viewport) to identify coffee shops in that area. To do this, we are going to use Microsoft's new Local Insights API to search for things such as businesses in a given area. There is a limitation to this implementation right now, in that Local Insights are only available for US addresses, but there are plans to roll this feature out across other countries and continents.

To show that we can still use mapping in services, we are going to create a PointsOfInterestService that accepts an HttpClient, which we will use to get the results of the REST call:

```
export class PointsOfInterestService {
    constructor(private http: HttpClient) {}
}
```

The REST call endpoint accepts a query that tells us what type of businesses we are interested in, the location to use to perform the search, and the map key. Again, our search functionality could be long-running, so we will return a Promise, this time of a custom PoiPoint that returns the latitude and longitude, as well as the name of the business:

```
export interface PoiPoint {
    lat: number,
    long: number,
    name: string
}
```

When we call the API, we are going to use `http.get`, which returns an observable. We are going to `pipe` the result and `map` it using `MapData`. We will `subscribe` to the result and parse the results down (note that we don't really know the returning type, so we will leave this as `any`). The returning type can contain multiple `resourceSets`, mostly for if we were going to have multiple types of query at once here, but we only have to concern ourselves with the initial `resourceSet`, which we will then use to extract the resources. The following code shows the format of the elements we are interested in from this search. When we have finished parsing our results, we are going to unsubscribe from the search subscription and call back on the `Promise` with the points we have just added:

```
public Search(location: location): Promise<PoiPoint[]> {
  const endpoint =
`https://dev.virtualearth.net/REST/v1/LocalSearch/?query=coffee&userLocatio
n=${location[0]},${location[1]}&key=${environment.mapKey}`;
  return new Promise<PoiPoint[]>((callback) => {
    const subscription: Subscription =
this.http.get(endpoint).pipe(map(this.MapData))
      .subscribe((x: any) => {
        const points: PoiPoint[] = [];
        if (x.resourceSets && x.resourceSets.length > 0 &&
x.resourceSets[0].resources) {
          x.resourceSets[0].resources.forEach(element => {
            if (element.geocodePoints && element.geocodePoints.length > 0) {
              const poi: PoiPoint = {
                lat: element.geocodePoints[0].coordinates[0],
                long: element.geocodePoints[0].coordinates[1],
                name: element.name
              };
              points.push(poi)
            }
          });
        }
        subscription.unsubscribe();
        callback(points);
      })
  });
}
```

In our query, we are simply going to search at a point—we can easily extend this to search in a bounding box restricted to our view, if we wanted to, by accepting the map bounding box and changing `userLocation` to `userMapView=${boundingBox{0}},${boundingBox{1}},${boundingBox{2}},${boundingBox{3}}` (where `boundingBox` is a rectangle). For further details about extending the search, see `https://docs.microsoft.com/en-us/previous-versions/mt832854(v=msdn.10)`.

Now that we have the map searching functionality and the database functionality done, wouldn't it be great to actually put a map on the screen? Let's take care of that now.

Adding Bing Maps to the screen

Like we covered previously, we are going to use two components to display the maps. Let's start with the `MapViewComponent`. The HTML template for this control is really straightforward:

```
<div #myMap style='width: 100%; height: 100%;'>
</div>
```

Yes, that really is all there is to our HTML. What goes on behind it is a bit more complicated, and this is where we are going to learn how Angular lets us hook into standard DOM events. We normally don't show the whole `@Component` element because it is pretty much boilerplate code, but in this case, we are going to have to do something a little bit different. Here's the first part of our component:

```
@Component({
  selector: 'atp-map-view',
  templateUrl: './map-view.component.html',
  styleUrls: ['./map-view.component.scss'],
  host: {
    '(window:load)' : 'Loaded()'
  }
})
export class MapViewComponent implements OnInit {
  @ViewChild('myMap') myMap: { nativeElement: string | HTMLElement; };

  constructor() { }

  ngOnInit() {
  }
}
```

In the `@Component` section, we hook the window load event up to the `Loaded` method. We will add this method shortly, but for now, it's important to know that this is how we hook a component up to an event from the host. Inside the component, we use an `@ViewChild` to hook up to the `div` in our template. Basically, this allows us to reference an element inside our view by name so that we can work with it in some arbitrary way.

The reason we added a `Loaded` method is because Bing Maps have a particularly nasty habit of not working properly in browsers such as Chrome or Firefox unless we hook the map up in the `window.load` event. We are going to host the map inside the `div` statement we added to the template using a series of map load options, which includes the map credentials and the default zoom level:

```
Loaded() {
  // Bing has a nasty habit of not working properly in browsers like
  // Chrome if we don't hook the map up
  // in the window.load event.
  const map = new Microsoft.Maps.Map(this.myMap.nativeElement, {
    credentials: environment.mapKey,
    enableCORS: true,
    zoom: 13
  });
  this.map.emit(map);
}
```

If we want to choose a particular type of map type to display, we can set this in the map load options as follows:

```
mapTypeId:Microsoft.Maps.MapTypeId.road
```

Our `MapViewComponent` is going to be hosted inside another component, so we will create an `EventEmitter` that we can use to notify the parent. We already added the emit code in our `Loaded` method, passing the map we just loaded back to the parent:

```
@Output() map = new EventEmitter();
```

Let's add the parent container now. Most of the template is just taken up with creating the Bootstrap containers with the rows and columns. Inside the `div` column, we are going to host the child component we just created. Again, we can see that we use the `EventEmitter`, so when the map is emitted, it triggers the `MapLoaded` event:

```
<div class="container-fluid h-100">
  <div class="row h-100">
    <div class="col-12">
      <atp-map-view (map)="MapLoaded($event)"></atp-map-view>
    </div>
  </div>
</div>
```

Most of the mapping container code should be familiar territory to us by now. We inject `FirebaseMapPinsService` and `PointsOfInterestService`, which we use to create a `MapEvents` instance in the `MapLoaded` method. In other words, when the `atp-map-view` component hits `window.load`, the populated Bing map comes back through:

```
export class MappingcontainerComponent implements OnInit {
  private map: Microsoft.Maps.Map;
  private mapEvents: MapEvents;
  constructor(private readonly firebaseMapPinService:
FirebaseMapPinsService,
              private readonly poi: PointsOfInterestService) { }

  ngOnInit() {
  }

  MapLoaded(map: Microsoft.Maps.Map) {
    this.map = map;
    this.mapEvents = new MapEvents(this.map, new
PinsModel(this.firebaseMapPinService), this.poi);
  }
}
```

A note on displaying the map—we really need to set the height of `html` and `body` so that it stretches to the full height of the browser window. Set this in the `styles.scss` file, as follows:

```
html,body {
  height: 100%;
}
```

The map events and setting pins

We have maps, and we have the logic to save points of interest to databases and to move them in memory. The one thing we don't have is the code to handle the user actually creating and managing the pins from the map itself. It's time to rectify that situation and add in a `MapEvents` class that will handle this for us. Just like the `MapGeocode`, `PinModel`, and `PinsModel` classes, this class is a standalone implementation. Let's start by adding the following code:

```
export class MapEvents {
  private readonly geocode: MapGeocode;
  private infoBox: Microsoft.Maps.Infobox;

  constructor(private map: Microsoft.Maps.Map, private pinsModel:
PinsModel, private poi: PointsOfInterestService) {

  }
}
```

`Infobox` is the box that appears when we add a point of interest to the screen. We could add a new one when each point of interest is added, but this would be a waste of resources. Instead, we are going to add a single `Infobox` and reuse it when we add new points on the screen. To do this, we are going to add a helper method that checks whether the `Infobox` has been set or not previously. If it has not been set before, we will instantiate a new instance of the `Infobox`, taking in the pin location, the title, and description. We will be supplying the name of the point as the description. We need to set the map instance that this will appear on using `setMap`. When we reuse this `Infobox`, all we need to do is set the same values in the options and then set the visibility to `true`:

```
private SetInfoBox(title: string, description: string, pin:
Microsoft.Maps.Pushpin): void {
  if (!this.infoBox) {
    this.infoBox = new Microsoft.Maps.Infobox(pin.getLocation(), { title:
title, description: description });
    this.infoBox.setMap(this.map);
  return;
  }
  this.infoBox.setOptions({
    title: title,
    description: description,
    location: pin.getLocation(),
    visible: true
  });
}
```

There are a couple of helper methods we still need to add to this class before we add the ability to select points from the map. The first one we are going to add takes the points of interest from the Local Insights search and adds them to the map. Here, we can see that the way that we add a pin is to create a green Pushpin, which then gets added onto our Bing map at the correct Location. We also add an event handler that reacts to a click on the pin and shows the Infobox using the method we just added:

```
AddPoi(pois: PoiPoint[]): void {
  pois.forEach(poi => {
    const pin: Microsoft.Maps.Pushpin = new Microsoft.Maps.Pushpin(new
Microsoft.Maps.Location(poi.lat, poi.long), {
      color: Microsoft.Maps.Color.fromHex('#00ff00')
    });
    this.map.entities.push(pin);
    Microsoft.Maps.Events.addHandler(pin, 'click', (x) => {
      this.SetInfoBox('Point of interest', poi.name, pin);
    });
  })
}
```

The next helper method is more complicated, so we will add it in stages. The AddPushPin code is going to be called when the user clicks on the map. The signature looks as follows:

```
AddPushPin(e: any): void {
}
```

The first thing that we are going to do in this method is create a Guid to use when we add a PinsModel entry and add a draggable Pushpin at the click location:

```
const guid: Guid = Guid.create();
const pin: Microsoft.Maps.Pushpin = new Microsoft.Maps.Pushpin(e.location,
{
  draggable: true
});
```

With this in place, we are going to call the ReverseGeocode method we wrote earlier. When we get the result from this, we will add our PinsModel entry and push the Pushpin onto the map before we show the Infobox:

```
this.geocode.GeoCode(e.location).then((geocode) => {
  this.pinsModel.Add(guid.toString(), geocode, e.location.latitude,
e.location.longitude);
  this.map.entities.push(pin);
  this.SetInfoBox('User location', geocode, pin);
});
```

We haven't finished with this method yet. As well as adding a `Pushpin`, we also have to be able to drag it so that the user can choose a new location for it when they drag the pin. We are going to use the `dragend` event to move the pin. Again, the hard work we put in earlier pays dividends, because we have a simple mechanism to `Move` the `PinsModel` and display our `Infobox`:

```
const dragHandler = Microsoft.Maps.Events.addHandler(pin, 'dragend', (args:
any) => {
  this.geocode.GeoCode(args.location).then((geocode) => {
    this.pinsModel.Move(guid.toString(), geocode, args.location.latitude,
args.location.longitude);
    this.SetInfoBox('User location (Moved)', geocode, pin);
  });
});
```

Finally, when the user clicks a pin, we want to remove the pin from the `PinsModel` and the map. When we added the event handlers for `dragend` and `click`, we saved the handlers to variables so that we can use them to remove the event handlers from the map events. Tidying up after ourselves is good practice, especially when dealing with things like event handlers:

```
const handler = Microsoft.Maps.Events.addHandler(pin, 'click', () => {
  this.pinsModel.Remove(guid.toString());
  this.map.entities.remove(pin);

  // Tidy up our stray event handlers.
  Microsoft.Maps.Events.removeHandler(handler);
  Microsoft.Maps.Events.removeHandler(dragHandler);
});
```

Well, that's our helper methods in place. All we need to do now is update the constructor to add the ability to `click` on the map to set a point of interest and search for Local Insights when the viewport that the user is looking at changes. Let's start with responding to the user clicking on the map:

```
this.geocode = new MapGeocode(this.map);
Microsoft.Maps.Events.addHandler(map, 'click', (e: any) => {
  this.AddPushPin(e);
});
```

We don't need to store the handler as a variable here because we are associating it with something that won't be removed at any stage while the application is live in the browser; namely, the map itself.

When the user moves the map around so that they can see other areas, we need to perform the Local Insights search and, based on the results that come back, add the points of interest. We attach an event handler to the map `viewchangeend` event to trigger this search:

```
Microsoft.Maps.Events.addHandler(map, 'viewchangeend', () => {
    const center = map.getCenter();
    this.poi.Search([center.latitude,
center.longitude]).then(pointsOfInterest => {
        if (pointsOfInterest && pointsOfInterest.length > 0) {
            this.AddPoi(pointsOfInterest);
        }
    })
})
```

We keep seeing that preparing methods beforehand can save us so much time later on. We are simply leveraging the `PointsOfInterestService.Search` method to do our Local Insights search for us, and then pumping the results into our `AddPoi` method if we get any back. If we don't want to perform the Local Insights search, we can simply remove this event handler and won't need to do any searching.

The only thing that we have left to do is handle the loading in of our pins from the database. The code here is a variation of the code we have seen already for adding the `click` and `dragend` handlers, but we don't need to perform the geocoding, since we already have the name of each point of interest. Therefore, we aren't going to reuse the `AddPushPin` method. Instead, we will opt to do this whole section inline. The load subscription looks as follows:

```
const subscription = this.pinsModel.Load().subscribe((data: PinModelData[])
=> {
    data.forEach(pinData => {
        const pin: Microsoft.Maps.Pushpin = new Microsoft.Maps.Pushpin(new
Microsoft.Maps.Location(pinData.lat, pinData.long), {
            draggable: true
        });
        this.map.entities.push(pin);
        const handler = Microsoft.Maps.Events.addHandler(pin, 'click', () => {
            this.pinsModel.Remove(pinData.id);
            this.map.entities.remove(pin);
        Microsoft.Maps.Events.removeHandler(handler);
            Microsoft.Maps.Events.removeHandler(dragHandler);
        });
        const dragHandler = Microsoft.Maps.Events.addHandler(pin, 'dragend',
(args: any) => {
            this.geocode.GeoCode(args.location).then((geocode) => {
                this.pinsModel.Move(pinData.id, geocode, args.location.latitude,
```

```
args.location.longitude);
        this.map.entities.push(pin);
      this.SetInfoBox('User location (moved)', geocode, pin);
        });
      });
    });
    subscription.unsubscribe();
    this.pinsModel.AddFromStore(data);
  });
```

The point to note with this code snippet is that, since we are dealing with a subscription, once we have completed the subscription, we `unsubscribe` from it. The subscription should return an array of `PinModelData` items that we iterate over, adding in the elements as needed.

That's it. We now have a working mapping solution in place. This was one of the chapters I was looking forward to writing the most because I love mapping applications. I hope you have as much fun with this as I have. Before we leave this chapter, though, if you want to prevent people from getting unsecured access to the data, you can apply that knowledge in the next section.

Securing the database

This section is an optional overview of what we would need to do to provide security for the database. As you may remember, when we created our Firestore database, we set it up so that access was available to anyone, completely unrestricted. That's fine while you're developing a small test application, but it's generally not what you are going to want to deploy as a commercial application.

We are going to change the configuration of our database so that we only allow read/write access if the authorization ID is set. To do this, select the **Rules** tab in the **Database** and add `if request.auth.uid != null;` to the rules list. The format of `match` `/{document=**}` simply means that this rule applies to any document in the list. It is possible to set up rules that would only apply to certain documents, but that doesn't make much sense in the context of an application like this.

Note that doing this means that we would have to add in authentication, just like we did in `Chapter 6`, *Building a Chat Room Application Using Socket.IO*. Setting this up is outside the scope of this chapter, but copying over the navigation and providing login features from the previous chapter should be straightforward:

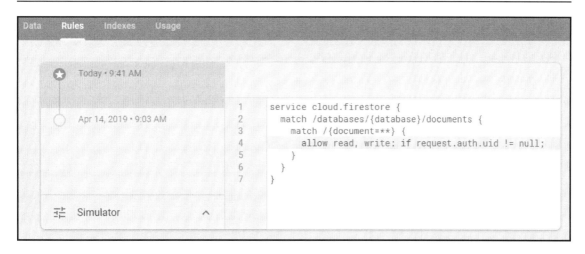

This has been quite a journey. We have gone through the process of signing up for different online services and brought mapping features into our code. At the same time, we have seen how we can scaffold an Angular application with TypeScript support, without having to generate and register services. You should now be able to take this code and look to add the mapping features that you really want.

Summary

In this chapter, we have reached the conclusion of projects that work with Angular, which we introduced using cloud services from Microsoft and Google in the form of Bing Maps and Firebase cloud services for storing data. We signed up to these services and obtained the relevant information from them in order to set up client access to them. In the course of writing our code, we have created classes to work with the Firestore database and interact with Bing Maps to do things such as search for addresses based on user clicks, leading to us adding pins to a map, as well as searching for coffee shops using Local Insights.

Continuing our journey of TypeScript, we introduced rest tuples. We also saw how to add code to Angular components to react to browser host events.

In the next chapter, we are going to revisit React. This time, we will be creating a limited microservice CRM that uses Docker to contain the various microservices.

Questions

1. How does Angular allow us to interact with a host element?
2. What are latitude and longitude?
3. What is the purpose of reverse geocoding?
4. What service are we using to store our data?

Building a CRM Using React and Microservices

8

In previous chapters where we used REST services, we concentrated on having a single site for dealing with REST calls. Modern applications frequently make use of microservices, potentially hosted inside a container-based system such as Docker.

In this chapter, we are going to look at how to create a set of microservices hosted in multiple Docker containers using Swagger to design our REST API. Our React client application will be responsible for drawing these microservices together to create a simple **Customer Relationship Management (CRM)** system.

The following topics will be covered in this chapter:

- Understanding Docker and containers
- What microservices are and what they are used for
- Decomposing monolithic architectures down into microarchitectures
- Sharing common server-side functionality
- Using Swagger to design APIs
- Hosting microservices in Docker
- Using React to connect to microservices
- Using routing in React

Technical requirements

The finished project can be downloaded from `https://github.com/PacktPublishing/Advanced-TypeScript-3-Programming-Projects/tree/master/Chapter08`.

After downloading the project, you will have to install the package requirements using the `npm install` command. Since the services are spread over a number of folders, you will have to install each service individually.

Understanding Docker and microservices

Since we are building a system that uses microservices hosted inside Docker containers, there is a bit of terminology and theory that we need to understand beforehand.

In this section, we are going to look at common Docker terms and what they mean before we move on to looking at what microservices are, what problems they are intended to solve, and how to think about breaking monolithic applications down into more modular services.

Docker terminology

If you are new to Docker, there is a whole slew of terminology surrounding it that you will come across. Knowing the terminology will help when we come to set up our servers, so let's start with the basics.

Container

This is probably a term you have come across if you have seen any Docker literature on the internet. A container is a running instance taking in the various pieces of software needed to run an application. This is the starting point for us. Containers are built from images, which you can either build yourself or download from a central Docker database. Containers can be opened up to other containers, the host operating system, or even to the wider world using ports and volumes. One of the big selling points of containers is that they are easy to set up and create and can be stopped and started very quickly.

Image

As we covered in the previous paragraph, a container starts off as an image. There are a huge number of images already available for use, but we can also create our own images. When we create an image, the creation steps are cached so that they can be reused easily.

Port

This should be familiar to you already. The term ports in Docker means exactly the same as ports does for OSes. These are TCP or UDP ports that are visible to the host operating system, or that are connected to the outer world. We will get to some interesting code later on in this chapter when we have applications use the same port number internally but expose them to the world using different port numbers.

Volume

The easiest way to visualize a volume is that it is similar to a shared folder. When a container is created, volumes are initialized and allow us to persist data, regardless of the container life cycle.

Registry

Effectively, a registry could be viewed as the App Store of the Docker world. It stores Docker images that can be downloaded, and local images can be pushed back to the registry in a similar fashion to pushing an app up to the App Store.

Docker Hub

Docker Hub is the original Docker registry, provided by Docker themselves. This registry stores a vast number of Docker images, some of which come from Docker and some of which have been built for them by software teams.

> In this chapter, we aren't going to cover installing Docker, as installing it and setting it up is a chapter in its own right, especially since installing Docker on Windows is a different experience to installing Docker on macOS or Linux. The commands that we will use to compose Docker applications and check the state of instances don't change though, so we will cover them as and when they are needed.

Microservices

It's hard to be involved in the corporate software world and not hear the term microservices. This is a style of architecture that breaks a so-called monolithic system down into a collection of services. The nature of this architecture is that services are tightly scoped and testable. Services should be loosely coupled so that dependencies between them are limited—it should be up to the end application to bring these services together. This loose coupling promotes the idea that they can be deployed independently and that services are generally tightly focused on business capabilities.

Despite what we may hear from marketing gurus and consultancies looking to sell services, microservices are not always a suitable choice for an application. Sometimes, it is better to stay with a monolithic application. If we can't break the application down using all the ideas outlined in the preceding paragraph then, chances are, the application is not a suitable candidate for microservices.

Unlike a lot of what we have covered in this book so far, such as patterns, microservices don't have an officially approved definition. You can't follow a checklist and say, *this is a microservice because it is doing a, b, and c*. Instead, the agreed view on what constitutes a microservice has evolved, based on seeing what works and what doesn't, into a series of characteristics. For our purposes, the important attributes of what constitutes a microservice include the following:

- The service can be deployed independently of other microservices. In other words, the service has no dependency on other microservices.
- The service is based on a business process. Microservices are meant to be granular, so having them organized around single business areas helps create large-scale applications out of small, focused components.
- The languages and technologies can be different across the services. This gives us the opportunity to leverage the best and most appropriate technologies where necessary. For instance, we might have one service hosted in-house while another service might be hosted in a cloud service such as Azure.
- The service should be small in size. That doesn't mean that it should not have much code to it; rather, it means that it is focused on one area only.

Designing our REST API using Swagger

When developing REST-driven applications, I find it really useful to use the facilities of Swagger (`https://swagger.io`). Swagger has many features that make it the go-to tool when we want to do things such as creating API documentation, creating code for APIs, and testing APIs.

We're going to use the Swagger UI to prototype the ability to retrieve a list of people. From this, we can generate documentation to go along with our API. While we could generate the code from this, we are going to use the tooling that's available to see what the *shape* of our final REST call will be, which we will use to roll our own implementation using the data model we created previously. The reason I like to do this is twofold. First, I like to craft small, clean data models, and I find the prototype gives me a visualization of the model. Secondly, there's a lot of generated code—an awful lot—and I find it easier to tie my data model to the database when I craft the code myself.

For this chapter, we are going to write the code ourselves, but we will use Swagger to prototype what we want to deliver.

The first thing we need to do is sign into Swagger:

1. From the home page, click **Sign In**. This brings up a dialog that asks which product we want to log into, that is, **SwaggerHub** or **Swagger Inspector**. **Swagger Inspector** is a great tool for testing our APIs, but since we are going to be developing the API, we will sign into **SwaggerHub**. The following screenshot shows how it looks:

2. If you don't have a Swagger account, you can create one from here either by signing up or by using a GitHub account. In order to create an API, we need to select **Create New** > **Create New API**. Choose **None** in the **Template** dropdown and fill it in, as follows:

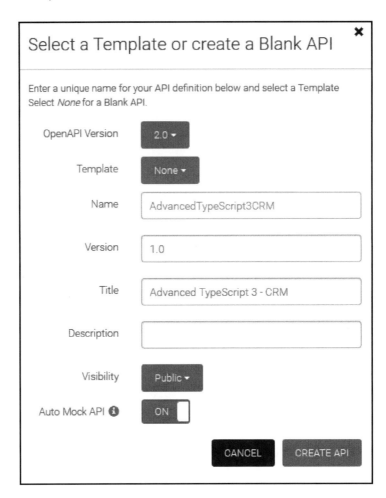

3. At this stage, we are ready to start filling in our API. What we are given out of the box is the following:

```
swagger: '2.0'
info:
  version: '1.0'
  title: 'Advanced TypeScript 3 - CRM'
  description: ''
paths: {}
# Added by API Auto Mocking Plugin
host: virtserver.swaggerhub.com
basePath: /user_id/AdvancedTypeScript3CRM/1.0
schemes:
  - https
```

Let's start building this API out. First of all, we are going to create the start of our API paths. Any paths we need to create go under a `paths` node. The Swagger editor validates inputs as we are building the API, so don't worry if it comes up with validation errors as we are filling it in. In our example here, we are going to create the API to retrieve an array of all the people we have added to our database. Therefore, we start off with this, our API endpoint, which replaces the `paths: {}` line:

```
paths:
  /people:
    get:
      summary: "Retrieves the list of people from Firebase"
      description: Returns a list of people
```

So, we have said that our REST call will be issued using a `GET` verb. Our API is going to return two statuses, `HTTP 200` and `HTTP 400`. Let's provide the beginnings of this by populating a `responses` node with these statuses. When we return a `400` error, we need to create the schema that defines what we will return over the wire. The `schema` returns an `object` that contains a single `message` string, as follows:

```
responses:
  200:
  400:
    description: Invalid request
    schema:
      type: object
      properties:
        message:
          type: string
```

Since our API is going to return an array of people, our schema is typed to an `array`. The `items` that make up the person map back to the model we discussed in the server code. So, by filling in our `schema` for the `200` response, we get this:

```
description: Successfully returned a list of people
schema:
  type: array
  items:
    type: object
    properties:
      ServerID:
        type: string
      FirstName:
        type: string
      LastName:
        type: string
      Address:
        type: object
        properties:
          Line1:
            type: string
          Line2:
            type: string
          Line3:
            type: string
          Line4:
            type: string
          PostalCode:
            type: string
          ServerID:
            type: string
```

This is what our `schema` looks like in the editor:

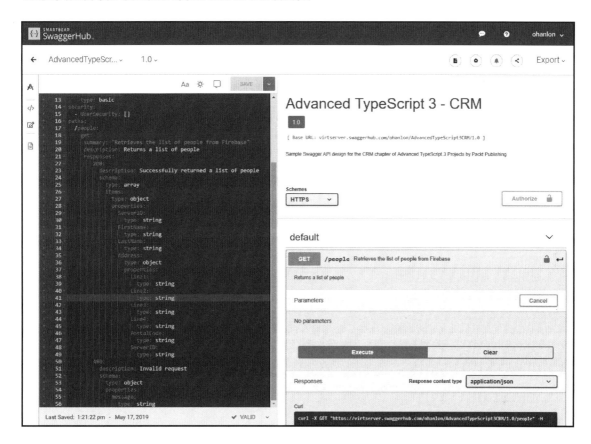

Now that we have seen how Swagger can be used to prototype our APIs, we can move onto the definition of the project that we want to build.

Creating a microservices application with Docker

The project we are going to write is a small part of a CRM system to maintain details about customers and add leads for those customers. The way the application works is that the user creates addresses; when they add in details about contacts, they will select the address from the list of addresses they have already created. Finally, they can create leads that use the contacts they have already added. The idea behind this system is that, previously, the application used one big database for this information—we are going to break this down into three discrete services.

Working alongside the GitHub code, this chapter should take about three hours to complete. When completed, the application should look as follows:

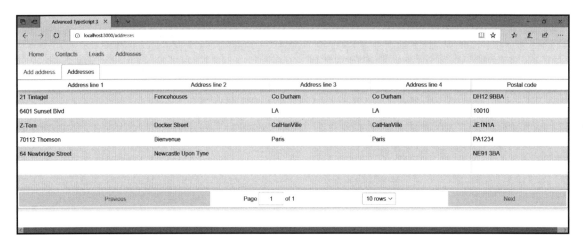

After doing this, we'll move on and see how to create apps for Docker and how this complements our project.

Getting started creating a microservices application with Docker

We are making a welcome return to React in this chapter. As well as using React, we will also be using Firebase and Docker, hosting Express and Node. REST communications between our React application and the Express microservices will be done with Axios.

If you are using Windows 10 for your development, install Docker Desktop for Windows, which is available here: `https://hub.docker.com/editions/community/docker-ce-desktop-windows`.

 In order to run Docker on Windows, you need to have Hyper-V virtualization installed.

If you want to install Docker Desktop on macOS, head to `https://hub.docker.com/editions/community/docker-ce-desktop-mac`.

 Docker Desktop on Mac runs on OS X Sierra 10.12 and newer macOS releases.

The CRM application that we are going to build demonstrates how we can take a number of microservices and bring them together into one cohesive application where the end user is unaware that our application is working with information from a wide number of data sources.

The requirements of our application are as follows:

- The CRM system will provide the ability to enter addresses.
- The system will let the user enter details about a person.
- When details are entered about a person, the user can choose a previously entered address.
- The system will let the user enter details about potential leads.
- Data will be saved to a cloud database.
- The people, leads, and address information will be retrieved from separate services.
- These separate services will be hosted by Docker.
- Our user interface will be created as a React system.

We have been steadily working toward being able to share functionality in our application. Our microservices are going to take this approach to the next level by sharing as much common code as possible and then just adding in the little bits and pieces that they need to customize the data they fetch and return to the client. We can do this because our services are similar in their requirements, so they can share a lot of common code.

Our microservice application starts off from the point of view of a monolithic application. That application has the people, addresses, and leads all managed by one system. We are going to treat this monolithic application with the contempt it deserves and break it down into smaller, discrete chunks, where each constituent part exists in isolation from other parts. Here, the leads, addresses, and people all exist in their own self-contained services.

The place that we are going to start is with our tsconfig file. In previous chapters, we had one service per chapter, with a single tsconfig file. We are going to mix things up here by having a root level tsconfig.json file. Our services will all use that as a common base:

1. Let's start by creating a folder called Services, which will serve as the base for our services. Under this, we are going to create separate Addresses, Common, Leads, and People folders, as well as our base tsconfig file.

2. When we have finished this step, our Services folder should look as follows:

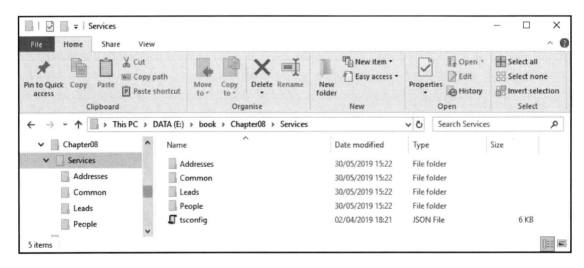

3. Now, let's add the tsconfig settings. These settings are going to be shared by all of the services we are going to host:

```
{
    "compileOnSave": true,
    "compilerOptions": {
        "target": "es5",
        "module": "commonjs",
        "removeComments": true,
        "strict": true,
        "esModuleInterop": true,
        "inlineSourceMap": true,
```

```
        "experimentalDecorators": true,
    }
}
```

You might have noticed that we haven't set up our output directory here. We're going to leave that to slightly later on. Before we get to that step, we are going to start adding in the common functionality that will be shared by our microservices. Our shared functionality is going to be added in the Common folder. Some of what we are going to add should look very familiar because we built similar server code in earlier chapters.

Our services are going to save to Firebase, so we are going to start off by writing our database code. The npm packages that we need to install to work with Firebase are firebase and @types/firebase. While we are adding these, we should also import guid-typescript and the basic node cors and express packages that we installed previously.

When each service saves data to the database, it will start with the same basic structure. We will have a ServerID that we are going to set ourselves using a GUID. The basic model that we are going to use starts off like this:

```
export interface IDatabaseModelBase {
    ServerID: string;
}
```

We are going to create an abstract base class that will work with instances of IDatabaseModelBase, giving us the ability to Get a record, GetAll the records, and Save a record. The beauty of working with Firebase is that, while it is a powerful system, the code that we have to write to accomplish each of these tasks is very short. Let's start off with the class definition:

```
export abstract class FirestoreService<T extends IDatabaseModelBase> {
    constructor(private collection: string) { }
}
```

As you can see, our class is generic, which tells us that each service will extend IDatabaseModelBase and use that in its specific database implementation. The collection is the name of the collection that will be written in Firebase. For our purposes, we are going to share one Firebase instance to store the different collections, but the beauty of our architecture is that we don't need to if we don't want to. We can use separate Firebase stores if we need to; in fact, this is generally what would happen in a production environment.

It's pointless us adding our GET methods if we don't have any data saved, so the first thing we are going to do is write our Save method. Unsurprisingly, our Save method is going to be asynchronous, so it will return a Promise:

```
public Save(item: T): Promise<T> {
    return new Promise<T>(async (coll) => {
        item.ServerID = Guid.create().toString();
        await
firebase.firestore().collection(this.collection).doc(item.ServerID).set(ite
m);
        coll(item);
    });
}
```

Something that might look strange is the async (coll) code. Since we are using the fat arrow (=>), we are creating a simplified function. Since this is a function, we add the async keyword to it to indicate that the code can have an await inside it. If we didn't mark this as async, then we would not be able to use the await inside.

Our code allocates a GUID to the ServerID before we call a chain of methods to set the data. Let's tackle the code in small chunks to see what each bit does. As we discussed in Chapter 7, *Angular Cloud-Based Mapping with Firebase*, Firebase offers more than just database services, so the first thing we need to do is access the database part. If we weren't following method chaining here, we could write this as follows:

```
const firestore: firebase.firestore.Firestore = firebase.firestore();
```

In Firestore, we don't save data in tables, we save it in named collections. Once we have firestore, we get CollectionReference. Following on from the preceding code snippet, we could rewrite this as follows:

```
const collection: firebase.firestore.CollectionReference =
firestore.collection(this.collection);
```

Once we have CollectionReference, we can get access to individual documents using the ServerID we set up earlier in the method. If we don't supply our own ID, one will be created for us:

```
const doc: firebase.firestore.DocumentReference =
collection.doc(item.ServerID);
```

Now, we need to set the data that we want to write to the database:

```
await doc.set(item);
```

This will save the data to a document in the appropriate collection in Firestore. I have to admit that, while I like the ability to type in code that can be broken down like this, method chaining means that I rarely do so if it's available. Where the next step in the chain logically follows on from the previous step, I will often chain the methods together because you cannot get to the next step without going through the previous steps, and it makes it easy for me to visualize the sequence of steps if I see them linked together.

Once the item is saved to the database, we are going to return the saved item, complete with `ServerID`, back to the calling code so that it can be used immediately. That's where this line comes in:

```
coll(item);
```

The next step in our `FirestoreService` is to add the `GET` method. This method, like the `Save` method, is an `async` method that returns a single instance of type `T`, wrapped inside a promise. Since we know the ID, the vast majority of our Firestore code is the same. The difference here is that we call `get()`, which we then use to return the data:

```
public async Get(id: string): Promise<T> {
    const qry = await
firebase.firestore().collection(this.collection).doc(id).get();
    return <T>qry.data();
}
```

Guess what? We also have an `async GetAll` method to write, this time returning an array of `T`. Since we want to retrieve multiple records, rather than just a single doc, we call `get()` on our `collection` instead. Once we have the records, we use a simple `forEach` to build up the array we need to return:

```
public async GetAll(): Promise<T[]> {
    const qry = await firebase.firestore().collection(this.collection).get();
    const items: T[] = new Array<T>();
    qry.forEach(item => {
        items.push(<T>item.data());
    });
    return items;
}
```

With our database code in place, let's see what this looks like in practice. We're going to start off in the `Addresses` service by creating an `IAddress` interface that extends `IDatabaseModelBase`:

```
export interface IAddress extends IDatabaseModelBase {
    Line1 : string,
    Line2 : string,
```

```
      Line3 : string,
      Line4 : string,
      PostalCode : string
   }
```

With `IAddress` in place, we can now create the class that ties our service to the `addresses` collection that we are going to store in Firebase. With all the hard work that we have put in, our `AddressesService` is as simple as this:

```
export class AddressesService extends FirestoreService<IAddress> {
   constructor() {
      super('addresses');
   }
}
```

You might wonder whether the code for the data models and database access are as easy with the other microservices. Let's see what our `People` interface and database service looks like:

```
export interface IPerson extends IDatabaseModelBase {
   FirstName: string;
   LastName: string;
   Address: IAddress;
}
export class PersonService extends FirestoreService<IPerson> {
   constructor() {
      super('people');
   }
}
```

You might also be wondering why we store the address information inside `IPerson`. It's tempting to think that we should start a reference to the address only and not duplicate data, especially if you are coming to the NoSQL architecture from the viewpoint of relational databases where records are linked together through foreign keys to create `pointers` to relationships. *Old-fashioned* SQL databases use foreign tables to minimize the redundancies in records so we don't end up creating duplicate data that's shared across multiple records. While that's a useful thing to have available, it does make querying and retrieving records more complicated because the information that we are interested in could well be scattered over several tables. By storing the address alongside the person, we reduce the number of tables we have to query to build up the person's information. This is based on the idea that we want to query records far more often than we want to change them so, if we needed to change the address, we would change the master address and then a separate query would run through all of the people records looking for addresses that needed to be updated. We will be achieving this because the `ServerID` record in the address part of the person record will match the `ServerID` in the master address.

We won't cover the `Leads` database code; you can read it in the source, and it is virtually identical to this. What we did was work out that our microservices would be, functionally, very similar so that we can take advantage of inheritance in a simple way.

Adding server-side routing support

As well as having a common way of working with the database, our incoming API requests are all going to be very similar in terms of endpoints. While writing this book, I tried to put together snippets of code that could be reused later on. One such snippet is the way we handle Express routing. The server-side code we put together in Chapter 4, *The MEAN Stack – Building a Photo Gallery*, was one such area, specifically the code for routing. We can bring this code in pretty much exactly as we wrote it all those chapters ago.

Here's a quick reminder of what the code looks like. First, we have our `IRouter` interface:

```
export interface IRouter {
  AddRoute(route: any): void;
}
```

Then, we have our routing engine—the code that we are going to plug directly into our server:

```
export class RoutingEngine {
  constructor(private routing: IRouter[] = new Array<IRouter>()) {
  }
  public Add<T1 extends IRouter>(routing: (new () => T1), route: any) {
    const routed = new routing();
    routed.AddRoute(route);
    this.routing.push(routed);
  }
}
```

So, what does this look like in practice? Well, here's the code to save an address that has been sent over from the client. When we receive an `/add/` request from the client, we extract the details from the body and cast it to an `IAddress`, which we then use to save to the addresses service:

```
export class SaveAddressRouting implements IRouter {
  AddRoute(route: any): void {
    route.post('/add/', (request: Request, response: Response) => {
      const person: IAddress = <IAddress>{...request.body};
      new AddressesService().Save(person);
      response.json(person);
    });
```

```
    }
  }
```

The code to get the address is very similar. We aren't going to dissect this method because it should look very familiar by now:

```
export class GetAddressRouting implements IRouter {
  AddRoute(route: any): void {
    route.get('/get/', async (request: Request, response: Response) => {
      const result = await new AddressesService().GetAll();
      if (result) {
        response.json(result);
      }
      response.send('');
    });
  }
}
```

The code for the `Leads` and `People` services are virtually identical. Please read the code from our GitHub repository to get familiar with it.

The Server class

Again, continuing with the theme of reusing code as much as possible, we are going to use a slightly modified version of the Express `Server` class we wrote, way back in Chapter 4, *The MEAN Stack – Building a Photo Gallery*. Again, we will quickly go through the code to re-familiarize ourselves with it. First, let's put the class definition and constructor in place. Our constructor is a slimmed-down version of the constructor from Chapter 4, *The MEAN Stack – Building a Photo Gallery*:

```
export abstract class Server {
  constructor(private port: number = 3000, private app: any = express(),
  protected routingEngine: RoutingEngine = new RoutingEngine()) {}
  }
}
```

We also want to add CORS support. While we could make this mandatory, I still like the idea that we can put control of whether we want to do this into the hands of the service developer, so we will keep this as a `public` method:

```
public WithCorsSupport(): Server {
  this.app.use(cors());
  return this;
}
```

In order for our actual server implementations to work, we need to give them the ability to add routing. We do this through the `AddRouting` method:

```
protected AddRouting(router: Router): void {
}
```

Now that we have our `AddRouting` method, we need code in place to start up our server:

```
public Start(): void {
  this.app.use(bodyParser.json());
  this.app.use(bodyParser.urlencoded({extended:true}));
  const router: Router = express.Router();
  this.AddRouting(router);
  this.app.use(router);
  this.app.listen(this.port, ()=> console.log(`logged onto server at
${this.port}`));
}
```

What you may have noticed is that we are missing one important piece of the puzzle. We have no database support in place in our server, but our service needs to initialize Firebase. In our server, we add in the following:

```
public WithDatabase(): Server {
  firebase.initializeApp(Environment.fireBase);
  return this;
}
```

Note that I have not included `Environment.fireBase` in the repository because it contains details about servers and keys that I use. This is a constant that contains the Firebase connection information. You can replace this with the connection information you set up when you created your Firebase database in the cloud. To add this, you will need to create a file in the `Common` folder called `Environment.ts` which contains code that looks like this:

```
export const Environment = {
  fireBase: {
    apiKey: <<add your api key here>>,
    authDomain: "advancedtypescript3-containers.firebaseapp.com",
    databaseURL: "https://advancedtypescript3-containers.firebaseio.com",
    projectId: "advancedtypescript3-containers",
    storageBucket: "advancedtypescript3-containers.appspot.com",
    messagingSenderId: <<add your sender id here>>
  }
}
```

Creating our Addresses service

We now have everything we need to create our actual services. Here, we will look at the `Addresses` service, understanding that the other services will follow the same pattern. Since we already have the data models, data access code, and routing in place, all we have to do is create our actual `AddressesServer` class. The `AddressesServer` class is as simple as this:

```
export class AddressesServer extends Server {
  protected AddRouting(router: Router): void {
    this.routingEngine.Add(GetAddressRouting, router);
    this.routingEngine.Add(SaveAddressRouting, router);
  }
}
```

We start the server like this:

```
new AddressesServer()
  .WithCorsSupport()
  .WithDatabase().Start();
```

The code is as easy as that. We are following a principle called **Don't Repeat Yourself (DRY)** as much as possible. This simply states that you should aim to retype as little code as possible. In other words, you should try to avoid having code that does exactly the same thing scattered about your code base. Sometimes, you can't avoid it and sometimes, it doesn't make sense to go to the trouble of creating a lot of code scaffolding for a one- or two-line piece of code, but when you have large functional areas, you should definitely try to avoid having to copy and paste it into multiple parts of your code. Part of the reason for this is if you have copied and pasted code and subsequently you find a bug in it, you are going to have to fix that bug in multiple places.

Using Docker to run our services

When we look at our services, we can see that we have an interesting problem; namely that they all use the same port to start up on. Obviously, we can't actually use the same port for each service, so have we caused ourselves a problem? Does this mean that we cannot start more than one service and, if so, does this blow our microservice architecture apart and mean that we should go back to a monolithic service?

Given the potential problems we have just discussed and the fact that this chapter introduces Docker, it should come as no surprise to learn that Docker is the answer to this. With Docker, we can spin up a container, deploy our code to it, and expose the service with a different endpoint. So, how do we do this?

In each service, we are going to add a couple of common files:

```
node_modules
npm-debug.log
```

The first file, called `.dockerignore`, chooses which files to ignore when copying or adding files to the container.

The next file we are going to add is called `Dockerfile`. This file describes the Docker container and how to build it up. `Dockerfile` works by building up layers of instructions that represent a step toward building up the container. The first layer downloads and installs Node in the container, specifically Node version 8:

```
FROM node:8
```

The next layer is used to set the default working directory. This directory is used for subsequent commands, such as RUN, COPY, ENTRYPOINT, CMD, and ADD:

```
WORKDIR /usr/src/app
```

In some online sources, you'll see that people create their own directories to use as the working directory. It's better to use a predefined, well-known location such as `/usr/src/app` as WORKDIR.

Since we have a working directory in place right now, we can start to set up the code. We want to copy the necessary files to download and install our npm packages:

```
COPY package*.json ./
RUN npm install
```

As a good practice, we copy the `package.json` and `package-lock.json` files before copying the code because the install caches the contents of the installation. As long as we don't change the `package.json` file, if the code is built again, we won't need to re-download the packages.

So, we have our packages installed, but we don't have any code in place. Let's copy the contents of our local folders into the working directory:

```
COPY . .
```

We want to expose the server port to the outside world, so let's add that layer now:

```
EXPOSE 3000
```

Finally, we want to start the server. To do this, we want to trigger npm start:

```
CMD [ "npm", "start" ]
```

 As an alternative to running CMD ["npm", "start"], we can bypass npm altogether and use CMD ["node", "dist/server.js"] (or whatever the server code is called). The reason we might want to consider doing this is that running npm starts the npm process, which then starts our server process, so using Node directly reduces the number of services that are running. Also, npm has a habit of silently consuming process exit signals, so Node has no idea that the process has exited unless npm tells it.

Now, if we want to start the address service, for instance, we run the following commands from the command line:

```
docker build -t ohanlon/addresses .
docker run -p 17171:3000 -d ohanlon/addresses
```

The first line builds the container image using Dockerfile and gives it a tag so that we can identify it in the Docker containers.

Once the image has been built, the next command runs the installation and publishes the container port to the host. This trick is the *magic* that makes our server code work—it exposes the internal port 3000 to the outside world as 17171. Note that we are using ohanlon/addresses in both cases to tie the container image to the one that we are going to run (you can replace this name with whatever you want).

The -d flag stands for detach, which means that our container runs silently in the background. This allows us to start the service and avoid tying up the command line.

If you want to find what images you have available, you can run the docker ps command.

Using docker-compose to compose and start the services

Rather than running up our images using docker build and docker run, we have something called docker-compose to compose and run multiple containers. With Docker composition, we can create our containers from multiple docker files or entirely through a file called docker-compose.yml.

We are going to use a combination of `docker-compose.yml` and the Docker files that we created in the previous section to create a composition that we can easily run up. In the root of the server code, create a blank file called `docker-compose.yml`. We are going to start off by specifying the compose format that the file conforms to. In our case, we are going to set it to `2.1`:

```
version: '2.1'
```

We are going to create three services inside our containers, so let's start by defining the services themselves:

```
services:
  chapter08_addresses:
  chapter08_people:
  chapter08_leads:
```

Now, each service is made up of discrete information, the first part of which details the build information that we want to use. This information comes under a build node and consists of the context, which maps to the directory our service lives under, and the Docker file, which defines how we build up the container. Optionally, we can set the `NODE_ENV` parameter to identify the node environment, which we are going to set to `production`. The last piece of our puzzle maps back to the `docker run` command where we set the port mapping; each service can set its own `ports` mapping. This is what the node looks like that goes under `chapter08_addresses`:

```
build:
  context: ./Addresses
  dockerfile: ./Dockerfile
environment:
  NODE_ENV: production
ports:
  - 17171:3000
```

When we put this all together, our `docker-compose.yml` file looks like this:

```
version: '2.1'

services:
  chapter08_addresses:
    build:
      context: ./Addresses
      dockerfile: ./Dockerfile
    environment:
      NODE_ENV: production
    ports:
      - 17171:3000
```

```
chapter08_people:
  build:
    context: ./People
    dockerfile: ./Dockerfile
  environment:
    NODE_ENV: production
  ports:
    - 31313:3000
chapter08_leads:
  build:
    context: ./Leads
    dockerfile: ./Dockerfile
  environment:
    NODE_ENV: production
  ports:
    - 65432:3000
```

 Before we can start the processes, we must compile our microservices. Docker is not responsible for building the application, so it is our responsibility to do this before we attempt to compose our service.

We now have multiple containers that can be started together using one compose file. In order to run our compose file, we use the docker-compose up command. When all of the containers have started, we can verify their status using the docker ps command, which gives us the following output:

We have now finished with the server-side code. We have everything in place that we need to create our microservices. What we want to do now is move on to creating the user interface that is going to interact with our services.

Creating our React user interface

We've spent a lot of time building Angular applications, so it's only fair that we return to building a React one. In just the same way that Angular can work with Express and Node, React can also work with them and, since we have the Express/Node side already in place, we are now going to create our React client. We will start off with the command to create our React application with TypeScript support:

```
npx create-react-app crmclient --scripts-version=react-scripts-ts
```

This creates a standard React application, which we will modify to suit our needs. The first thing that we need to do is bring in support for Bootstrap, this time using the `react-bootstrap` package. While we are at it, we might as well install the following dependencies as well—`react-table`, `@types/react-table`, `react-router-dom`, `@types/react-router-dom`, and `axios`. We will be using these throughout this chapter, so installing them now will save a bit of time later on.

Throughout this book, we have been using `npm` to install dependencies, but this isn't the only option available to us. `npm` has the advantage of being the default package manager for Node (it is called Node Package Manager, after all), but Facebook introduced its own package manager back in 2015, called Yarn. Yarn was created to address issues in the version of `npm` that existed at the time. Yarn uses its own set of lock files, instead of the default `package*.lock` that `npm` uses. Which one you use really depends on your personal preferences and evaluating whether the features they provide are something you need. For our purposes, `npm` is a suitable package manager, so that's what we will continue to use.

Using Bootstrap as our container

We want to use Bootstrap to render the entirety of our display. Fortunately, this is a trivial task and revolves around a minor modification being made to our `App` component. In order to render out our display, we will wrap our content inside a container, like this:

```
export class App extends React.Component {
  public render() {
    return (
      <Container fluid={true}>
        <div />
      </Container>
    );
  }
}
```

Now, when we render our content, it will automatically be rendered inside a container that stretches to the full width of the page.

Creating a tabbed user interface

Before we add in our navigation elements, we are going to create the components that we will link to when the user clicks on one of the links. We will start with `AddAddress.tsx`, which we will add code into to add an address. We start off by adding the class definition:

```
export class AddAddress extends React.Component<any, IAddress> {
}
```

The default state for our component is an empty `IAddress`, so we add the definition for it, and set the component state to our default:

```
private defaultState: Readonly<IAddress>;
constructor(props:any) {
  super(props);
  this.defaultState = {
    Line1: '',
    Line2: '',
    Line3: '',
    Line4: '',
    PostalCode: '',
    ServerID: '',
  };
  const address: IAddress = this.defaultState;
  this.state = address;
}
```

Before we add our code to render out our form, we need to add in a couple of methods. As you may remember from our last look at React, we learned that we have to explicitly update the state if the user changes anything in the display. Just like we did last time, we are going to write an `UpdateBinding` event handler, which we will call when the user changes any value on the display. We will see this pattern repeated throughout all of our `Addxxx` components. As a refresher, the ID tells us what field is being updated by the user, which we then use to set the appropriate field in the state with the update value. Given this information, our `event` handler looks like this:

```
private UpdateBinding = (event: any) => {
  switch (event.target.id) {
    case `address1`:
      this.setState({ Line1: event.target.value});
      break;
    case `address2`:
```

```
      this.setState({ Line2: event.target.value});
      break;
    case `address3`:
      this.setState({ Line3: event.target.value});
      break;
    case `address4`:
      this.setState({ Line4: event.target.value});
      break;
    case `zipcode`:
      this.setState({ PostalCode: event.target.value});
      break;
  }
}
```

The other supporting method we need to add in triggers the REST call to our address service. We are going to use the Axios package to transmit a POST request to the add address endpoint. Axios gives us promise-based REST calls so that we can, for example, issue the call and wait for it to come back before we continue processing. We are going to opt for a simple code model here and send our request over in a fire-and-forget fashion so we don't have to wait for any results to come back. For the sake of simplicity, we are going to immediately reset the state of the UI, ready for the user to add another address.

Now that we have added these methods in, we are going to code up our render method. The definition looks like this:

```
public render() {
  return (
    <Container>
    </Container>
  );
}
```

The Container element maps back to the good old container class we are used to from Bootstrap. What is missing from this is the actual input elements. Each piece of input is grouped inside Form.Group so that we can add Label and Control, like this:

```
<Form.Group controlId="formGridAddress1">
  <Form.Label>Address</Form.Label>
  <Form.Control placeholder="First line of address" id="address1"
value={this.state.Line1} onChange={this.UpdateBinding} />
</Form.Group>
```

As another reminder, the current value of the binding is rendered to our display inside the one-way binding, represented by value={this.state.Line1}, and any input from the user triggers an update to the state through the UpdateBinding event handler.

The `Button` code that we add to save our state looks like this:

```
<Button variant="primary" type="submit" onClick={this.Save}>
  Submit
</Button>
```

Putting it all together, this is what our `render` method looks like:

```
public render() {
  return (
    <Container>
      <Form.Group controlId="formGridAddress1">
        <Form.Label>Address</Form.Label>
        <Form.Control placeholder="First line of address" id="address1"
value={this.state.Line1} onChange={this.UpdateBinding} />
      </Form.Group>
      <Form.Group controlId="formGridAddress2">
        <Form.Label>Address 2</Form.Label>
        <Form.Control id="address2" value={this.state.Line2}
onChange={this.UpdateBinding} />
      </Form.Group>
      <Form.Group controlId="formGridAddress2">
        <Form.Label>Address 3</Form.Label>
        <Form.Control id="address3" value={this.state.Line3}
onChange={this.UpdateBinding} />
      </Form.Group>
      <Form.Group controlId="formGridAddress2">
        <Form.Label>Address 4</Form.Label>
        <Form.Control id="address4" value={this.state.Line4}
onChange={this.UpdateBinding} />
      </Form.Group>
      <Form.Group controlId="formGridAddress2">
        <Form.Label>Zip Code</Form.Label>
        <Form.Control id="zipcode" value={this.state.PostalCode}
onChange={this.UpdateBinding}/>
      </Form.Group>
      <Button variant="primary" type="submit" onClick={this.Save}>
        Submit
      </Button>
    </Container>
  )
}
```

So, is everything good with this code? Well, no, there is one small problem with the `Save` code. If the user clicked the button, nothing would be saved to the database because the state is not visible in the `Save` method. When we do `onClick={this.Save}`, we are assigning a callback to the `Save` method. What happens internally is that the `this` context is lost, so we cannot use it to get the state. Now, we have two fixes for this; one we have seen a lot of already, which is to use the fat arrow `=>` to capture the context so that our method can cope with it.

The other way to solve this problem (and the reason we have deliberately coded the `Save` method to not use the fat arrow, so we can see this method in operation) is to add the following code to the constructor to bind the context in:

```
this.Save = this.Save.bind(this);
```

Well, that's our code in place to add an address in. I hope you will agree that it's a simple enough piece of code; time and again, people create unnecessarily complicated code where, in general, simplicity is a much more attractive option. I am a great fan of making code as simple as possible. There is a habit in the industry of trying to make code more complicated than it needs to be, simply to impress other developers. I urge people to avoid that temptation as clean code is much more impressive.

The user interface we use for managing our addresses is tabbed, so we have one tab responsible for adding the address, while the other tab displays a grid containing all of the addresses we have currently added in. It's now time for us to add the tab and grid code. We are going to create a new component called `addresses.tsx`, which does this for us.

Again, we start off by creating our class. This time, we are going to set the `state` to an empty array. We do this because we are going to populate it later on from our address microservice:

```
export default class Addresses extends React.Component<any, any> {
  constructor(props:any) {
    super(props);
    this.state = {
      data: []
    }
  }
}
```

In order to load the data from our microservice, we need a method to handle this for us. We are going to make use of Axios again, but this time we are going to use the promise features to set the state when it is returned from the server:

```
private Load(): void {
  axios.get("http://localhost:17171/get/").then(x =>
  {
    this.setState({data: x.data});
  });
}
```

The question now, is when do we want to call the `Load` method? We don't want to try to get the state during the constructor as that will slow down the construction of the component, so we need another point to retrieve this data. The answer to this lies in the React component life cycle. Components go through several methods when they are being created. The order that they go through is as follows:

1. `constructor();`
2. `getDerivedStateFromProps();`
3. `render();`
4. `componentDidMount();`

The effect we are going to go for is to display the component using `render`, then use binding to update the values to display in the table. That tells us that we want to load our state inside `componentDidMount`:

```
public componentWillMount(): void {
  this.Load();
};
```

We do have another potential point to trigger the update. If the user adds an address and then switches the tab back to the one displaying the table, we'll want to automatically retrieve the updated list of addresses. Let's add a method to cope with this:

```
private TabSelected(): void {
  this.Load();
}
```

It's time for us to add our `render` method. To keep things simple, we are going to add this in two stages; the first is to add the `Tab` and `AddAddress` components. In the second stage, we'll add the `Table`.

Adding the tab requires us to bring in the *Reactified* Bootstrap tab component. Inside our `render` method, add the following code:

```
return (
  <Tabs id="tabController" defaultActiveKey="show"
onSelect={this.TabSelected}>
    <Tab eventKey="add" title="Add address">
      <AddAddress />
    </Tab>
    <Tab eventKey="show" title="Addresses">
      <Row>
      </Row>
    </Tab>
  </Tabs>
)
```

We have a `Tabs` component, which contains two individual `Tab` items. Each tab is given an `eventKey`, which we can use to set the default active key (in this case, we set it to `show`). When a tab is selected, we trigger the loading of the data. We will see that our `AddAddress` component has been added in the `Add Address` tab.

All that we have left to do here is add the table that we are going to use to display the list of addresses. We are going to create a list of columns that we want to display in our table. We use the following syntax to create the columns list, where `Header` is the title that will be displayed at the top of the column. `accessor` tells React what property to pick off the data row:

```
const columns = [{
  Header: 'Address line 1',
  accessor: 'Line1'
}, {
  Header: 'Address line 2',
  accessor: 'Line2'
}, {
  Header: 'Address line 3',
  accessor: 'Line4'
}, {
  Header: 'Address line 4',
  accessor: 'Line4'
}, {
  Header: 'Postal code',
  accessor: 'PostalCode'
}]
```

Finally, we need to add the table in our `Addresses` tab. We are going to use the popular `ReactTable` component to display the table. Put the following code inside the `<Row></Row>` section to add it:

```
<Col>
  <ReactTable data={this.state.data} columns={columns}
    defaultPageSize={15} pageSizeOptions = {[10, 30]} className="-striped -
highlight" /></Col>
```

There are a number of interesting parameters in here. We bind `data` to `this.state.data` to automatically update it when the state changes. The columns that we created are bound to the `columns` attribute. I like the fact that we can control how many rows a person sees per page using `defaultPageSize`, and the fact that we can let the user choose to override the number of rows using `pageSizeOptions`. We set `className` to `-striped -highlight` so that the display is striped between gray and white, with row highlighting used to show which row the mouse is over when the mouse moves over the table.

Using a select control to select an address when adding a person

When the user wants to add a person, they only need to type in their first and last name. We display a selection box to the user, which is populated with the list of previously entered addresses. Let's see how we handle a more complicated scenario like this with React.

The first thing we need to do is create two separate components. We have an `AddPerson` component to type the first name and last name in, and we have an `AddressChoice` component, which retrieves and displays the complete list of addresses for the user to select from. We will start with the `AddressChoice` component.

This component uses a custom `IAddressProperty`, which provides us with access back to the parent component so that we can trigger the update to the currently selected address when this component changes value:

```
interface IAddressProperty {
  CurrentSelection : (currentSelection:IAddress | null) => void;
}
export class AddressesChoice extends React.Component<IAddressProperty,
Map<string, string>> {
}
```

We have told React that our component accepts `IAddressProperty` as the props to our component and has `Map<string, string>` as the state. When we retrieve the list of addresses from the server, we populate this map with the addresses; the key is used to hold `ServerID`, and the value holds a formatted version of the address. As the logic behind this looks a little bit complicated, we will start with the method to load the addresses, and then we will go back to the constructor:

```
private LoadAddreses(): void {
  axios.get("http://localhost:17171/get/").then((result:AxiosResponse<any>)
=>
  {
    result.data.forEach((person: any) => {
      this.options.set(person.ServerID, `${person.Line1} ${person.Line2}
${person.Line3} ${person.Line4} ${person.PostalCode}`);
    });
    this.addresses = { ...result.data };
    this.setState(this.options);
  });
}
```

We start off by issuing a call to the server to get the complete list of addresses. When we get the list back, we are going to iterate over the addresses to build up the formatted map that we just discussed. We fill the state with the formatted map and copy the unformatted address into a separate addresses field; the reason we do this is that while we want to display the formatted version to the display, we want to send the unformatted version back to the caller when the selection changes. There are other ways that we could have achieved this, but this is a useful little hack that keeps things simple.

With the load functionality in place, we can now add our constructor and fields:

```
private options: Map<string, string>;
private addresses: IAddress[] = [];
constructor(prop: IAddressProperty) {
  super(prop);
  this.options = new Map<string, string>();
  this.Changed = this.Changed.bind(this);
  this.state = this.options;
}
```

Note that we have a changed binding in here, in keeping with the `bind` code we discussed in the previous section. Loading the data happens, again, in `componentDidMount`:

```
public componentDidMount() {
  this.LoadAddreses();
}
```

We are ready to build our render method now. To simplify the visualization of what goes on inside the building up of the entries that make up the selection items, we separate that code out into a separate method. This simply iterates over the list of `this.options` to create options to be added to the `select` control:

```
private RenderList(): any[] {
  const optionsTemplate: any[] = [];
  this.options.forEach((value, key) => (
    optionsTemplate.push(<option key={key} value={key}>{value}</option>)
  ));
  return optionsTemplate;
}
```

Our render method uses a select `Form.Control`, which displays `Select...` as the first option and then renders out the list from `RenderList`:

```
public render() {
  return (<Form.Control as="select" onChange={this.Changed}>
    <option>Select...</option>
    {this.RenderList()}
  </Form.Control>)
}
```

Eagle-eyed readers will notice that we have referenced a `Changed` method twice now, without actually adding it. This method takes the selection value and uses it to look up the unformatted address and, if it finds it, uses the `props` to trigger the `CurrentSelection` method:

```
private Changed(optionSelected: any) {
  const address = Object.values(this.addresses).find(x => x.ServerID ===
optionSelected.target.value);
  if (address) {
    this.props.CurrentSelection(address);
  } else {
    this.props.CurrentSelection(null);
  }
}
```

In our `AddPerson` code, `AddressesChoice` is referenced in the render like this:

```
<AddressesChoice CurrentSelection={this.CurrentSelection} />
```

We aren't going to cover the rest of the content inside `AddPerson`. I would suggest following the downloaded code to see this in place. We also aren't going to cover the other components; this chapter could turn into a hundred-page monster if we were to continue dissecting the other components, especially since they largely follow the same formats as the controls we have just covered.

Adding our navigation

The last bit of code we want to add to our client code base is the ability to handle client-side navigation. We saw how to do this when we covered Angular, so it's time for us to see how to display different pages based on the link the user selects. We are going to use a combination of Bootstrap navigation and React route manipulation. We start off by creating a router that contains our navigation:

```
const routing = (
  <Router>
    <Navbar bg="light">
      <Navbar.Collapse id="basic-navbar-nav">
        <Nav.Link href="/">Home</Nav.Link>
        <Nav.Link href="/contacts">Contacts</Nav.Link>
        <Nav.Link href="/leads">Leads</Nav.Link>
        <Nav.Link href="/addresses">Addresses</Nav.Link>
      </Navbar.Collapse>
    </Navbar>
  </Router>
)
```

We have left a home page in place so that we can add appropriate documentation and images if we wanted to *jazz* it up to make it look like a commercial CRM system. The other `href` elements will tie back to the router to show the appropriate React components. Inside the `Router`, we add `Route` entries that map the `path` to the `component` so that, if the user selects `Addresses`, for instance, the `Addresses` component will be shown:

```
<Route path="/" component={App} />
<Route path="/addresses" component={Addresses} />
<Route path="/contacts" component={People} />
<Route path="/leads" component={Leads} />
```

Our `routing` code now looks like this:

```
const routing = (
  <Router>
    <Navbar bg="light">
      <Navbar.Collapse id="basic-navbar-nav">
        <Nav.Link href="/">Home</Nav.Link>
        <Nav.Link href="/contacts">Contacts</Nav.Link>
        <Nav.Link href="/leads">Leads</Nav.Link>
        <Nav.Link href="/addresses">Addresses</Nav.Link>
      </Navbar.Collapse>
    </Navbar>
    <Route path="/" component={App} />
    <Route path="/addresses" component={Addresses} />
    <Route path="/contacts" component={People} />
    <Route path="/leads" component={Leads} />
  </Router>
)
```

In order to add our navigation, complete with routing, we do the following:

```
ReactDOM.render(
  routing,
  document.getElementById('root') as HTMLElement
);
```

That's it. We now have a client application that can talk to our microservices and orchestrate their results together so that they work together, even though their implementations are independent of each other.

Summary

At this point, we have created a series of microservices. We started off by defining a series of shared functionality, which we used as a basis for creating specialist services. These services all used the same port in Node.js, which would have presented us with a problem, but we solved this problem by creating a series of Docker containers to start up our services and redirected the internal ports to different external ports. We saw how to create the relevant Docker files and Docker compose files to start up the services.

Then, we created a React-based client application that used a more advanced layout by introducing tabs to separate viewing results from the microservices from the ability to add records to the services. Along the way, we also used Axios to manage our REST calls.

When it came to REST calls, we saw how we could use Swagger to define our REST API and talked about whether or not to use the API code that Swagger provided inside our services.

In the next chapter, we are going to move away from React and look at how to create a Vue client that works with TensorFlow to automatically perform image classification.

Questions

1. What is a Docker container?
2. What do we use to group Docker containers together to start them up, and what commands can we use to start them?
3. How do we map an internal port to a different external port with Docker?
4. What features does Swagger provide for us?
5. What do we need to do if a method can't see state in React?

Further reading

- If you want to know more about Docker, *Docker Quick Start Guide* by Earl Waud (`https://www.packtpub.com/in/networking-and-servers/docker-quick-start-guide`) is a good place to start.
- If you are running Docker on Windows, *Docker on Windows - Second Edition* (`https://www.packtpub.com/virtualization-and-cloud/docker-windows-second-edition`) by Elton Stoneman is a great help.
- At this stage, I would hope that your appetite for microservices has been well and truly whetted. If that's the case, *Microservices Development Cookbook* by Paul Osman (`https://www.packtpub.com/in/application-development/microservices-development-cookbook`) should be just what you need to carry on.

Image Recognition with Vue.js and TensorFlow.js

9

One of the hottest topics in computing at the moment is machine learning. In this chapter, we are going to step into the world of machine learning and look at using the popular `TensorFlow.js` package to perform image classification, as well as to detect poses. As a break from Angular and React, we will move on to Vue.js to provide our client implementation.

The following topics will be covered in this chapter:

- What machine learning is and how it relates to AI
- How to install Vue
- Creating an application with Vue
- Showing a home page with the Vue template
- Using routing in Vue
- What **Convolutional Neural Networks** (**CNNs**) are
- How models are trained in TensorFlow
- Building an image classification class using pre-trained TensorFlow models
- The image types that TensorFlow supports for image classification and pose detection
- Using pose detection to show body joints

Technical requirements

The finished project can be downloaded from `https://github.com/PacktPublishing/Advanced-TypeScript-3-Programming-Projects/tree/master/chapter09`. This project uses TensorFlow, so the following additional components will be used in this chapter:

- `@tensorflow-models/mobilenet`
- `@tensorflow-models/posenet`
- `@tensorflow/tfjs`

We will also use Bootstrap with Vue, so we will need to install the following Bootstrap components:

- `bootstrap`
- `bootstrap-vue`

After downloading the project, you will have to install the package requirements using the `npm install` command.

What is machine learning and how does TensorFlow fit in?

It's very hard nowadays to get away from the idea of artificially intelligent machines. People have become accustomed to having access to tools such as Siri, Alexa, and Cortana, which create the appearance that the technology understands us and is able to interact with us. These voice-activated systems use natural language processing to recognize sentences such as, *What's the weather like in Kos today?*

The magic behind these systems is machine learning. To pick one of these systems, we will quickly look at what Alexa does behind the scenes before we look at how machine learning relates to AI.

When we ask Alexa a question, *she* recognizes *her* name so that she knows that she should start listening to what comes after to start processing. This is the software equivalent of tapping someone on their shoulder to get their attention. Alexa then records the following sentence until a point is reached where Alexa can transmit the recording via the internet to the Alexa voice service. This incredibly sophisticated service parses the recording as best it can (sometimes, heavy accents can confuse the service). The service then acts on the parsed recording and sends the results back to your Alexa device.

As well as answering questions about the weather, there is an exhausting number of Alexa skills that users can use, and Amazon encourages developers to create skills that go beyond what they have time to come up with. This means that it's as easy to order a pizza as it is to check the latest racing results.

This preamble leads us to the point where we start to touch on what machine learning has to do with Alexa. The software behind Alexa uses machine learning to continually update itself, so every time it makes a mistake, this is fed back in so that the system is *smarter* the next time around and doesn't make that mistake in the future.

As you can imagine, interpreting speech is a hugely complicated task. It's something that we, as humans, learn from an early age, and the analogy with machine learning is quite breathtaking because we also learn speech through repetition and reinforcement. So, when a baby randomly says *dada*, the baby has learned to make the sounds, but does not know the correct context for the sound yet. Reinforcement, usually provided by the parents pointing to themselves, is used to link the sound to a person. Similar reinforcement takes place when we use picture books; when we teach a baby the word *cow*, we point to a picture of a cow. That way, the baby learns to associate the word with the picture.

Since speech interpretation is so complicated, it takes a huge amount of processing power, and it also requires a huge pre-trained dataset. Imagine how frustrating it would be if we had to teach Alexa everything. This is partly why machine learning systems are only really coming into their own now. We now have enough infrastructure in place to offload the computations to reliable, powerful, and dedicated machines. Additionally, we now have internet that is, by and large, powerful and fast enough to cope with the vast amounts of data that is being transmitted to these machine learning systems. We certainly wouldn't have been able to do half of what we can do now if we were still running on 56K modems.

What is machine learning?

We know that computers are good at yes and no answers, or 1s and 0s, if you like. This means that a computer fundamentally cannot reply with an *-ish* answer, so it cannot say yes-ish to a question. Bear with me for a moment, as this will become clear shortly.

At its most basic level, we can say that machine learning boils down to teaching computers to learn in the same way that we do. They learn to interpret data from all sorts of sources and use this learning to classify that data. The machine will learn from successes and failures, which will, in turn, make it more accurate and capable of making even more complex inferences.

Getting back to the idea of computers working with yes or no answers, when we come up with an answer that amounts to *well, it depends*, we are largely coming up with multiple answers based on the same input—the equivalent of multiple routes through to yes or no answers. Machine learning systems are becoming much better at learning, so the algorithms behind them are able to draw on more and more data, along with more and more reinforcement to make deeper connections.

Behind the scenes, machine learning applies an incredible array of algorithms and statistical models so that systems can perform set tasks without having to be given detailed instructions on how to accomplish those tasks. This level of inference is light years away from the way we have traditionally built applications, and this draws on the fact that, given the right mathematical models, computers are very, very good at spotting patterns. Along with that, they are doing a huge number of related tasks simultaneously, meaning that the mathematical models underpinning the learning can take the results of their calculations back in as feeds to themselves in order to build a better understanding of the world.

At this point, we must mention that AI and machine learning are not the same. Machine learning is an application of AI based on the ability to automatically learn without being programmed to deal with a particular task. The success of machine learning is based on having a sufficient amount of data for the system to learn for itself. There are a number of algorithm types that can be applied. Some are known as unsupervised learning algorithms, while others are known as supervised learning algorithms.

Unsupervised algorithms take in data that has not been classified or labeled previously. The algorithms are run on such datasets to look for underlying or hidden patterns, which can be used to create inferences.

A supervised learning algorithm takes its previous learning and applies it to new data using labeled examples. These labeled examples help it learn the correct answers. Behind the scenes, there is a training dataset that learning algorithms use to refine their knowledge and learn from. The greater the level of training data, the more likely the algorithm is to be able to produce correct answers.

There are other types of algorithms, including reinforcement learning algorithms and semi-supervised learning algorithms, but these are outside the scope of this book.

What is TensorFlow and how does it relate to machine learning?

We have talked about what machine learning is and that it could seem very daunting if were to try and implement it ourselves. Fortunately, there are libraries that help us create our own machine learning implementations. Originally created by the Google Brain team, TensorFlow is one such library designed to support large-scale machine learning and numerical computation. Initially, TensorFlow was written as a hybrid Python/C++ library, where Python provided the frontend API for building learning applications and the C++ side executed them. TensorFlow brings a number of machine learning and neural networking (sometimes called **deep learning**) algorithms together.

Given the success of the original Python implementation, we now have an implementation of TensorFlow (properly called `TensorFlow.js`) written in TypeScript that we can use in our applications. This is the version we are going to use in this chapter.

Project overview

The project we are going to write in this chapter is the one that excited me the most when I was writing the proposal for this book. I have a long-term love affair with all things AI; the topic fascinates me. With the rise of frameworks such as `TensorFlow.js` (I'll be shortening this to just TensorFlow), the ability to perform sophisticated machine learning has never been more readily available outside of academia. As I said, this chapter really got me excited, so we aren't going to use just one machine learning operation—we are going to use image classification to determine what is in a picture and we will use pose detection to draw the key points, such as the major joints and major facial landmarks of a person.

Working alongside the GitHub code, this topic should take about an hour to complete and, when you have finished it, it should look like this:

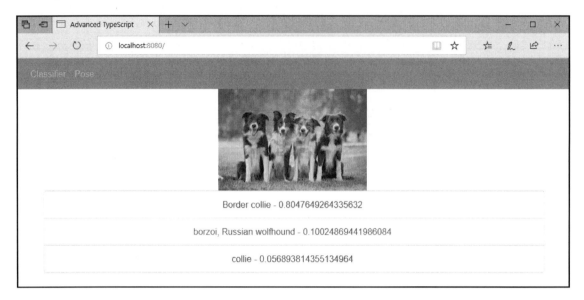

Now that we know what project we are going to build, we are ready to start the implementation. In the next section, we are going to start off by installing Vue.

Getting started with TensorFlow in Vue

If you do not already have Vue installed, the first step is to install the Vue **Command-Line Interface (CLI)**. This is installed using npm with the following command:

```
npm install -g @vue/cli
```

Creating our Vue-based application

Our TensorFlow application is going to run entirely in the client browser. This means that we need to write an application to host the TensorFlow functionality. We are going to use Vue to provide our client, so the following steps are needed to automatically build our Vue application.

Creating our client is as simple as running the vue create command, as follows:

```
vue create chapter09
```

This starts off the process of creating the application. There are a number of decision points that need to happen when going through the client creation process, starting off with choosing whether to accept the defaults or to manually select the features we want to add. Since we want to add TypeScript support, we need to choose the **Manually select features** preset. The following screenshot shows the steps that we will go through to select the features for our Vue application:

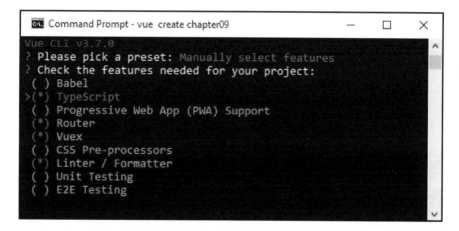

There are a number of features that we could add to our project, but we are only interested in a few of them, so deselect **Babel** and choose to add **TypeScript**, **Router**, **VueX**, and **Linter / Formatter** from the list. Selection/deselection is accomplished by using the spacebar:

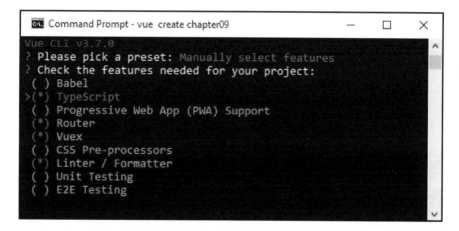

When we press *Enter*, a number of other options will be presented. Pressing *Enter* will set the default value for the first three options. When we get to the option for selecting the **linter** (short for **Lexical INTERpreter**), choose **TSLint** from the list, and then keep pressing *Enter* for the other options. A linter is a tool that automatically parses your code, looking for potential issues. It does this by looking at our code to see if it breaches a set of predefined rules, which could indicate that there are bugs or code-styling issues.

When we have gone all the way through this process, our client will be created; this will take some time to complete as there is a lot of code being downloaded and installed:

Now that our application has been created, we can run it by running `npm run serve` in the root of the client folder. Unlike Angular and React, the browser won't display the page by default, so we will need to open the page for ourselves using `http://localhost:8080`. When we do so, the page will look like this:

We are going to make our life easier when we write the image classifier since we are going to reuse some of the existing infrastructure that the Vue CLI created for us by modifying the home page to show our image classifier in action.

Showing a home page with the Vue template

In a similar way to React giving us the special `.jsx`/`.tsx` extensions to allow us to put our code and web page together, Vue provides us with single-file components that are created as `.vue` files. These files allow us to mix our code and web templates together to build up our page. Let's open up our `Home.vue` page and analyze it before we go on to create our first TensorFlow component.

We can see that our `.vue` component is broken up into two separate parts. There's a template section that defines the layout of the HTML that will be displayed on the screen, and there's a separate script section where we include our code. Since we are using TypeScript, the language for our `script` section is `ts`.

The script section starts off by defining the `import` section in much the same way that we would see in a standard `.ts` file. Where we see @ in the import, this tells us that the import path is relative to the `src` directory, so the `HelloWorld.vue` component is located in the `src/components` folder:

```ts
<script lang="ts">
import { Component, Vue } from 'vue-property-decorator';
import HelloWorld from '@/components/HelloWorld.vue';
</script>
```

The next thing we need to do is create a class that extends from the `Vue` class. What we are doing with this is using `@Component` to create a component registration called `Home` that can be used elsewhere:

```
@Component
export default class Home extends Vue {}
```

There is something else that we need to do. Our template is going to reference an external `HelloWorld` component. We must decorate our class with the components that the template is going to use, like this:

```
@Component({
  components: {
    HelloWorld,
  },
})
export default class Home extends Vue {}
```

The template is very straightforward. It consists of a single `div` class that we are going to render the `HelloWorld` component into:

```
<template>
  <div class="home">
    <HelloWorld />
  </div>
</template>
```

From the previous code template, we can see that, unlike React, Vue does not give us an explicit `render` function to deal with rendering HTML and state. Instead, the build-up of rendering is a lot closer to the Angular model, in which a template is parsed into content that can be served up.

 The reason that we mentioned Angular here is because Vue.js started off being developed by Evan You, who was working on the AngularJS project at Google; he wanted to create a more performant library. While AngularJS was a great framework, it did require a complete buy-in to the Angular ecosystem in order to work with it (the Angular team is working to rectify this). So, while Vue leverages Angular features such as templates, it has a very light touch in that you can just add a script tag to your existing code and start slowly migrating your existing code base over to Angular.

Vue borrows concepts from React such as the use of the Virtual DOM (as we discussed when we introduced React). Vue also uses a virtual DOM but implements it in a slightly different fashion, primarily with Vue only re-rendering out components that have a change, where React, by default, would also re-render child components.

What we want to do now is modify the `HelloWorld` component so that we can work with TensorFlow. But, before we do that, we need to write a couple of supporting classes that will do the heavy lifting with TensorFlow. These aren't big classes in terms of code, but they are extremely important. Our `ImageClassifier` class starts off with a standard class definition, as follows:

```
export class ImageClassifier {
}
```

The next step is optional, but it has a major impact on the stability of our application if it is running on a Windows client. Underneath the cover, TensorFlow uses WebGLTextures, but there is a problem with creating WebGLTextures on Windows platforms. To get around this issue, our constructor needs to be modified to look like this:

```
constructor() {
  tf.ENV.set('WEBGL_PACK', false);
}
```

Since we can run the image classification any number of times, we are going to add a private variable that represents the standard `MobileNet` TensorFlow:

```
private model: MobileNet | null = null;
```

Introducing MobileNet

At this point, we need to take a small detour into the world of CNNs. `MobileNet` is a CNN model, so having a little understanding of what a CNN is helps us to understand how it relates to the problem we are solving here. Don't worry, we aren't going to dig into the mathematics behind CNNs, but knowing a little bit about what they do will help us appreciate what they bring to the table for us.

CNN classifiers work by taking in an input image (potentially from a video stream), processing the image, and classifying it under predefined categories. In order to understand how they work, we need to take a step back and think about the problem from a computer's point of view. Suppose we have a picture of a horse. To a computer, that picture is just a series of pixels, so if we were to show a picture of a slightly different horse, the computer cannot say that they match just by comparing pixels.

A CNN breaks the images down into pieces (say, into 3x3 grids of pixels) and compares those pieces. Simplistically speaking, what it is looking for is the number of matches that it can make with these pieces. The greater the number of matches, the greater the confidence that we have a match. This is a very simplified description of what a CNN does, which involves a number of steps and filters, but it should serve to provide an understanding of why we would want to use a CNN such as MobileNet in TensorFlow.

MobileNet is a specialist CNN that, among other things, provides us with image classification that has been trained against images in the ImageNet database (http://www.image-net.org/). When we load the model, we are loading a pre-trained model that has been created for us. The reason we are using a pre-trained network is that it has been trained on a large dataset on the server. We would not want to run image classification training in the browser because it would require too much load being carried over from the server to the browser in order to perform the training. So, no matter how powerful your client PC is, copying over the training datasets will be too much.

We have mentioned MobileNetV1 and MobileNetV2 without going into what they are and what datasets they were trained on. Basically, the MobileNet models were developed by Google and trained on the ImageNet dataset, a dataset containing 1.4 million images broken down into 1,000 classes of images. The reason these are called MobileNet models is because they were trained with mobile devices in mind, so they are designed to run on low power and/or low storage devices.

 With a pre-trained model, we can use it as it is or we could customize it to use it for transfer learning.

The Classify method

Now that we understand a little bit about CNNs, we are ready to put this knowledge into practice. We are going to create an asynchronous classification method. TensorFlow can work with a number of formats when it needs to detect images, so we are going to generalize our method to only accept the appropriate types:

```
public async Classify(image: tf.Tensor3D | ImageData | HTMLImageElement |
    HTMLCanvasElement | HTMLVideoElement):
      Promise<TensorInformation[] | null> {
}
```

Only one of these types is specific to TensorFlow—the `Tensor3D` type. All the other types are standard DOM types, so this can be easily consumed in a web page without having to jump through numerous hoops to convert the image into a suitable format.

We haven't introduced our `TensorInformation` interface yet. When we receive classifications back from `MobileNet`, we receive a classification name and a confidence level for the classification. This comes back as `Promise<Array<[string, number]>>` from the classification operation, so we convert this into something more meaningful for our consuming code:

```
export interface TensorInformation {
  className: string;
  probability: number;
}
```

We now know that we are going to be returning an array of classifications and a probability (the confidence level). Getting back to our `Classify` method, we need to load `MobileNet` if it has not previously been loaded. This operation can take a while, which is why we cache it so that we don't have to reload it the next time we call this method:

```
if (!this.model) {
  this.model = await mobilenet.load();
}
```

We have accepted the defaults for the `load` operation. There are a number of options that we could have supplied if we needed to:

- `version`: This sets the `MobileNet` version number, and defaults to 1. Right now, there are two values that can be set: 1 means that we use `MobileNetV1`, and 2 means that we use `MobileNetV2`. Practically, for us, the difference between versions relates to the accuracy and performance of the model.
- `alpha`: This can be set to `0.25`, `0.5`, `0.75`, or `1`. Surprisingly, this has nothing to do with the `alpha` channel on an image. Instead, it refers to the width of the network that will be used, effectively trading accuracy for performance. The higher the number, the greater the accuracy. Conversely, the higher the number, the slower the performance. The default for the `alpha` is 1.
- `modelUrl`: If we wanted to work with a custom model, we could supply this here.

If the model loads successfully, then we can now perform the image classification. This is a straightforward call to the `classify` method, taking in the `image` that has been passed into our method. Following the completion of this operation, we return the array of classification results:

```
if (this.model) {
  const result = await this.model.classify(image);
  return {
    ...result,
  };
}
```

The `model.classify` method returns three classifications by default, but if we wanted to, we could pass a parameter to return a different number of classifications. If we wanted to retrieve the top five results, we would change the `model.classify` line, as follows:

```
const result = await this.model.classify(image, 5);
```

Finally, in the unlikely event that the model failed to load, we return `null`. With this in place, our completed `Classify` method looks like this:

```
public async Classify(image: tf.Tensor3D | ImageData | HTMLImageElement |
    HTMLCanvasElement | HTMLVideoElement):
      Promise<TensorInformation[] | null> {
  if (!this.model) {
    this.model = await mobilenet.load();
  }
  if (this.model) {
    const result = await this.model.classify(image);
    return {
      ...result,
    };
  }
  return null;
}
```

TensorFlow really can be that simple. Obviously, behind the scenes, a great deal of complexity has been hidden, but that is the beauty of well-designed libraries. They should shield us from the complexities while leaving us with room to get into the more complex operations and customization if we need to.

So, that's our image classification component written. How do we use it in our Vue application, though? In the next section, we are going to see how we modify the `HelloWorld` component to use this class.

Modifying the HelloWorld component to support image classification

When we created our Vue application, the CLI helpfully created a `HelloWorld.vue` file for us containing the `HelloWorld` component. We are going to take advantage of the fact that we already have this component, and we are going to use it to classify a pre-loaded image. If we wanted to, we could use it to load images using a file upload component and drive the classifications when this changes.

Now, let's take a look at what our `HelloWorld` TypeScript code looks like. Obviously, we are going to start with a class definition. Just like we saw earlier, we have marked this with the `@Component` decorator to say that this is a component:

```
@Component
export default class HelloWorld extends Vue {
}
```

We have two member variables that we want to declare in our class. We know that we want to use the `ImageClassifier` class that we have just written, so we will bring that one in. We also want to create an array of the `TensorInformation` results from the classification operation. The reason that we are going to store them as a class-level value is that we are going to have to bind to this when the operation finishes:

```
private readonly classifier: ImageClassifier = new ImageClassifier();
private tensors : TensorInformation[] | null = null;
```

Before we finish writing our class, we need to see what our template will look like. We start off with the `template` definition:

```
<template>
  <div class="container">
  </div>
</template>
```

As we can see, we are using Bootstrap, so we are going to use a `div` container to lay out our content. The first thing we are going to add to our container is an image. I have chosen to use an image of a group of Border Collie dogs here, largely because I am a fan of dogs. In order for us to read this image inside TensorFlow, we need to set `crossorigin` to `anonymous`. Pay particular attention to `ref="dogId"` in this part because we are going to need it again shortly:

```
<img crossorigin="anonymous" id="img"
src="https://encrypted-tbn0.gstatic.com/images?q=tbn:ANd9GcQ0ucPLLnB4Pu1kME
s2uRZISegG5W7Icsb7tq27blyry0gnYhVOfg" alt="Dog" ref="dogId" >
```

Following the image, we are going to add further Bootstrap support with the `row` and `col` classes:

```
<div class="row">
  <div class="col">
  </div>
</div>
```

Inside this row, we are going to create a Bootstrap list. We saw that Vue has its own Bootstrap support, so we are going to use its version for list support, `b-list-group`:

```
<b-list-group>
</b-list-group>
```

Now, we finally get to the meat of the template. The reason that we exposed the array of tensors in our class was so that we could iterate over each result in the array when it is populated. In the following code, we create a dynamic number of `b-list-group-item` by using `v-for` to automatically iterate over each tensor item. This creates the `b-list-group-item` entry, but we still need to display the individual `className` and `probability` items. With Vue, we bind text items such as this using `{{ <<item>> }}`:

```
<b-list-group-item v-for="tensor in tensors" v-bind:key="tensor.className">
  {{ tensor.className }} - {{ tensor.probability }}
</b-list-group-item>
```

 The reason we have added `v-bind:key` alongside `v-for` is because Vue provides something it calls an **in-place patch** by default. This means that Vue uses this key as a hint to uniquely track the item so that it can keep the values up to date on changes.

That's it; our template is complete. As we can see, the following is a simple template, but there's a lot going on with it. We have a Bootstrap container showing an image and, following that, letting Vue dynamically bind in the `tensor` details:

```
<template>
  <div class="container">
    <img crossorigin="anonymous" id="img" src="https://encrypted-
      tbn0.gstatic.com/imagesq=tbn:ANd9GcQ0ucPLLnB4Pu1kMEs2uRZ
      ISegG5W7Icsb7tq27blyry0gnYhVOfg" alt="Dog" ref="dogId" >
    <div class="row">
      <div class="col">
        <b-list-group>
          <b-list-group-item v-for="tensor in tensors"
              v-bind:key="tensor.className">
            {{ tensor.className }} - {{ tensor.probability }}
          </b-list-group-item>
```

```
        </b-list-group>
      </div>
    </div>
  </div>
</template>
```

Getting back to our TypeScript code, we are going to write the method that takes the image and then uses it to call our `ImageClassifier.Classify` method:

```
public Classify(): void {
}
```

Since we are loading an image onto our client, we have to wait for the page to render with the image so that we can retrieve it. We are going to call our `Classify` method from the constructor so, as it runs while the page is being created, we need to use a little trick to wait for the image to load. Specifically, we are going to use a Vue function called `nextTick`. It is important to understand that updates to the DOM happen asynchronously. When a value changes, the change isn't rendered immediately. Instead, Vue requests a DOM update, which is then triggered by a timer. So, by using `nextTick`, we wait for the next DOM update tick and perform the relevant operation:

```
public Classify(): void {
  this.$nextTick().then(async () => {
  });
}
```

 The reason why we mark the `async` function inside the `then` block is that we are going to perform an await inside this section, which means that we have to scope this as `async` as well.

In the template, we defined our image with a `ref` statement because we want to access this from inside our class. To do that, we query the map of `ref` statements that Vue maintains for us here, and since we have set our own reference up with `dogId`, we can now access the image. This trick saves us from having to use `getElementById` to retrieve our HTML element:

```
/* tslint:disable:no-string-literal */
const dog = this.$refs['dogId'];
/* tslint:enable:no-string-literal */
```

When we built our Vue application, the CLI automatically set up TSLint rules for us. One of these rules related to accessing elements via string literals. We disable the rule temporarily by using `tslint:disable:no-string-literal`. To re-enable the rule, we use `tslint:enable:no-string-literal`. There is an alternative way to disable this rule for a single line, which is to use `/* tslint:disable-next-line:no-string-literal */`. The approach you take doesn't really matter; what matters is the end result.

Once we have a reference to the dog image, we can now cast the image to `HTMLImageElement` and use this in the call to our `Classify` method in the `ImageClassifier` class:

```
if (dog !== null && !this.tensors) {
  const image = dog as HTMLImageElement;
  this.tensors = await this.classifier.Classify(image);
}
```

When the call to `Classify` comes back, as long as the model has loaded and successfully found classifications, it will populate our onscreen list through the power of binding.

Throughout our examples, I have tried to keep our code base as clean and as simple as possible. The code has been separated into separate classes just so we can create small and powerful pieces of functionality. To see why I like to do this, this is what our `HelloWorld` code looks like:

```
@Component
export default class HelloWorld extends Vue {
  private readonly classifier: ImageClassifier = new ImageClassifier();
  private tensors: TensorInformation[] | null = null;

  constructor() {
    super();
    this.Classify();
  }
  public Classify(): void {
    this.$nextTick().then(async () => {
      /* tslint:disable:no-string-literal */
      const dog = this.$refs['dogId'];
      /* tslint:enable:no-string-literal */
      if (dog !== null && !this.tensors) {
        const image = dog as HTMLImageElement;
        this.tensors = await this.classifier.Classify(image);
      }
    });
```

```
    }
  }
```

In total, including `tslint` formatters and white space, this code is only 20 lines long. Our `ImageClassifier` class is only 22 lines long, and that's an `ImageClassifier` class that could be used elsewhere without modification. By keeping classes simple, we decrease the number of ways that they could go wrong and we increase our chances of being able to reuse them. More importantly, we stick to the rather unfriendly named **Keep It Simple, Stupid** (**KISS**) principle, which states that systems work best if they are inherently as simple as they can possibly be.

Now that we have seen image classification in action, we can think about adding pose detection to our application. Before we do so, we need to look at a couple of other Vue areas that are going to be important to us.

The Vue application entry point

Something that we haven't touched on yet is what the entry point to our Vue application is. We have seen the `Home.vue` page, but that is just a component that gets rendered somewhere else. We need to take a step back and see how our Vue application actually handles loading itself and showing the relevant components. While we are doing this, we will also touch on routing in Vue so that we can see how that all hangs together.

Our starting point is found inside the `public` folder. In there, we have an `index.html` file, which we can think of as being the master template for our application. It's a fairly standard HTML file—we might want to give it a more suitable `title` (here, we're going with `Advanced TypeScript - Machine Learning`):

```
<!DOCTYPE html>
<html lang="en">
  <head>
    <meta charset="utf-8">
    <meta http-equiv="X-UA-Compatible" content="IE=edge">
    <meta name="viewport" content="width=device-width,
      initial-scale=1.0">
    <link rel="icon" href="<%= BASE_URL %>favicon.ico">
    <title>Advanced TypeScript - Machine Learning</title>
  </head>
  <body>
    <noscript>
      <strong>We're sorry but chapter09 doesn't work properly without
        JavaScript enabled. Please enable it to continue.</strong>
```

```
    </noscript>
    <div id="app"></div>
    <!-- built files will be auto injected -->
  </body>
</html>
```

The important element here is the `div` with its `id` property set to `app`. This is the element into which we are going to render our components. The way we do this is controlled from the `main.ts` file. Let's start by adding Bootstrap support, both by adding the Bootstrap CSS files and by registering the `BootstrapVue` plugin using `Vue.use`:

```
import 'bootstrap/dist/css/bootstrap.css';
import 'bootstrap-vue/dist/bootstrap-vue.css';
Vue.use(BootstrapVue);
```

Even though we have Bootstrap support in place, we don't have anything that hooks our components into `app div`. The reason why we add this support is to create a new Vue application. This accepts a router, a Vue store that is used to contain things such as Vue state and mutations, and a `render` function, which is called when the component is being rendered. The `App` component that's passed into our `render` method is the top-level `App` component that we will use to render all the other components into. When the Vue application finishes being created, it is mounted into the `app` div from `index.html`:

```
new Vue({
  router,
  store,
  render: (h) => h(App),
}).$mount('#app');
```

Our `App.vue` template consists of two separate areas. Before we add those areas, let's define the `template` element and containing `div` tag:

```
<template>
  <div id="app">
  </div>
</template>
```

Inside this `div` tag, we are going to add our first logical section—our good old friend, the navigation bar. Since these come in from the Vue Bootstrap implementation, they are all prefixed with `b-`, but they should need no dissection now, as they should be very familiar by this point:

```
<b-navbar toggleable="lg" type="dark" variant="info">
  <b-collapse id="nav-collapse" is-nav>
    <b-navbar-nav>
      <b-nav-item to="/">Classifier</b-nav-item>
      <b-nav-item to="/pose">Pose</b-nav-item>
    </b-navbar-nav>
  </b-collapse>
</b-navbar>
```

When the user navigates to a page, we need to display the appropriate component. Under the cover, the component that is displayed is controlled by the Vue router, but we need somewhere to display it. This is accomplished by using the following tag below our navigation bar:

```
<router-view/>
```

This is what our `App` template looks like when it has been completed. As we can see, if we want to route to other pages, we will need to add separate `b-nav-item` entries to this list. If we wanted to, we could dynamically create this navigation list using `v-for` in a similar way to what we saw when we were building up the classifications with the image classifier view:

```
<template>
  <div id="app">
    <b-navbar toggleable="lg" type="dark" variant="info">
      <b-collapse id="nav-collapse" is-nav>
        <b-navbar-nav>
          <b-nav-item to="/">Classifier</b-nav-item>
          <b-nav-item to="/pose">Pose</b-nav-item>
        </b-navbar-nav>
      </b-collapse>
    </b-navbar>
    <router-view/>
  </div>
</template>
```

When we first started looking at routing, all those chapters ago, you possibly thought that routing was a highly complicated thing to add to our applications. By now, you should be a lot more comfortable with routing and it isn't going to be much of a surprise that it is straightforward and simple to add routing support in Vue. We start off by registering the Router plugin inside Vue using the following command:

```
Vue.use(Router);
```

With this in place, we are now ready to build routing support. We export an instance of Router that can be used in our new Vue call:

```
export default new Router({
});
```

We are now at the point where we need to add our routing options. The first option we are going to set up is the routing mode. We are going to use the HTML5 history API to manage our links:

```
mode: 'history',
```

 We could use URL hashing for routing. This works in all the browsers that Vue supports and is a good choice if the HTML5 history API is unavailable. Alternatively, there is an abstract routing mode that works across all JavaScript environments, including Node. If the browser API is not present, no matter what we set the mode to, the router will automatically be forced to use this.

The reason we want to use the history API is that it allows us to modify the URL without triggering full-page refreshes. Since we know that we only want to replace components, rather than replacing the whole index.html page, we end up leveraging this API to only reload the component parts of the page, without doing a full-page reload.

We also want to set the base URL of our application. If we wanted to override this location to serve everything from the deploy folder, for instance, then we would set this to /deploy/:

```
base: process.env.BASE_URL,
```

While it is all well and good setting up the routing mode and the base URL, we are missing out on the important part here—setting the routes themselves. At a minimum, each route contains a path and a component. The path relates to the path in the URL, and the component identifies what component will be displayed as a result of that path. Our routes look like this:

```
routes: [
  {
    path: '/',
    name: 'home',
    component: Home,
  },
  {
    path: '/pose',
    name: 'Pose',
    component: Pose,
  },
  {
    path: '*',
    component: Home,
  }
],
```

 We have a special path match in our route. If the user types in a URL that doesn't exist, then we use * to capture that and redirect it to a particular component. We must put this as the last entry because otherwise, it would take precedence over the exact matches. The eagle-eyed reader will notice that, strictly speaking, we don't need the first path because our routing would still show the Home component due to our * fallback.

One thing we added to our route was a reference to a component that doesn't exist yet. We're going to address that now by adding the Pose component.

Adding pose detection capabilities

Before we start addressing pose detection, we are going to add a component that will play host to the relevant functionality. As this is our first component *from scratch*, we'll also cover it from scratch. Inside our views folder, create a file called Pose.vue. This file is going to contain three logical elements, so we will start off by adding those and setting up our template to use Bootstrap:

```
<template>
  <div class="container">
  </div>
```

```
</template>
<script lang="ts">
</script>
<style scoped>
</style>
```

 The only one of these that we haven't looked at so far is the `style` section. Scoped styles allow us to apply styling that just applies to the current component. We will apply local styling shortly, but first, we need to set up the image that we are going to display.

For our example code, I have selected a picture that is 1,200 pixels wide and 675 pixels high. This information is important because, when we do our pose detection, we are going to draw these points on the image, which means that we need to do a little bit of styling arrangement to put a canvas in place on which we can draw the points that match the locations on the image. We start off with two containers to hold our image:

```
<div class="outsideWrapper">
  <div class="insideWrapper">
  </div>
</div>
```

We are now going to add some CSS inside our style-scoped section to hardwire the dimensions in place. We start by setting the outside wrapper to have the dimensions I have just described. We then position our inside wrapper relative to our outer one, and set the width and height to 100% so that they fill the bounds exactly:

```
.outsideWrapper{
  width:1200px; height:675px;
}
.insideWrapper{
  width:100%; height:100%;
  position:relative;
}
```

Going back to `insideWrapper`, we need to add our image inside this. The image I chose for our example was a neutral pose, showing the key body points. The format of our image tag should look familiar, having done this already with the image classification code:

```
<img crossorigin="anonymous" class="coveredImage" id="img"
src="https://www.yogajournal.com/.image/t_share/MTQ3MTUyNzM1MjQ1MzEzNDg2/mo
untainhp2_292_37362_cmyk.jpg" alt="Pose" ref="poseId" >
```

In the same `insideWrapper` `div` tag, just below our image, we need to add a canvas. We will use the canvas when we want to draw the key body points. The key thing with this is that the width and height of the canvas match the container dimensions exactly:

```
<canvas ref="posecanvas" id="canvas" class="coveringCanvas" width=1200
height=675></canvas>
```

At this point, our `template` looks like this:

```
<template>
  <div class="container">
    <div class="outsideWrapper">
      <div class="insideWrapper">
        <img crossorigin="anonymous" class="coveredImage"
          id="img" src="https://www.yogajournal.com/.image/t_share/
          MTQ3MTUyNzM1MjQ1MzEzNDg2/mountainhp2_292_37362_cmyk.jpg"
          alt="Pose" ref="poseId" >
        <canvas ref="posecanvas" id="canvas"
          class="coveringCanvas" width="1200" height="675"></canvas>
      </div>
    </div>
  </div>
</template>
```

We have added classes to the image and canvas, but we haven't added their definitions. We could use one class to cover both, but I'm happy enough for us to have separate ones in place to set the width and height to 100%, and to position them absolutely inside the container:

```
.coveredImage{
  width:100%; height:100%;
  position:absolute;
  top:0px;
  left:0px;
}
.coveringCanvas{
  width:100%; height:100%;
  position:absolute;
  top:0px;
  left:0px;
}
```

Our completed, the styling section will look like this:

```
<style scoped>
  .outsideWrapper{
    width:1200px; height:675px;
  }
```

```
.insideWrapper{
  width:100%; height:100%;
  position:relative;
}
.coveredImage{
  width:100%; height:100%;
  position:absolute;
  top:0px;
  left:0px;
}
.coveringCanvas{
  width:100%; height:100%;
  position:absolute;
  top:0px;
  left:0px;
}
</style>
```

We have a couple of helper classes that we need to write at this point—one to do the pose detection, and the other to draw the points on the image.

Drawing the key points on the canvas

Whenever we detect a pose, we receive a number of key points back with it. Each key point is made up of a position (the x and y coordinates), the score (or confidence), and the actual part that the key point represents. We want to loop over the points and draw them on the canvas.

As always, let's start off with our class definition:

```
export class DrawPose {
}
```

We only need to get the canvas element once as it's not going to change. This indicates that we could pass this as our canvas and, because we are interested in the two-dimensional element of the canvas, we can extract the drawing context directly from the canvas. With this context, we clear off any previously drawn elements on the canvas and set a fillStyle color to #ff0300, which we will use to color in our pose points:

```
constructor(private canvas: HTMLCanvasElement, private context =
canvas.getContext('2d')) {
  this.context!.clearRect(0, 0, this.canvas.offsetWidth,
this.canvas.offsetHeight);
  this.context!.fillStyle = '#ff0300';
}
```

In order to draw our key points, we write a method that loops over each `Keypoint` instance and calls `fillRect` to draw the point. The rectangle is offset from the *x* and *y* coordinates by 2.5 pixels so that drawing a 5-pixel rectangle actually draws a rectangle that is roughly centered on the point:

```
public Draw(keys: Keypoint[]): void {
  keys.forEach((kp: Keypoint) => {
    this.context!.fillRect(kp.position.x - 2.5,
                           kp.position.y - 2.5, 5, 5);
  });
}
```

Once finished, our `DrawPose` class looks like this:

```
export class DrawPose {
  constructor(private canvas: HTMLCanvasElement, private context =
    canvas.getContext('2d')) {
      this.context!.clearRect(0, 0, this.canvas.offsetWidth,
        this.canvas.offsetHeight);
      this.context!.fillStyle = '#ff0300';
  }

  public Draw(keys: Keypoint[]): void {
    keys.forEach((kp: Keypoint) => {
      this.context!.fillRect(kp.position.x - 2.5,
                             kp.position.y - 2.5, 5, 5);
    });
  }
}
```

Using pose detection on the image

Earlier, we created an `ImageClassifier` class to perform our image classification. In keeping with the spirit of this class, we are now going to write a `PoseClassifier` class to manage the physical pose detection:

```
export class PoseClassifier {
}
```

We are going to set up two private members for our class. The model is a `PoseNet` model, which will be populated when we call the relevant load method. `DrawPose` is the class we just defined:

```
private model: PoseNet | null = null;
private drawPose: DrawPose | null = null;
```

Before we go any further into our pose detection code, we should start to get an understanding of what pose detection is, some of the things it is good for, and what some of the constraints are.

A brief aside about pose detection

We are using the term **pose detection** here, but this is also known as **pose estimation**. If you have not come across pose estimation, this simply refers to a computer vision operation where human figures are detected, either from an image or from a video. Once the figure(s) have been detected, the model is able to determine roughly where the key joints and body segments (such as the left ear) are.

The growth of pose detection has been rapid, and it has some obvious usages. For instance, we could use pose detection to perform motion capture for animation; studios are increasingly turning to motion capture to capture live-action performances and convert them into 3D images. Another usage lives in the field of sports; in fact, sports have many potential usages of motion capture. Suppose you are a pitcher in a major league baseball team. Pose detection could be used to determine whether your stance was correct at the point of releasing the ball; perhaps you were leaning over too far, or your elbow positioning was incorrect. With pose detection, it becomes easier for coaches to work with players to correct potential problems.

At this point, it's worth noting that pose detection is not the same as person recognition. I know it seems obvious, but there are people who have been confused by this technology into thinking that this somehow identified who a person is. That's a completely different form of machine learning.

How does PoseNet work?

Even with camera-based input, the process of performing pose detection does not change. We start with an input image (a single still of a video is good enough for this). The image is passed through a CNN to do the first part and identify where the people are in the scene. The next step takes the output from the CNN, passes it through a pose decoding algorithm (we'll come back to this in a moment), and uses this to decode poses.

The reason we said *pose decoding algorithm* was to gloss over the fact that we actually have two decoding algorithms. We can detect single poses, or if there are multiple people, we can detect multiple poses.

We have opted to go with the single pose algorithm because it is the simpler and faster algorithm. If there are multiple people in the picture, there is potential for the algorithm to merge key points from different people together; therefore, things such as occlusion could mean that the algorithm detects person 2's right shoulder as person 1's left elbow. In the following image, we can see how the elbow of the girl on the right obscures the left elbow of the person in the middle:

Occlusion is when one part of an image hides another part.

The key points that are detected by `PoseNet` are as follows:

- Nose
- Left eye
- Right eye
- Left ear
- Right ear
- Left shoulder
- Right shoulder
- Left elbow
- Right elbow
- Left wrist
- Right wrist
- Left hip
- Right hip
- Left knee
- Right knee
- Left ankle
- Right ankle

We can see where these are placed in our application. When it has finished detecting the points, we get an overlay of images, such as this:

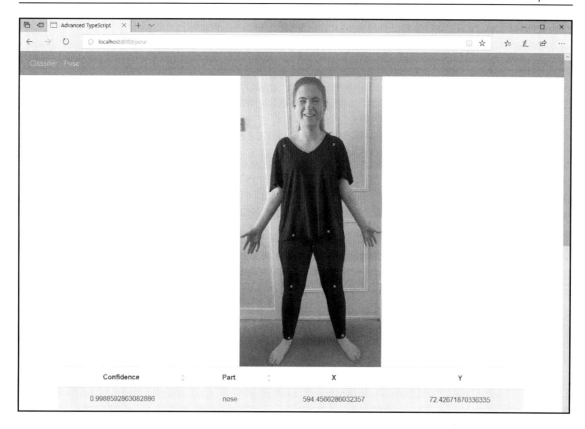

Confidence	Part	X	Y
0.9988592863082886	nose	594.4566286032357	72.42671870336335

Back to our pose detection code

Getting back to our `PoseClassifier` class, our constructor deals with exactly the same WebGLTexture issue that we discussed for our `ImageClassifier` implementation:

```
constructor() {
  // If running on Windows, there can be issues
  // loading WebGL textures properly.
  // Running the following command solves this.
  tf.ENV.set('WEBGL_PACK', false);
}
```

We are now going to write an asynchronous `Pose` method that returns either an array of `Keypoint` items, or `null` if the `PoseNet` model fails to load or find any poses. As well as accepting an image, this method will also accept the canvas that provides the context that we are going to draw our points on:

```
public async Pose(image: HTMLImageElement, canvas: HTMLCanvasElement):
Promise<Keypoint[] | null> {
  return null;
}
```

In the same way that `ImageClassifier` retrieved the `MobileNet` model as a cached operation, we are going to retrieve the `PoseNet` model and cache it. We will take this opportunity to instantiate the `DrawPose` instance as well. The point behind performing logic such as this is to ensure that this is something that we only do once, no matter how many times we call this method. Once the model is not null, the code prevents us from attempting to load `PoseNet` again:

```
if (!this.model) {
  this.model = await posenet.load();
  this.drawPose = new DrawPose(canvas);
}
```

When we load the model, we can supply the following option:

- **Multiplier**: This is the float multiplier for the number of channels (the depth) for all convolution operations. Choose from 1.01, 1.0, 0.75, or 0.50. There is a trade-off of speed and accuracy here, with the larger values being more accurate.

Finally, if the model loads successfully, we are going to call `estimateSinglePose` with our image to retrieve the `Pose` prediction, which also contains the `keypoints` that we will draw:

```
if (this.model) {
  const result: Pose = await this.model.estimateSinglePose(image);
  if (result) {
    this.drawPose!.Draw(result.keypoints);
    return result.keypoints;
  }
}
```

Again, putting this all together to show how we don't have to write huge amounts of code to accomplish all this work, and how separating the code out into small, self-contained logical chunks, makes our code so much simpler to understand, as well as easier to write. This is the full `PoseClassifier` class:

```
export class PoseClassifier {
  private model: PoseNet | null = null;
  private drawPose: DrawPose | null = null;
  constructor() {
    // If running on Windows, there can be
    // issues loading WebGL textures properly.
    // Running the following command solves this.
    tf.ENV.set('WEBGL_PACK', false);
  }

  public async Pose(image: HTMLImageElement, canvas:
    HTMLCanvasElement): Promise<Keypoint[] | null> {
      if (!this.model) {
        this.model = await posenet.load();
        this.drawPose = new DrawPose(canvas);
      }

      if (this.model) {
        const result: Pose = await
            this.model.estimateSinglePose(image);
        if (result) {
          this.drawPose!.Draw(result.keypoints);
          return result.keypoints;
        }
      }
      return null;
  }
}
```

Completing our pose detection component

Getting back to our `Pose.vue` component, we now have to fill in the `script` section. We are going to need the following `import` statements and class definition for our component (remember that I promised we would build this class up from scratch). Again, we can see the use of `@Component` to give us a component registration. We see this time and time again with Vue components:

```
import { Component, Vue } from 'vue-property-decorator';
import {PoseClassifier} from '@/Models/PoseClassifier';
import {Keypoint} from '@tensorflow-models/posenet';
```

```
@Component
export default class Pose extends Vue {
}
```

We have reached the point where we can write our `Classify` method, which will retrieve the image and canvas when they have been created and pass this through to the `PoseClassifier` class. We need a couple of private fields to hold the `PoseClassifier` instance and the returned `Keypoint` array:

```
private readonly classifier: PoseClassifier = new PoseClassifier();
private keypoints: Keypoint[] | null;
```

Inside our `Classify` code, we are going to employ the same life cycle trick of waiting for `nextTick` before we retrieve the image referenced as `poseId`, and the canvas referenced as `posecanvas`:

```
public Classify(): void {
  this.$nextTick().then(async () => {
    /* tslint:disable:no-string-literal */
    const pose = this.$refs['poseId'];
    const poseCanvas = this.$refs['posecanvas'];
    /* tslint:enable:no-string-literal */
  });
}
```

Once we have the image reference, we cast them to the appropriate `HTMLImageElement` and `HTMLCanvasElement` types, before we call the `Pose` method and populate our `keypoints` member with the resulting values:

```
if (pose !== null) {
  const image: HTMLImageElement = pose as HTMLImageElement;
  const canvas: HTMLCanvasElement = poseCanvas as HTMLCanvasElement
  this.keypoints = await this.classifier.Pose(image, canvas);
}
```

At this point, we can run the application. It's very satisfying seeing the `keypoints` results being overlaid onto the image, but we can go further. With just a little bit of extra effort, we can display the `keypoints` results in a Bootstrap table. Go back to our template and add the following `div` statements to add a Bootstrap row and column below the image:

```
<div class="row">
  <div class="col">
  </div>
</div>
```

Since we have already exposed the `keypoints` results, we can simply create a Vue Bootstrap table using `b-table`. We set the binding to the items using `:items`, setting it to the `keypoints` results that we defined in our class. This means that, whenever the `keypoints` entry gets new values, the table will be updated to display these values:

```
<b-table striped hover :items="keypoints"></b-table>
```

Refreshing our application adds the table below the image, with the table looking like this:

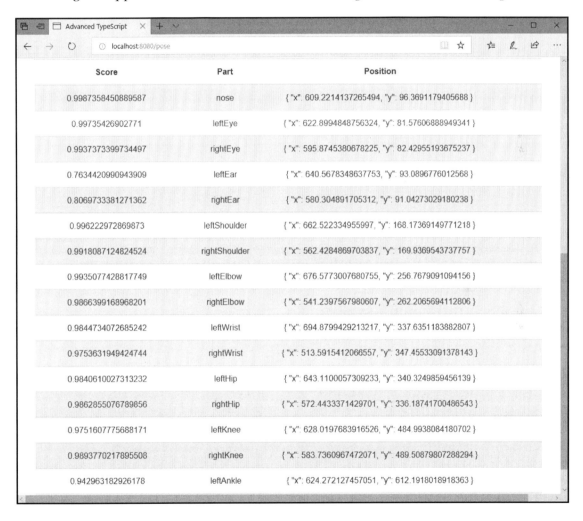

While this is a reasonable start, it would be good if we could take a bit more control of the table. Right now, the fields are picked up and automatically formatted by `b-table`. With a small change, we can separate the `Position` instance out into two separate entries and make the `Score` and `Part` fields sortable.

In our `Pose` class, we will create a `fields` entry. The `fields` entry maps the score entry to use the `Confidence` label and sets it to be `sortable`. The `part` field maps to a `label` value of `Part` and is also set to be `sortable`. We break `position` into two separate mapped entries labeled `x` and `y`, respectively:

```
private fields =
    {'score':
      { label: 'Confidence', sortable: true},
     'part':
      { label: 'Part', sortable: true},
     'position.x':
      {label:'X'},
     'position.y': {label: 'Y'}};
```

The last thing we need to do is hook the `fields` entry into `b-table`. We do this using the `:fields` property, like this:

```
<b-table striped hover :items="keypoints" :fields="fields"></b-table>
```

Refreshing our application shows us the effect of such little changes. This is a much more attractive screen, and the fact that the user can sort the `Confidence` (originally called `score`) and `Part` fields with such little effort shows just how powerful Vue really is:

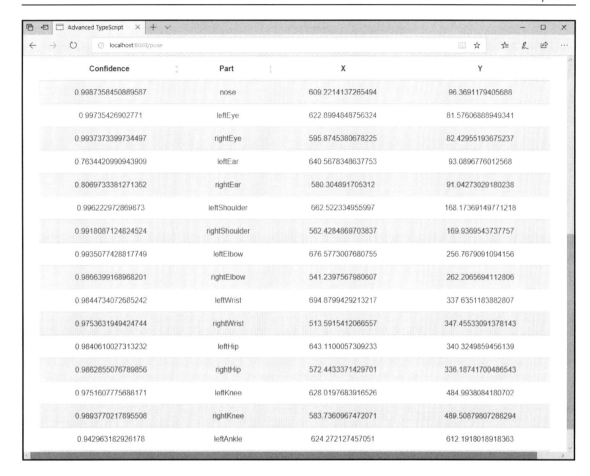

Confidence	Part	X	Y
0.9987358450889587	nose	609.2214137265494	96.3691179405688
0.99735426902771	leftEye	622.8994848756324	81.57606888949341
0.9937373399734497	rightEye	595.8745380678225	82.42955193675237
0.7634420990943909	leftEar	640.5678348637753	93.0896776012568
0.8069733381271362	rightEar	580.304891705312	91.04273029180238
0.996222972869873	leftShoulder	662.522334955997	168.17369149771218
0.9918087124824524	rightShoulder	562.4284869703837	169.9369543737757
0.9935077428817749	leftElbow	676.5773007680755	256.7679091094156
0.9866399168968201	rightElbow	541.2397567980607	262.2065694112806
0.9844734072685242	leftWrist	694.8799429213217	337.6351183882807
0.9753631949424744	rightWrist	513.5915412066557	347.45533091378143
0.9840610027313232	leftHip	643.1100057309233	340.3249859456139
0.9862855076789856	rightHip	572.4433371429701	336.18741700486543
0.9751607775688171	leftKnee	628.0197683916526	484.9938084180702
0.9893770217895508	rightKnee	583.7360967472071	489.50879807288294
0.942963182926178	leftAnkle	624.272127457051	612.1918018918363

That's it—we have reached the end of introducing TensorFlow and Vue. We have steered clear of the mathematical aspects behind CNNs because although they can appear intimidating at first glance, they aren't really as bad as all of that, but there are a lot of parts to a typical CNN. There is also a lot more that we can do with Vue; for such a small library, it is incredibly powerful, and this combination of small size and power is one of the reasons that it is becoming ever more popular.

Summary

In this chapter, we have taken our first steps into writing machine learning applications using the popular `TensorFlow.js` library. As well as learning about what machine learning is, we have also seen how it fits into the AI space. While we wrote our classes to hook up to `MobileNet` and pose detection libraries, we also covered what CNNs are.

As well as looking at `TensorFlow.js`, we have started a journey into using Vue.js, the up-and-coming client side library that is rapidly gaining popularity alongside Angular and React. We saw how to use .vue files and how to hook our TypeScript alongside the web templates, including using Vue's binding syntax.

In the next chapter, we are going to take a radical step sideways and see how we can incorporate TypeScript alongside ASP.NET Core to build a music library combining C# with TypeScript.

Questions

1. What languages was TensorFlow originally released in?
2. What is supervised machine learning?
3. What is `MobileNet`?
4. How many classifications are returned to us by default?
5. What command do we use to create our Vue application?
6. How do we denote a component in Vue?

Further reading

Packt has an extensive number of TensorFlow books and videos, should you want to improve your knowledge of TensorFlow. These books aren't just limited to `TensorFlow.js`, so there is an incredible depth of topics that go back to the original implementation of TensorFlow. Here are some of the ones I recommend:

- *TensorFlow Reinforcement Learning Quick Start Guide* (https://www.packtpub.com/in/big-data-and-business-intelligence/tensorflow-reinforcement-learning-quick-start-guide): Get up and running with training and deploying intelligent and self-learning agents using Python by Kaushik Balakrishnan: ISBN 978-1789533583.

- *TensorFlow Machine Learning Projects* (`https://www.packtpub.com/big-data-and-business-intelligence/tensorflow-machine-learning-projects`): Build 13 real-world projects with advanced numerical computations using the Python ecosystem by Ankit Jain and Amita Kapoor: ISBN 978-1789132212.
- *Hands-On Computer Vision with TensorFlow 2* (`https://www.packtpub.com/in/application-development/hands-computer-vision-tensorflow-2`): Leverage deep learning to create powerful image processing apps with TensorFlow 2.0 and Keras by Benjamin Planche and Eliot Andres: ISBN 978-1788830645.

As well as TensorFlow, we have also looked at using Vue, so the following will also be helpful for furthering your knowledge:

- *Vue CLI 3 Quick Start Guide* (`https://www.packtpub.com/in/web-development/vue-cli-3-quick-start-guide`) by Ajdin Imsirovic: ISBN 978-1789950342

Building an ASP.NET Core Music Library

10

This chapter marks a change in direction for us. In previous chapters, we concentrated on using TypeScript as our main development language. In this chapter, we are going to look at how we can use TypeScript inside Microsoft's ASP.NET Core in order to learn how to mix ASP.NET Core, C#, and TypeScript to make an artist-search program where we can search for musicians and retrieve details about their music.

The following topics will be covered in this chapter:

- Installing Visual Studio
- Understanding why we have ASP.NET Core MVC
- Creating an ASP.NET Core application
- Understanding why we have `Program.cs` and `Startup.cs`
- Adding TypeScript support to an ASP.NET application
- Using the `fetch` promise in TypeScript

Technical requirements

This chapter requires .NET Core Framework version 2.1 or higher. The easiest way to install this framework is to download and install Visual Studio; Microsoft provides a fully functional Community Edition, which you can get at `https://visualstudio.microsoft.com/downloads/`.

The finished project can be downloaded from `https://github.com/PacktPublishing/Advanced-TypeScript-3-Programming-Projects/tree/master/Chapter10`.

.NET applications don't tend to use npm to download packages; instead, they use NuGet to manage .NET packages. Building the source code will download the packages automatically.

Introducing ASP.NET Core MVC

Microsoft has a long and relatively chequered history with web frameworks. I first started developing server-based applications back in the late 1990s with their **Active Server Pages** technology, now known as classic **ASP**. This technology allowed the developer to create dynamic web pages based on user requests and send the resulting web pages back to the client. This technology required a special **Internet Information Services (IIS)** plugin for it to work, so it was entirely Windows-based and was a strange mix of the proprietary VBScript language and HTML. This meant that we often saw code that looked like this:

```
<%
Dim connection
Set connection = Server.CreateObject("ADODB.Connection")
Response.Write "The server connection has been created for id " &
Request.QueryString("id")
%>
<H1>Hello World</H1>
```

The fact that the language was so verbose for mixing dynamic content with HTML, and the underlying types were not type-safe, meant that developing with ASP was particularly error-prone, and debugging was challenging, to say the least.

The next step in the evolution of ASP was formally released in 2002 and was known as ASP.NET (or ASP.NET Web Forms). This was based on Microsoft's new .NET Framework and radically changed the way that we built web applications. Using this, we could build applications using languages such as C# or VB.NET and combine user controls in our web pages in order to create small self-contained components that slotted into our web pages. This was a great move on Microsoft's part, but there were still some fundamental issues that people spent a lot of time working around. The biggest issue was the fact that the web page was inherently mixed with the logic because the actual server-side implementation was handled using code behind. There was also a strict page compilation cycle, so the default architecture was based on the idea that there would be a round trip between the client and the server. Again, this could be worked around (and frequently was), but as a default architecture, it left a lot to be desired. Also, this technology was tied into the Windows platform, so it didn't get the reach that it could have. Even though .NET and C# were standardized so that other implementations could be created, Web Forms was a proprietary technology.

Recognizing the limitations of the Web Forms model, a team inside Microsoft decided to work on a form of ASP that would no longer be bound by the code-behind limitations of Web Forms. This was a major step forward because it opened the architecture up to developers so that they could follow object-oriented best practices better, including separation of concerns. All of a sudden, Microsoft had given developers a fighting chance of developing applications that followed SOLID design principles. This framework, known as ASP.NET MVC, allows us to develop applications following the **Model View Controller** (**MVC**) pattern. This is a powerful pattern because it allows us to separate code out into separate logical areas. MVC stands for the following:

- **Model**: This is the business layer that represents the logic that drives the behavior of the application
- **View**: This is the display that the user sees
- **Controller**: This handles the inputs and interactions

The following diagram shows the interactions in the MVC pattern:

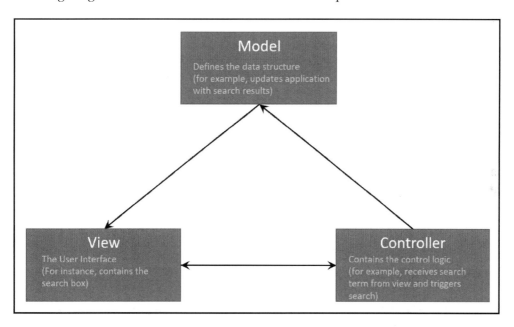

This architecture represents yet another major step forward for us when we want to develop full-stack web applications; however, it still suffers from the problem that it relies on Windows to host it.

Indirectly, from this diagram, we can work out that ASP.NET represents code that runs both on the client and on the server. This means that we don't need a server-side instance of Node running, so we can leverage the power and features of the .NET stack with this architecture.

Something that came as a surprise to a lot of people was the fact that Microsoft began to shift its focus away from Windows—long considered a cash cow for the company—and moved toward a more open model where the operating system their applications ran on became much less important. This has reflected a shift in its core priorities where cloud operations, through their superlative Azure offerings, have very much become the focus. If Microsoft stayed with its web architecture as it stood, then it would be missing out on a lot of the opportunities that were opening up; therefore, it started a multi-year rearchitecting of .NET Framework to remove its reliance on Windows and to make it platform-agnostic for developers using it.

This has resulted in Microsoft releasing ASP.NET Core MVC, which removes the reliance on Windows altogether. From one code base, we can now target Windows or Linux. All of a sudden, the number of servers that we can host our code on has gone through the roof, and the cost of running the servers has potentially gone down. At the same time, with each successive version of Core that Microsoft releases, they are tuning and honing the performance to give considerable boosts in the request server statistics. Also, the fact that we can develop these applications for free, and target Linux hosting as well, means that this technology is a lot more exciting for start-ups. I thoroughly expect the number of start-ups getting on the ASP.NET Core MVC bandwagon to grow significantly over the next couple of years as cost barriers are reduced.

Providing the project overview

The project we are building in this chapter is quite different from any of the ones we have written so far. This project sees us moving away from pure TypeScript and toward working with mixed programming languages, namely C# and TypeScript, as we see how to incorporate TypeScript into an ASP.NET Core web application. The application itself uses the Discogs music API so that our users can search for artists and retrieve details of their discography and artwork. The search part is accomplished using pure ASP.NET with C#, while the artwork retrieval is accomplished using TypeScript.

As long as you work alongside the code in the GitHub repository, this chapter should take about 3 hours to complete, which will not seem like much as we try out the code together! The finished application will look like this:

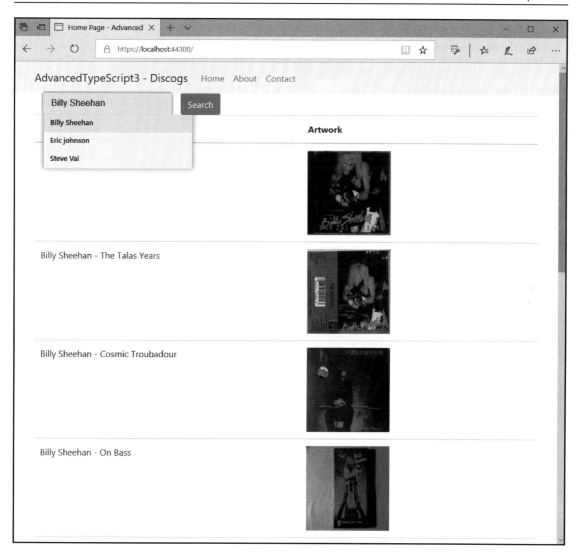

So, let's get on with it!

Getting started creating a music library with ASP.NET Core, C#, and TypeScript

I'm a big music fan. I have played guitar for years, which has led to me listening to a lot of musicians. Keeping track of all the music they have produced can be a very complex task, so I have long been interested in publicly available APIs that let us search for all things musician-related. The public API that I think provides us with the widest set of choices for querying for albums, artists, tracks, and more is the Discog library.

In this chapter, we are going to take advantage of this API and write an application that leverages ASP.NET Core in order to show you how we can use C# and TypeScript cooperatively.

In order to run this application, you will need to set up an account at **Discogs**, as follows:

1. Start off at `https://www.discogs.com/users/create` and sign up for an account.
2. While we could create a **Discogs** API application if we wanted to, especially if we wanted to take advantage of features such as authentication and having access to the full API, all we need for our purposes is to generate a personal access token by clicking the **Generate token** button, as shown in the following screenshot:

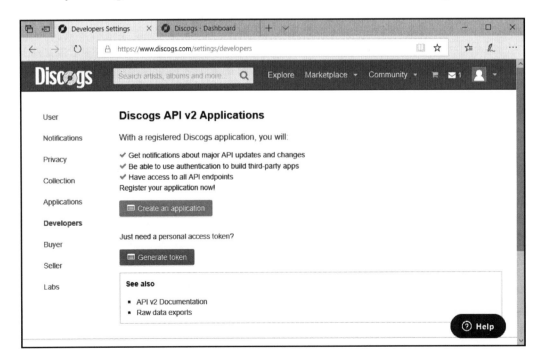

Now that we have signed up to **Discogs** and generated our token, we are ready to create our ASP.NET Core application.

Creating our ASP.NET Core application with Visual Studio

In previous chapters, we created our applications from the command line. With Visual Studio, however, the normal practice is to create our application visually.

Let's see how this is done:

1. Open Visual Studio and select **Create a New Project** to start the wizard for creating new projects. We are going to create an **ASP.NET Core Web Application**, as follows:

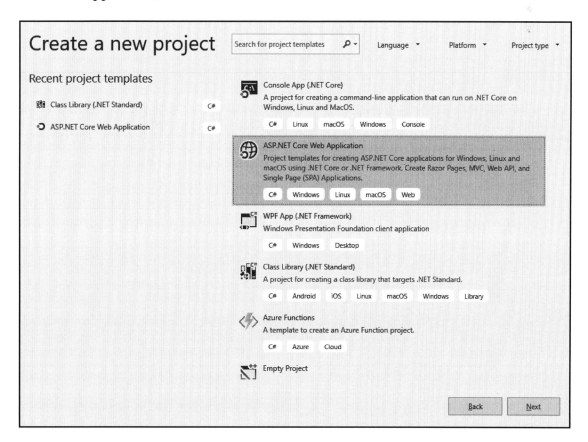

Older versions of .NET were only capable of running on Windows platforms. While .NET is an excellent framework, and C# is a wonderful language, this lack of cross-platform capability meant that .NET was only ever favored by companies with Windows desktops or Windows servers available. A while back, Microsoft decided to address this deficiency by stripping .NET back and rearchitecting it from the ground up as something that could run cross-platform. This has broadened the reach of .NET immensely and is known as .NET Core. What this means to us is that we can develop on one platform and deploy our application to another platform. Internally, .NET Core applications have platform-specific code that gets hidden behind a single .NET API so, for example, we can do file access without worrying about how the underlying operating system handles files.

2. We need to choose where we are going to put our code. My local Git repository is based under `E:\Packt\AdvancedTypeScript3`, so targeting that as my location tells Visual Studio to create the necessary files in a folder under that directory. In this case, Visual Studio will create a solution called `Chapter10`, which will contain all of our files. Click **Create** to create all the files we need:

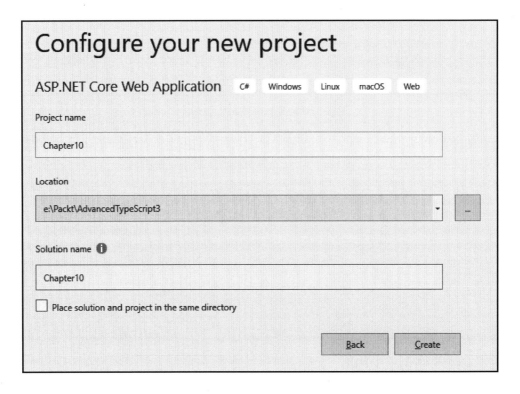

3. Once Visual Studio has finished creating our solution, it should have the following files available. As we develop our application, we will discuss the more important files and look at how we can use them:

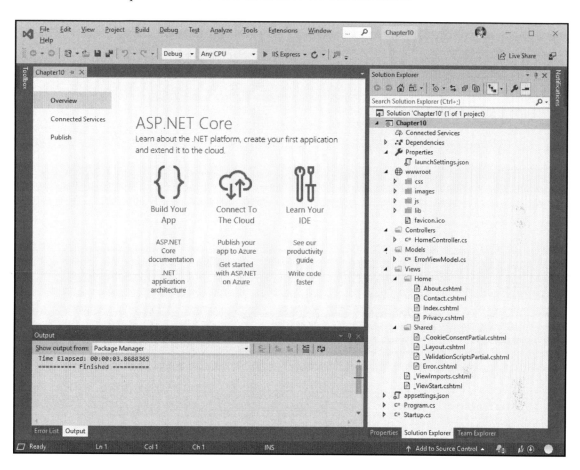

4. We can also build and run our application (pressing *F5* will do this), resulting in the application starting up like this:

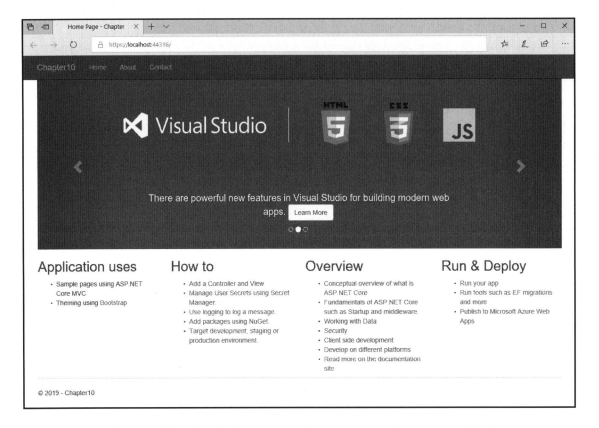

Having created our application, in the next section, we are going to cover the important points of the generated code, starting with the startup and program files before we start to amend it and bring in our search functionality.

Understanding the application structure

Behavior-wise, the starting point for our application is the `Startup` class. The purpose of this file is to set up the system during the startup process, so we take care of features such as configuring how cookies will be handled by our application and adding HTTP support. While this class is largely boilerplate in terms of functionality, we will come back to it later on in order to add support for the Discogs client we are going to write. The questions are, where does this functionality get called from? What actually starts our physical application? The answer to these questions is the `Program` class. If we quickly break this code down, we will see how the startup functionality is brought in and how it helps to build our hosting application.

.NET-executable applications start with a `Main` method. Sometimes, this is hidden from developers, but there is always one somewhere. This is the standard entry point for executable applications, and our web application is no different. This static method simply calls the `CreateWebHostBuilder` method, passing in any command-line arguments before calling **Build and Run** to build the host and run it:

```
public static void Main(string[] args)
{
   CreateWebHostBuilder(args).Build().Run();
}
public static IWebHostBuilder CreateWebHostBuilder(string[] args) =>
   WebHost.CreateDefaultBuilder(args)
      .UseStartup<Startup>();
```

The use of `=>` here is not the same as using the fat arrow. What this does, in this particular context, is replace the `return` keyword, so if you have a method with a single `return` operation, this can be simplified. The equivalent code, complete with the `return` statement, would look like this:

```
public static IWebHostBuilder CreateWebHostBuilder(string[] args)
{
    return WebHost.CreateDefaultBuilder(args).UseStartup<Startup>();
}
```

`CreateDefaultBuilder` is used to configure our service host with options such as setting up the Kestrel web engine, loading configuration information, and setting up logging support. The `UseStartup` method tells the default builder that our `Startup` class is the one that it needs to use to start the service.

The Startup class

So, what does our `Startup` class actually look like? Well, in a similar fashion to the way we have been developing with TypeScript, C# starts with the class definition:

```
public class Startup
{
}
```

Unlike JavaScript, C# does not have a special `constructor` keyword. Instead, C# uses the name of the class to represent the constructor. Note that, just like JavaScript when we create our constructor, we don't give it a return type (we'll see how C# deals with return types shortly). Our constructor is going to receive a configuration entry to allow us to read the configuration. We expose this as a C# property using the following `get;` property:

```
public Startup(IConfiguration configuration)
{
  Configuration = configuration;
}
public IConfiguration Configuration { get; }
```

When the runtime starts up our host process, the `ConfigureServices` method is called. This is the point where we would hook in any services that we need; in this code, I've added an `IDiscogsClient`/`DiscogsClient` registration, which adds this particular combination to the IoC container so that we can inject it into other classes later on. We have already seen an example of the dependency injection happening in this class with the configuration being supplied to the constructor.

Don't worry that we haven't seen `IDiscogsClient` and `DiscogsClient` yet. We will soon be adding the class and interface to our code. Here, we are registering them with the service collection so that they can be injected into classes automatically. As you may remember from what we said earlier in this book, a singleton will only give one instance of a class, regardless of where it is used. This is very similar to when we generated services in Angular, where we were registering the services as singletons:

```
public void ConfigureServices(IServiceCollection services)
{
  services.Configure<CookiePolicyOptions>(options =>
  {
    options.CheckConsentNeeded = context => true;
    options.MinimumSameSitePolicy = SameSiteMode.None;
  });

  services.AddHttpClient();
  services.AddSingleton<IDiscogsClient, DiscogsClient>();
```

```
services.AddMvc().SetCompatibilityVersion(
    CompatibilityVersion.Version_2_1);
}
```

 Something to note here is that the place where we set the return type differs from TypeScript. Like we saw in our TypeScript, we set the return type at the very end of the method declaration. With C#, the return type is set before the name so we know that ConfigureServices has a void return type.

The syntax on AddSingleton shows that C# also supports generics, so the syntax should not be scary to us. While there is a lot of parity in the language, TypeScript has some interesting differences here in that there aren't dedicated any or never types, for instance. If we wanted our C# type to do something similar to any, it would have to use the object type instead.

Now that the underlying services have been configured, the last step for this class is to configure the HTTP request pipeline. This simply means that this tells the application how to respond to HTTP requests. In this code, we can see that we already have support for static files enabled. This is very important for us because we are going to rely on static file support to hook our TypeScript (well, the compiled JavaScript version) so that it coexists with our C# application. We can also see that routing has been set up for our requests:

```
public void Configure(IApplicationBuilder app, IHostingEnvironment env)
{
    if (env.IsDevelopment())
    {
        app.UseDeveloperExceptionPage();
    }
    else
    {
        app.UseExceptionHandler("/Home/Error");
        app.UseHsts();
    }

    app.UseHttpsRedirection();
    app.UseStaticFiles();
    app.UseCookiePolicy();

    app.UseMvc(routes =>
    {
        routes.MapRoute(
                name: "default",
                template: "{controller=Home}/{action=Index}/{id?}");
    });
}
```

It's all very well creating the C# infrastructure to fire up our application, but if we don't have anything to display, then we are wasting our time. It is time for us to look at the base files that are going to be served up.

The files that make up the base views

The entry point for our view is the special `_ViewStart.cshtml` file. This file defines the common layout that the application will display. Rather than adding the contents to this file directly, we place the contents in a file called `_Layout.cshtml` and refer to this (minus the file extension) when setting the `Layout` file, like this:

```
@{
    Layout = "_Layout";
}
```

 Files that end with `.cshtml` have a special meaning to ASP.NET. This tells the application that these files are a combination of C# and HTML, which the underlying engine will have to compile before serving the result to the browser. We should be very familiar with this concept by now, having seen similar behavior with both React and Vue.

Now that we have covered the view entry point, we need to consider `_Layout` itself. The default ASP.NET implementation currently uses Bootstrap 3.4.1 so, as we go through this file, we're going to make the necessary changes for using Bootstrap 4. Let's start with the header as it currently stands:

```
<!DOCTYPE html>
<html>
<head>
    <meta charset="utf-8" />
    <meta name="viewport" content="width=device-width,
      initial-scale=1.0" />
    <title>@ViewData["Title"] - Chapter10</title>

    <environment include="Development">
        <link rel="stylesheet"
          href="~/lib/bootstrap/dist/css/bootstrap.css" />
        <link rel="stylesheet" href="~/css/site.css" />
    </environment>
    <environment exclude="Development">
        <link rel="stylesheet"
          href="https://stackpath.bootstrapcdn.com/bootstrap/3.4.1/
                css/bootstrap.min.css"
          asp-fallback-href="~/lib/bootstrap/dist/
                            css/bootstrap.min.css"
```

```
          asp-fallback-test-class="sr-only"
          asp-fallback-test-property="position"
          asp-fallback-test-value="absolute" />
        <link rel="stylesheet" href="~/css/site.min.css"
          asp-append-version="true" />
      </environment>
  </head>
```

This header looks like a fairly normal header, but there are a few little quirks in it. In the title, we are picking up `Title` from `@ViewData`. We use `@ViewData` to transfer data between the controller and the view, so if we looked in the `index.cshtml` file (for instance), the top part of the file would say this:

```
@{
    ViewData["Title"] = "Home Page";
}
```

What this section does, in combination with our layout, is set our `title` tag to `Home Page` `- Chapter 10`. The `@` symbol tells the compiler that ASP.NET's templating engine, called Razor, will have to do something with that piece of code.

The next part of our header splits the logic of what style sheets to include based on whether or not we are in the development environment. If we are running a development build, we get one set of files, whereas the release version gets the minified versions.

We are going to simplify our header by serving up Bootstrap from the CDN, regardless of whether or not we are in development mode, and change our title slightly:

```
<head>
  <meta charset="utf-8"/>
  <meta name="viewport" content="width=device-width,
    initial-scale=1.0"/>
  <title>@ViewData["Title"] - AdvancedTypeScript 3 - Discogs</title>

  <link rel="stylesheet" href="https://maxcdn.bootstrapcdn.com/
    bootstrap/4.0.0/css/bootstrap.min.css"
    integrity="sha384-
      Gn5384xqQ1aoWXA+058RXPxPg6fy4IWvTNh0E263XmFcJlSAwiGgFAW/dAiS6JXm"
        crossorigin="anonymous">
  <environment include="Development">
    <link rel="stylesheet" href="~/css/site.css"/>
  </environment>
  <environment exclude="Development">
    <link rel="stylesheet" href="~/css/site.min.css"
      asp-append-version="true"/>
  </environment>
</head>
```

The next section of our page layout is the body element. We are going to break this down section by section. Starting with the body element, we are going to look at the navigation element first:

```
<body>
    <nav class="navbar navbar-inverse navbar-fixed-top">
        <div class="container">
            <div class="navbar-header">
                <button type="button" class="navbar-toggle"
                    data-toggle="collapse"
                    data-target=".navbar-collapse">
                    <span class="sr-only">Toggle navigation</span>
                    <span class="icon-bar"></span>
                    <span class="icon-bar"></span>
                    <span class="icon-bar"></span>
                </button>
                <a asp-area="" asp-controller="Home"
                    asp-action="Index" class="navbar-brand">Chapter10</a>
            </div>
            <div class="navbar-collapse collapse">
                <ul class="nav navbar-nav">
                    <li><a asp-area="" asp-controller="Home"
                        asp-action="Index">Home</a></li>
                    <li><a asp-area="" asp-controller="Home"
                        asp-action="About">About</a></li>
                    <li><a asp-area="" asp-controller="Home"
                        asp-action="Contact">Contact</a></li>
                </ul>
            </div>
        </div>
    </nav>

</body>
```

This is, by and large, a familiar navigation component (albeit in Bootstrap 3 format). Converting the navigation component into Bootstrap 4 gives us the following:

```
<nav class="navbar navbar-expand-lg navbar-light bg-light">
    <div class="container">
        <a class="navbar-brand" asp-area="" asp-controller="Home"
            asp-action="Index">AdvancedTypeScript3 - Discogs</a>
        <div class="navbar-header">
            <button class="navbar-toggler" type="button"
                data-toggle="collapse"
                data-target="#navbarSupportedContent"
                aria-controls="navbarSupportedContent"
                aria-expanded="false"
```

```
        aria-label="Toggle navigation">
        <span class="navbar-toggler-icon"></span>
      </button>
    </div>
    <div class="navbar-collapse collapse">
      <ul class="nav navbar-nav">
        <li>
          <a class="nav-link" asp-area="" asp-controller="Home"
            asp-action="Index">Home</a>
        </li>
        <li>
          <a class="nav-link" asp-area="" asp-controller="Home"
            asp-action="About">About</a>
        </li>
        <li>
          <a class="nav-link" asp-area="" asp-controller="Home"
            asp-action="Contact">Contact</a>
        </li>
      </ul>
    </div>
  </div>
</nav>
```

Here, the unfamiliar areas lie inside the a links. The `asp-controller` class links the view to the `controller` class; by convention, these class names expand out into `<<name>>Controller`, so `Home` becomes `HomeController`. There is an associated `asp-action`, which relates to the method inside the controller class that we will call. Clicking the `About` link will call the `About` method inside `HomeController.cs`:

```
public IActionResult About()
{
  ViewData["Message"] = "Your application description page.";
  return View();
}
```

This method sets a message that will be written onto the `About` page, and then returns that view. ASP.NET is smart enough to use `View()` to work out that it should return the `About.cshtml` page for this because this is the `About` action. This is where we start to see the controller part join to the view part in MVC.

Getting back to the _Layout file, the next section that we are interested in is the following section, where we render in the body contents using @RenderBody:

```
<div class="container body-content">
    @RenderBody()
    <hr />
    <footer>
        <p>&copy; 2019 - Chapter10</p>
    </footer>
</div>
```

The view that we have chosen to display from our controller will be rendered at the point that @RenderBody is declared, so we can assume that the purpose of this command is to act as the placeholder to put the relevant view in. We are going to change this slightly to use our Bootstrap knowledge properly and to add a more meaningful footer. Consider the following code:

```
<div class="container">
  <div class="row">
    <div class="col-lg-12">
      @RenderBody()
    </div>
  </div>
  <hr/>
  <footer>
    <p>&copy; 2019 - Advanced TypeScript3 - Discogs Artist search</p>
  </footer>
</div>
```

We don't need to cover the rest of this file because we really need to start looking at the model and the view we're going to render in, but please read the source code from GitHub and make the relevant JavaScript changes in this file so that you are using Bootstrap 4 in place of Bootstrap 3.

We are now ready to start writing the model part of our MVC code base. We will do this by writing the model that will send the request to the Discogs API and get and transform the results into something that can be sent to the client.

Creating a Discogs model

You will remember that we added a registration for an `IDiscogsClient` model earlier on. We hadn't actually added any code at that point, so our application would fail to compile. We are now going to create the interface and implementation. `IDiscogClient` is a model, so we are going to create it inside our model directory. To create the interface and model in Visual Studio, we need to right-click on the `Models` folder to bring up a context menu. Inside the menu, select **Add** > **Class....** The following screenshot shows this:

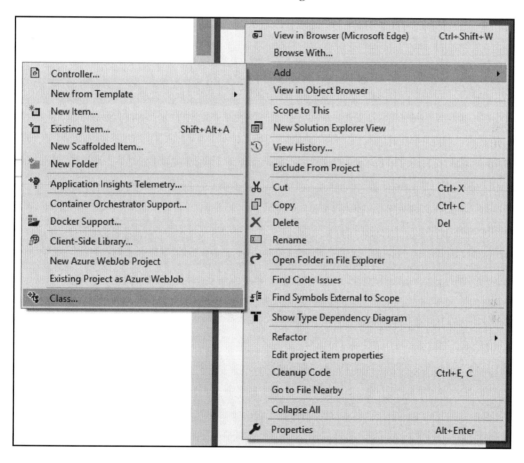

This brings up the following dialog, where we can create the class or associated interface:

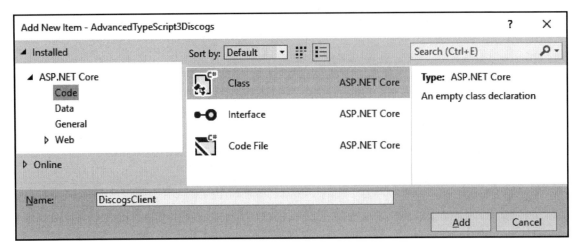

For the sake of brevity, we can create both the interface and the class definition inside the same file. I've separated them out in the GitHub code, but there's no need to do that for our classes here. First, we have the interface definition, as follows:

```
public interface IDiscogsClient
{
    Task<Results> GetByArtist(string artist);
}
```

The use of `Task<Results>` in our definition is similar to specifying a promise that returns a particular type in TypeScript. What we are saying here is that our method will run asynchronously and, at some point, it will return a `Results` type.

Setting up the Results type

The data that we get back from Discogs comes back as a hierarchy of fields. Ultimately, we want to have code in place that will convert and return the results, similar to the following:

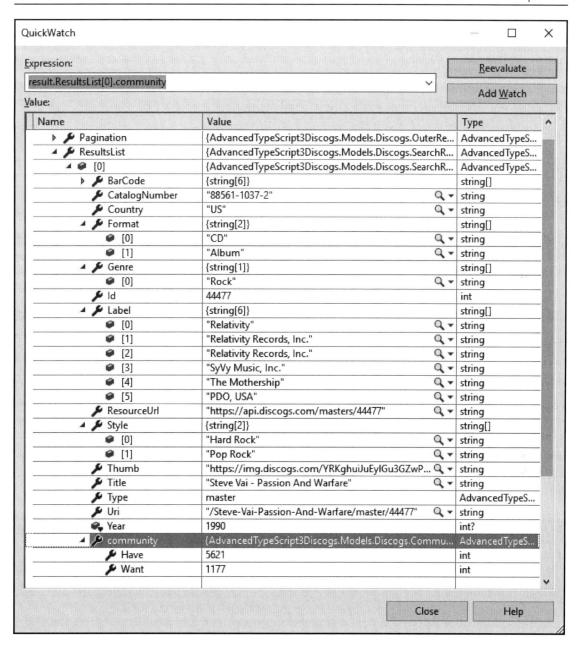

Behind the scenes, we are going to convert the JSON result from our call into a set of types. The top-level type is the `Results` type, which we are going to return out of our `GetByArtist` call. This hierarchy is shown in the following diagram:

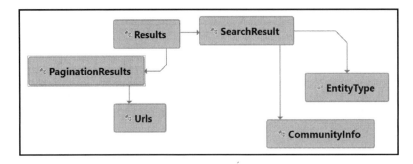

In order to see what the mappings look like, we are going to build the `CommunityInfo` type from scratch. This class will be used in our `SearchResult` class to provide the community fields that we selected in the previous **QuickWatch** screenshot. Create a class called `CommunityInfo` and add the following line at the top of the file:

```
using Newtonsoft.Json;
```

We are adding this line because there are features from here that we want to use; specifically, we want to use `JsonProperty` to map the name of a C# property onto one that is present in the JSON result. We have two fields that `CommunityInfo` needs to return—one that identifies how many people `want` the music title, and another that identifies how many people `have` it. We are going to follow standard C# naming conventions and use Pascal casing for property names (this means that the first letter is capitalized). Since the property name uses Pascal casing, we are going to use the `JsonProperty` attribute to map that name to the appropriate REST property name, so the `Want` property will be mapped to `want` in the result:

```
public class CommunityInfo
{
    [JsonProperty(PropertyName = "want")]
    public int Want { get; set; }
    [JsonProperty(PropertyName = "have")]
    public int Have { get; set; }
}
```

We aren't going to go through all the classes and properties. I would definitely recommend reading the GitHub code for more details, but this should definitely help to clarify what the project structure is.

Writing our DiscogsClient class

When we write our `DiscogsClient` class, we already have the contract that it will be based on, along with the interface definition. This tells us that our class starts off like this:

```
public class DiscogsClient : IDiscogsClient
{
  public async Task<Results> GetByArtist(string artist)
  {
  }
}
```

The definition of our class looks slightly different to our interface because we didn't have to say that `GetByArtist` was `public` or that the method was `async`. When we use `async` in a method declaration, we are setting a compilation expectation that the method will have the `await` keyword inside it. This should be very familiar to us from our TypeScript use of async/await.

When we call the Discogs API, it always starts off with the `https://api.discogs.com/` URL. In order to make life a little bit easier for us in our code base, we are going to define this as a constant in the class:

```
private const string BasePath = "https://api.discogs.com/";
```

Our class is going to talk to a REST endpoint. This means that we must be able to access HTTP from our code. In order to do this, our constructor will have a class that implements the `IHttpClientFactory` interface that's been injected into it. The client factory will implement a pattern called the factory pattern to build an appropriate `HttpClient` instance for us to use when we need it:

```
private readonly IHttpClientFactory _httpClientFactory;
public DiscogsClient(IHttpClientFactory httpClientFactory)
{
  _httpClientFactory = httpClientFactory ?? throw new
    ArgumentNullException(nameof(httpClientFactory));
}
```

This rather strange-looking syntax in the constructor simply states that we are going to set the member variable with the HTTP client factory that we pass in. If the client factory is null, `??` means that the code falls through to the next statement, which will throw an exception stating that the argument is null.

So, what does our `GetByArtist` method look like? The first thing we want to do is check whether or not we have passed an artist into the method. If we haven't, then we're going to return an empty `Results` instance:

```
if (string.IsNullOrWhiteSpace(artist))
{
  return new Results();
}
```

In order to create our HTTP request, we need to build our request address up. While we are building our address, we are going to append the path from `GetByArtist` with the `BasePath` string we defined as a constant. Suppose we wanted to search for `Peter O'Hanlon` as the artist. We would build up our search string so that we would escape the text that the user has entered to prevent dangerous requests from being sent; therefore, we would end up building an HTTP request string that looks like that shown at `https://api.discogs.com/database/search?artist=Peter O%27Hanlonper_page=10`. We have limited the number of results to 10 in order to keep well within the Discogs request limit. We start with the helper method that appends the two strings together:

```
private string GetMethod(string path) => $"{BasePath}{path}";
```

With the helper in place, we can build up the GET request. As we discussed previously, we need to change the artist so that potentially dangerous search terms are sanitized. With `Uri.EscapeDataString`, we have replaced the apostrophe in my name with its equivalent ASCII value of `%27`:

```
HttpRequestMessage request = new HttpRequestMessage(HttpMethod.Get,
GetMethod($"database/search?artist={Uri.EscapeDataString(artist)}&per_page=
10"));
```

With the request created, we need to add a couple of headers to it. We need to add an `Authorization` token and a `user-agent` because Discogs is expecting to receive them. The `Authorization` token takes the format of `Discogs token=<<token>>`, where `<<token>>` is the token we created earlier when we signed up. The `user-agent` just needs to be something meaningful, so we set it to `AdvancedTypeScript3Chapter10`:

```
request.Headers.Add("Authorization", "Discogs
token=MyJEHLsbTIydAXFpGafrrphJhxJWwVhWExCynAQh");
request.Headers.Add("user-agent", "AdvancedTypeScript3Chapter10");
```

The final part of our puzzle is to use the factory to create `HttpClient`. When this has been created, we call `SendAsync` to send our request to the Discogs server. When this comes back, we read the `Content` response and when this comes back, we need to convert the type using `DeserializeObject`:

```
using (HttpClient client = _httpClientFactory.CreateClient())
{
  HttpResponseMessage response = await client.SendAsync(request);
  string content = await response.Content.ReadAsStringAsync();
  return JsonConvert.DeserializeObject<Results>(content);
}
```

When we put this all together, our class looks like this:

```
public class DiscogsClient : IDiscogsClient
{
  private const string BasePath = "https://api.discogs.com/";
  private readonly IHttpClientFactory _httpClientFactory;
  public DiscogsClient(IHttpClientFactory httpClientFactory)
  {
    _httpClientFactory = httpClientFactory ?? throw new
               ArgumentNullException(nameof(httpClientFactory));
  }

  public async Task<Results> GetByArtist(string artist)
  {
    if (string.IsNullOrWhiteSpace(artist))
    {
      return new Results();
    }
    HttpRequestMessage request = new HttpRequestMessage(HttpMethod.Get,
      GetMethod($"database/search?artist=
        {Uri.EscapeDataString(artist)}&per_page=10"));
    request.Headers.Add("Authorization", "Discogs
      token=MyJEHLsbTIydAXFpGafrrphJhxJWwVhWExCynAQh");
    request.Headers.Add("user-agent", "AdvancedTypeScript3Chapter10");
    using (HttpClient client = _httpClientFactory.CreateClient())
    {
      HttpResponseMessage response = await client.SendAsync(request);
      string content = await response.Content.ReadAsStringAsync();
      return JsonConvert.DeserializeObject<Results>(content);
    }
  }
  private string GetMethod(string path) => $"{BasePath}{path}";
}
```

We mentioned that there was a rate limit. What does that actually mean, though?

Discogs rate limitations

Discog limits the number of requests that can be issued from a single IP. For authenticated requests, Discog limits the rate of requests to 60 per minute. For unauthenticated requests, for most cases, the number of requests that can be sent is 25 per minute. The number of requests is monitored using a moving window.

We have our Discogs API model written; now, it's time for us to look at wiring our model to our controller.

Wiring up our controller

We are going to use the power of dependency injection to pass the Discogs client model that we just wrote in:

```
public class HomeController : Controller
{
  private readonly IDiscogsClient _discogsClient;
  public HomeController(IDiscogsClient discogsClient)
  {
    _discogsClient = discogsClient;
  }
}
```

As you may remember, when we were setting up the navigation, we set asp-action to Index. When we perform a search, our view is going to pass the search string over to Index and call the GetByArtist method. When we get the result of the search back, we set ViewBag.Result with the results list. Finally, we serve up View, which will be the Index page:

```
public async Task<IActionResult> Index(string searchString)
{
  if (!string.IsNullOrWhiteSpace(searchString))
  {
    Results client = await _discogsClient.GetByArtist(searchString);
    ViewBag.Result = client.ResultsList;
  }

  return View();
}
```

But what does our view look like? We now need to set up the Index view.

Adding the Index view

At the top of the file, we set the `ViewData` to `Title`. We saw what this did back when we looked at `_Layout.cshtml`, but it's worth repeating that the value that we set here is used to help build the title in our master layout page. When we run our application, this sets the title to `Home Page - AdvancedTypeScript 3 - Discogs`:

```
@{
    ViewData["Title"] = "Home Page";
}
```

The user interacts with our application through a search control. It's time for us to add it in. We are going to add a `div` ID, which we will call `pageRoot`, that will contain a `form` element:

```
<div id="pageRoot">
  <form asp-controller="Home" asp-action="Index" class="form-inline">
  </form>
</div>
```

Again, we can see that we are using the full power of ASP.NET to our advantage here. Our form is MVC-aware, so we tell it that we are using `HomeController` (remembering the conventions for controllers) by using `asp-controller`. We set the action to `Index`, so we are going to call the same `Index` method that we do when we navigate to this page. The reason that we can do this is that we still want to show the current page when we have finished searching so that the user can search for a different artist if necessary. Our `Index` method is clever enough to know whether or not we have passed a search string to trigger the search, so when the user triggers a search inside our form, the search string will be provided and this will trigger the search itself.

Inside the form, we need to add an input search field and a button that triggers the `submit` form when pressed. The class elements in here are just used to make our `button` and `input` fields into Bootstrap versions:

```
<div class="form-group mx-sm-3 mb-10">
  <input type="text" name="SearchString" class="form-control"
    placeholder="Enter artist to search for" />
</div>
<button type="submit" class="btn btn-primary">Search</button>
```

With this in place, this is what our search section looks like:

```
<div id="pageRoot">
  <form asp-controller="Home" asp-action="Index" class="form-inline">
    <div class="form-group mx-sm-3 mb-10">
      <input type="text" name="SearchString" class="form-control"
        placeholder="Enter artist to search for" />
    </div>
    <button type="submit" class="btn btn-primary">Search</button>
  </form>
</div>
```

If we were to run the application right now, we would see the following. If we were to enter the details of an artist and press the **Search** button, the search would be triggered, but no data would be displayed on the screen:

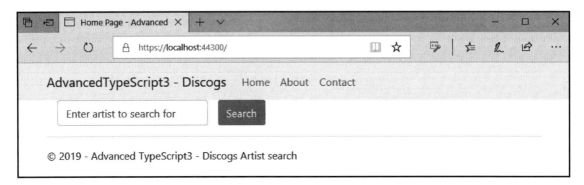

Now that we have search results coming back, we need to get the result out of the ViewBag that we added our result to. It's easy to become confused by ViewBag and ViewData, so it's worth talking about these for a second as they both serve the same purpose of bidirectionally passing data between the controller and the view, only slightly differently:

- When we added the results of the search, we set this as ViewBag.Result. If we were to take a look at the source code for ViewBag, though, we wouldn't actually find a property called **Result**. The reason for this is down to the fact that ViewBag is dynamic; in other words, it allows us to create arbitrary values that can be shared between the controller and the view, which can be called anything. In general, using ViewBag is a reasonable option, but since it is dynamic, it does not have the benefit of the compiler detecting whether or not there are errors, so it's vital that you make sure that the property you set in the controller is given exactly the same name as the property you set in the view.

- ViewData, however, relies on the use of a dictionary (similar to map in TypeScript), where we potentially have a number of key/value pairs holding the data. Internally, the value is an object, so this would have implications if we were setting the value in the view and passing it back to the controller as we would have to cast the object to the appropriate type. The effect of this is that setting ViewBag.Counter = 1 in the view means that we could treat ViewBag.Counter as an integer directly in our controller, but setting ViewData["Counter"] = 1 in the view means we would have to cast ViewData["Counter"] to an integer before we could do anything with it. The cast would look something like this:

```
int counter = (int)ViewData["Counter"];
```

For our purposes, we could have used either approach because the responsibility for setting the result lies with our controller, but I'm happy going with ViewBag to set our result. So, how do we go about adding the data in? We know that our Index page is a .cshtml file, so we can mix C# and HTML together. The way we denote the C# section is to use @{ }, so in order to render out the results, we need to check that there is a value in ViewBag.Result (note that C# uses !=, instead of the JavaScript format of !==, to test that the result is not null). The code that we write to render our result out starts off like this:

```
@{ if (ViewBag.Result != null)
   {
   }
}
```

Inside our result, we are going to create a Bootstrap table, with Title and Artwork as two columns. The HTML markup of the table that we're going to build starts off like this:

```
<table class="table">
  <thead>
    <tr>
      <th>Title</th>
      <th>Artwork</th>
    </tr>
  </thead>
  <tbody>
  </tbody>
</table>
```

Inside our table body (tbody), we are going to have to loop over each item in our result and write the relevant value out. The first thing that we have to do is create a variable called index. We are going to put this in place now, in anticipation of the point where we need to add an image with a unique name (we'll cover that in the next section).

Next, we are going to use `foreach` to iterate over every item in `ViewBag.Result`. For each item, we are going to create a new table row using `<tr></tr>` and, inside the row, we will write out two table data cells (`<td></td>`) containing the title and the resource URL, as follows:

```
<tbody>
  @{
    int index = 0;
  }
  @foreach (var item in ViewBag.Result)
  {
    <tr>
      <td>@item.Title</td>
      <td>@item.ResourceUrl</td>
    </tr>
    index++;
  }
</tbody>
```

If we run our application now, we will get results back, and these results will be written to the table:

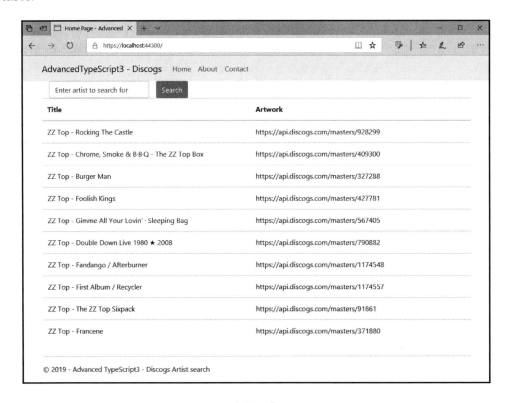

Obviously, the artwork element is wrong. That's not a picture, so we need to put something in place to go off and retrieve the pictures themselves, which requires our code to make another REST call for each result. We want this to happen when the results have been returned, so we are going to turn to client-side functionality now when we see how we can leverage TypeScript to get the image results for us.

Adding TypeScript to our application

The starting point for our TypeScript—pretty much as always—is our tsconfig.json file. We are going to create this to be as slimline as possible. We are going to set this particular outDir here because the creation of our project set a number of files in wwwroot. In the wwwroot/js folder, ASP.NET has already created a site.js file, so we are going to target our script to live alongside it:

```
{
  "compileOnSave": true,
  "compilerOptions": {
    "lib": [ "es2015", "dom" ],
    "noImplicitAny": true,
    "noEmitOnError": true,
    "removeComments": true,
    "sourceMap": true,
    "target": "es2015",
    "outDir": "wwwroot/js/"
  },
  "exclude": [
    "wwwroot"
  ]
}
```

We are going to use a single method to call the Discogs API to retrieve the relevant image. We aren't going to rely on any TypeScript packages loaded from an external source to make our API call because JavaScript provides us with the fetch API, which allows us to make REST calls without any dependencies.

We start off by adding a file called `discogHelper.ts`, which will contain the function we are going to call from our ASP.NET application. The reason we are adding this as a TypeScript method is that we want this to run on the client, rather than on the server side. This decreases the time taken to get the initial results loaded onto the client screen because we are going to let the client fetch and asynchronously load the images for us.

The signature of our function looks like this:

```
const searchDiscog = (request: RequestInfo, imgId: string): Promise<void>
=> {
  return new Promise((): void => {
  }
}
```

The `RequestInfo` parameter will accept the URL of the image request on the server. This follows the fact that Discog does not return full details about a particular music title, so the album artwork is not available at this point. Instead, it returns the REST call that we have to make to retrieve the full details, which we can then parse out to retrieve the artwork. For example, Steve Vai's Passion and Warfare album information returns the `ResourceUrl` of the `https://api.discogs.com/masters/44477` link. That becomes the URL that we pass in as our `request` to retrieve the full details, including the artwork.

The second parameter that we accept is the `id` of the `img` object. When we iterate over our initial search results to build the table of results, as well as add the album title, we also include a uniquely identified image, which we pass into our function. This allows us to dynamically update `src` when we have finished retrieving details about the album. Sometimes, this can lead to an amusing effect in the client because some albums take longer to retrieve than others, so it is entirely possible that the list of images updates out of sequence, meaning that later images are populated sooner than earlier ones. This is nothing to worry about because we are deliberately doing this to show that our client code is truly asynchronous.

> If we really wanted to worry about making our images display sequentially, we would change our function to accept an array of requests and image placeholders, issue our calls, and only update the images once all the REST calls had finished.

Unsurprisingly, the `fetch` API uses a promise called `fetch` for us to make our call. This accepts the request and, optionally, a `RequestInit` object that allows us to pass custom settings to our call, including the HTTP verb we want to apply and any headers we want to set:

```
fetch(request,
  {
    method: 'GET',
    headers: {
      'authorization': 'Discogs
          token=MyJEHLsbTIydAXFpGafrrphJhxJWwVhWExCynAQh',
      'user-agent': 'AdvancedTypeScript3Chapter10'
    }
  })
```

 Guess what? We are using the same `authorization` and `user-agent` headers here that we set in the C# code.

We have already said that the `fetch` API is promise-based, so we can rightly expect that the `fetch` call waits to complete before it returns the result. In order to get our image, we are going to perform a couple of transformations. The first transformation is to convert the response into a JSON representation:

```
.then(response => {
  return response.json();
})
```

The conversion operation is asynchronous, so the next stage of our transformation can occur in its own `then` block as well. At this point, if all has gone well, we should have a response body. We retrieve the `HTMLImageElement` using the image ID that we passed into our function. If this is a valid image, then we set `src` to the first `uri150` result we get back, which gives us the address of the 150 x 150 px image from the server:

```
.then(responseBody => {
  const image = <HTMLImageElement>document.getElementById(imgId);
  if (image) {
    if (responseBody && responseBody.images &&
        responseBody.images.length > 0) {
      image.src = responseBody.images["0"].uri150;
    }
  }
})
```

Putting this all together, our search function looks like this:

```
const searchDiscog = (request: RequestInfo, imgId: string): Promise<void>
=> {
  return new Promise((): void => {
    fetch(request,
      {
        method: 'GET',
        headers: {
          'authorization': 'Discogs
            token=MyJEHLsbTIydAXFpGafrrphJhxJWwVhWExCynAQh',
          'user-agent': 'AdvancedTypeScript3Chapter10'
        }
    })
    .then(response => {
      return response.json();
    })
    .then(responseBody => {
      const image = <HTMLImageElement>document.getElementById(imgId);
      if (image) {
        if (responseBody && responseBody.images &&
            responseBody.images.length > 0) {
          image.src = responseBody.images["0"].uri150;
        }
      }
    }).catch(x => {
      console.log(x);
    });
  });
}
```

 Discogs allows us to issue JSONP requests, which means that we have to pass a callback query string parameter. In order to issue a JSONP request, we would have to install the Fetch JSONP package from `https://github.com/camsong/fetch-jsonp`. This requires changing the signature of the `fetch` call to `fetchJsonp` instead. Apart from that, the rest of our functions look the same.

By now, we should be comfortable with the use of `async/await` inside promises. If we wanted a slightly less verbose function, we could change the code to this:

```
const searchDiscog = (request: RequestInfo, imgId: string): Promise<void>
=> {
  return new Promise(async (): void => {
    try
    {
      const response = await fetch(request,
```

```
    {
      method: 'GET',
      headers: {
        'authorization': 'Discogs
           token=MyJEHLsbTIydAXFpGafrrphJhxJWwVhWExCynAQh',
        'user-agent': 'AdvancedTypeScript3Chapter10'
      }
    });
    const responseBody = await response.json();
    const image = <HTMLImageElement>document.getElementById(imgId);
    if (image) {
      if (responseBody && responseBody.images &&
          responseBody.images.length > 0) {
        image.src = responseBody.images["0"].uri150;
      }
    }
  }
  catch(ex) {
    console.log(ex);
  }
});
}
```

In the next section, we are going to address how we call our TypeScript functionality from
ASP.NET.

Calling our TypeScript functionality from ASP.NET

Going back to our ASP.NET code, we can now hook up the searchDiscog function for
retrieving our images. The first thing we need to do is include the reference to the search
script:

```
<script src="~/js/discogHelper.js"></script>
```

With this in place, we can now expand our image section to include the search script:

```
<td>
  <img id="img_@index" width="150" height="150" />
  <script type="text/javascript">
      searchDiscog('@item.ResourceUrl', 'img_@index');
  </script>
</td>
```

Putting this all together, our `Index` page now looks like this:

```
@{
    ViewData["Title"] = "Home Page";
}
<div id="pageRoot">
    <form asp-controller="Home" asp-action="Index" class="form-inline">
        <div class="form-group mx-sm-3 mb-10">
            <input type="text" name="SearchString" class="form-control"
                placeholder="Enter artist to search for" />
        </div>
        <button type="submit" class="btn btn-primary">Search</button>
    </form>
</div>
@{ if (ViewBag.Result != null)
    {
        <script src="~/js/discogHelper.js"></script>
        <table class="table">
            <thead>
                <tr>
                    <th>Title</th>
                    <th>Artwork</th>
                </tr>
            </thead>
            <tbody>
                @{
                    int index = 0;
                }
                @foreach (var item in ViewBag.Result)
                {
                    <tr>
                        <td>@item.Title</td>
                        <td>
                            <img id="img_@index" width="150" height="150" />
                            <script type="text/javascript">
                                searchDiscog('@item.ResourceUrl', 'img_@index');
                            </script>
                        </td>
                    </tr>
                    index++;
                }
            </tbody>
        </table>
    }
}
```

Now, when we run the application, both the title and the image will be returned after we have performed a search. Rerunning the same search now gives us this:

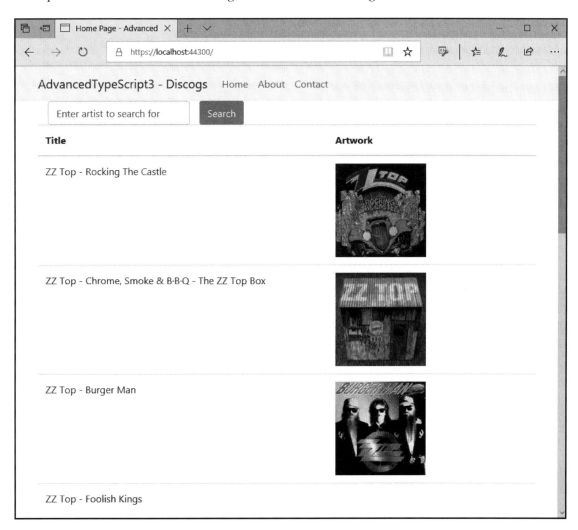

And that's it. We have an ASP.NET Core MVC application that we can use to search for artists and retrieve titles and artwork. All of this was achieved using a combination of ASP.NET MVC, HTML, Bootstrap, C#, and TypeScript.

Summary

In this, our last chapter, we moved over to developing an application using ASP.NET Core, C#, and TypeScript. We took this opportunity to learn about what Visual Studio generates for us when it creates an ASP.NET Core web application. We discovered that ASP.NET Core emphasizes the use of the MVC pattern to help us segregate the responsibilities of our code. In order to build this application, we signed up to the Discogs site and registered a token to let us start retrieving artists' details using C#. From the artist results, we created some TypeScript functionality that called out to the same site to retrieve album artwork.

While building the application, we covered how to mix C# and HTML code in the same .cshtml file, which constitutes the view. We wrote our own model to perform the artist search and we looked at how to update the controller to tie the model and the view together.

I hope you have enjoyed your journey with TypeScript and hope that we have enhanced your knowledge to the point where you want to use it more and more. TypeScript is a wonderful language and is always a joy to use, so please, go and have as much fun with it as I do. I look forward to seeing your work.

Questions

1. Why does TypeScript look similar to C#?
2. What C# method starts our program?
3. How does ASP.NET Core differ from ASP.NET?
4. What are the rate limitations of Discog?

Further reading

ASP.NET Core is a huge topic and would take far more time to cover than we have in this short chapter. Bearing that in mind, I recommend the following books for you to continue your ASP.NET journey:

- *ASP.NET Core 2 Fundamentals* (https://www.packtpub.com/in/web-development/aspnet-core-2-fundamentals): Build cross-platform apps and dynamic web services with this server-side web application framework by Onur Gumus and Mugilan T. S. Ragupathi. ISBN: 978-1789538915

- *Mastering ASP.NET Core 2.0* (`https://www.packtpub.com/in/application-development/mastering-aspnet-core`): MVC patterns, configuration, routing, deployment, and more by Ricardo Peres. ISBN: 978-1787283688

- *Building Microservices with .NET Core 2.0* (`https://www.packtpub.com/in/application-development/building-microservices-net-core-20-second-edition`): Transitioning monolithic architectures using microservices with .NET Core 2.0 using C# 7.0 by Gaurav Aroraa. ISBN: 978-1788393331

- *Learning ASP.NET Core 2.0* (`https://www.packtpub.com/application-development/learning-aspnet-core-20`): Build modern web apps with ASP.NET Core 2.0, MVC, and EF Core 2 by Jason De Oliveira and Michel Bruchet. ISBN: 978-1788476638

Assessments

Chapter 1

1. Using union types, we can write a method that accepts either the `FahrenheitToCelsius` class or the `CelsiusToFahrenheit` class:

```
class Converter {
    Convert(temperature : number, converter : FahrenheitToCelsius |
CelsiusToFahrenheit) : number {
        return converter.Convert(temperature);
    }
}

let converter = new Converter();
console.log(converter.Convert(32, new CelsiusToFahrenheit()));
```

2. To accept a key/value pair, we need to use a map. Adding our records to it would look something like this:

```
class Commands {
    private commands = new Map<string, Command>();
    public Add(...commands : Command[]) {
        commands.forEach(command => {
            this.Add(command);
        })
    }
    public Add(command : Command) {
        this.commands.set(command.Name, command);
    }
}

let command = new Commands();
command.Add(new Command("Command1", new Function()), new
Command("Command2", new Function()));
```

We have actually added two methods here. If we want to add multiple commands in one go, we can use REST parameters to accept the array of commands.

3. We can use a decorator to automatically log when our `Add` method is called. Our `log` method, for example, could look like this:

```
function Log(target : any, propertyKey : string | symbol,
descriptor : PropertyDescriptor) {
    let originalMethod = descriptor.value;
    descriptor.value = function() {
        console.log(`Added a command`);
        originalMethod.apply(this, arguments);
    }
    return descriptor;
}
```

We are only going to add this to the following `Add` method because the `Add` method that accepts the REST parameters calls this one anyway:

```
@Log
public Add(command : Command) {
    this.commands.set(command.Name, command);
}
```

Don't forget that we use the @ symbol to denote that this is a decorator.

4. To add a row with six medium columns of equal size, we use six `div` statements with the class set to `col-md-2`, like this:

```
<div class="row">
  <div class="col-md-2">
  </div>
  <div class="col-md-2">
  </div>
  <div class="col-md-2">
  </div>
  <div class="col-md-2">
  </div>
  <div class="col-md-2">
  </div>
  <div class="col-md-2">
  </div>
</div>
```

Remember, from our discussion on Bootstrap, that the number of columns in a row should equal 12.

Chapter 3

1. React provides us with special file types, `.jsx` (for JavaScript) or `.tsx` (for TypeScript), to create a file that can be *transpiled* down to JavaScript, so React takes the elements that look like HTML and renders them as JavaScript instead.

2. Both `class` and `for` are reserved keywords in JavaScript. Since `.tsx` files seemingly mix JavaScript and HTML together inside the same method, we need aliases to specify the CSS class and the control a `label` is associated with. React provides `className` to specify the class that should be applied to an HTML element and `htmlFor` to specify what control the label is associated with.

3. When we created our validators, we were creating reusable pieces of code that could be used to actually perform specific types of validation; for example, checking to ensure that a string was a minimum length. Since these were designed to be reusable, we had to separate them from our validation code, which was where we actually applied the validation.

4. By replacing `[0-9]` with `\d`, we convert
   `^(?:\\((?:[0-9]{3})\\)|(?:[0-9]{3}))[-. ]?(?:[0-9]{3})[-.]?(?:[0-9]{4})$` into the following
   expression: `^(?:\\((?:\d{3})\\)|(?:\d{3}))[-. ]?(?:\d{3})[-.]?(?:\d{4})$`

5. With a hard delete, we remove the physical record from the database. With soft deletes, we leave the record in place, but we apply a marker to it that means the record is no longer active.

Chapter 4

1. The MEAN stack consists of four major components:
   - **MongoDB**: MongoDB is a NoSQL database that became the de facto standard in building database support into client/server applications with Node. There are other database options available, but MongoDB is a very popular choice.
   - **Express**: Express wraps up a log of the complications of working with server-side code under Node and makes it easier to use. For instance, if we want to deal with HTTP requests, Express makes this trivial, as opposed to writing the equivalent Node code.

- **Angular**: Angular is the client-side framework that makes creating powerful web frontends easier.
- **Node**: Node (or Node.js) is the runtime environment for our application on the server.

2. We supply a prefix to make our component unique. Suppose we had a component that we wanted to call `label`; obviously, this will clash with the built-in HTML label. To avoid this clash, our component selector would be `atp-label`. Since HTML controls never use hyphens, we guarantee that we aren't going to *collide* with existing control selectors.

3. To start our Angular application, we run the following command in the top-level Angular folder:

```
ng serve --open
```

4. In the same way that our own language is broken down and structured into words and punctuation, we can break visual elements down into structures such as color and depth. As an example, the language tells us what colors mean, so if we see a button with one color on one screen in our application, it should have the same underlying usage across other screens in our application; we wouldn't use a green button to signify **OK** on one dialog and then **Cancel** on another. The idea behind a design language is that elements should be consistent. So, if we create our application as a Material application, it should be familiar to someone using Gmail (for instance).

5. We create services using the following command:

```
ng generate service <<servicename>>
```

This can be shortened to the following:

```
ng g s <<servicename>>
```

6. Whenever a request comes into our server, we need to determine how to handle the request the best, which means that we have to route it to the appropriate piece of functionality to handle the request. Express routing is the mechanism we use to accomplish this.

7. RxJS implements the observer pattern. This pattern has an object (known as the **subject**) that keeps track of an array of dependencies (known as the **observers**) and notifies them of *interesting* behaviors, such as state changes.

8. **CORS** stands for **Cross-Origin Request Sharing**. With CORS, we let *known* external locations have access to restricted operations on our site. In our code, since Angular is running from a different site to our web server (`localhost:4200`, as opposed to `localhost:3000`), we need to enable CORS support to post, otherwise we won't return anything when we make requests from Angular.

Chapter 5

1. GraphQL is not intended to fully replace REST clients. It can act as a cooperative technology, so it could very well consume multiple REST APIs itself to produce graphs.

2. A mutation is an operation that is intended to change the data in the graph in some way. We might want to add new items to the graph, update items, or delete items. It is important to remember that the mutation is just changing the graph – if the change has to be persisted to where the graph got the information from, then it is the graph's responsibility to call out to underlying services to make those changes.

3. In order to pass a value to a subcomponent, we need to use `@Input()` to expose a field for binding from the parent. In our code example, we set up a `Todo` item like so:

   ```
   @Input() Todo: ITodoItem;
   ```

4. With GraphQL, a resolver represents an instruction on how to turn an operation into data; they are organized as a one-to-one mapping to the fields. The schema, on the other hand, represents a number of resolvers.

5. To create a singleton, the first thing that we need to do is create our class with a private constructor. A private constructor means that the only place that we can instantiate our class is from inside the class itself:

   ```
   export class Prefill {
     private constructor() {}
   }
   ```

The next thing we need to do is add a field to hold a reference to the class instance and then offer a public static property to access that instance. The public property will take care of instantiating the class if it's not already available so that we'll always be able to access it:

```
private static prefill: Prefill;
public static get Instance(): Prefill {
  return this.prefill || (this.prefill = new this());
}
```

Chapter 6

1. Using `io.emit`, we can send a message to all connected clients.

2. If we wanted to send a message to all the users in a particular room, we would use something like the following, where we say what room we are sending the message to and then use `emit` to set the `event` and `message`:

```
io.to('room').emit('event', 'message');
```

3. To send the message to all users, except for the sender, we need to broadcast it:

```
socket.broadcast.emit('broadcast', 'my message');
```

4. There are certain event names that we cannot use as a message because they have been restricted due to them having a special meaning to Socket.IO. These are `error`, `connect`, `disconnect`, `disconnecting`, `newListener`, `removeListener`, `ping`, and `pong`.

5. Socket.IO is made up of a number of different cooperating technologies, one of which is called Engine.IO. This provides the underlying transport mechanism. The first type of connection it takes, when connecting, is an HTTP long poll, which is a fast and efficient transport mechanism to open. During idle periods, Socket.IO attempts to determine whether or not the transport can be changed over to a socket and, if it can use a socket, it seamlessly and invisibly upgrades the transport to use sockets. As far as the client is concerned, they connect quickly, and messages are reliable since the Engine.IO part establishes connections, even if firewalls and load balancers are present.

Chapter 7

1. In the `@Component` definition, we use `host` to map the host event that we want to work with to the relevant Angular method. In our `MapViewComponent`, for instance, we used the following component definition to map the `window load` event to a `Loaded` method:

```
@Component({
  selector: 'atp-map-view',
  templateUrl: './map-view.component.html',
  styleUrls: ['./map-view.component.scss'],
  host: {
    '(window:load)' : 'Loaded()'
  }
})
```

2. Latitude and longitude are geographic terms that are used to identify exactly where something is on the planet. Latitude tells us how far north or south something is from the equator, with the equator being 0; a positive number means we are north of the equator, while a negative number means we are going south from the equator. Longitude tells us how far east or west we are from the vertically centered line of the Earth which, by convention, runs through Greenwich in London. Again, if we are moving east, the numbers are positive, while moving west means the numbers are negative.
3. The act of converting a location, represented by latitude and longitude, into an address is called reverse geocoding.
4. We use a Firestore database, part of Google's Firebase cloud service, to save our data.

Chapter 8

1. A container is a running instance that takes in the various pieces of software that's needed to run the application. This is the starting point for us; containers are built from images, which you can either build yourself or download from a central Docker database. Containers can be opened up to other containers, such as the host operating system, or even to the wider world using ports and volumes. One of the big selling points with a container is that it is easy to set up and create and can be stopped and started very quickly.

2. When we were starting up Docker containers, we discussed two methods of achieving this. The first approach involves using a combination of `docker build` and `docker run` to start the services:

```
docker build -t ohanlon/addresses .
docker run -p 17171:3000 -d ohanlon/addresses
```

The use of `-d` signifies that it do not block the console as it detach and run silently in the background. This allows us to run a group of these commands together. In the download, you will find a batch file that I created to start them like this on Windows.

The second approach, and the one that I would recommend, uses Docker composition. In our example, we created a `docker-compose.yml` file that we used to group our microservices together. To run our composition file, we need to use the following command:

```
docker-compose up
```

3. If we use `docker run` to start our container, we can specify the port inside it using the `-p` switch. The following example remaps port 3000 to 17171:

```
docker run -p 17171:3000 -d ohanlon/addresses
```

When we use Docker composition, we specify the port remapping inside the `docker-compose.yml` file.

4. Swagger provides many useful features for us. We can use it for things such as creating API documentation, prototyping APIs, and using it to auto-generate our code, as well as for API testing.

5. When a React method cannot see the state, we have two options. We can either change it to use the fat arrow, `=>`, so that the `this` context is automatically captured, or we can use the JavaScript `bind` feature to bind to the correct context.

Chapter 9

1. While TensorFlow is now available with TypeScript/JavaScript support, it was originally released as a Python library. The backend of TensorFlow was written to use high-performance C++.

2. Supervised machine learning takes previous learning and uses this to work against new data. It uses labeled examples for this so that it learns correct answers. Behind this, there are training datasets that supervised algorithms work against to refine their knowledge.

3. MobileNet is a specialist **Convolutional Neural Network** (**CNN**) that, among other things, provides pre-trained image classification models.

4. The MobileNet `classify` method defaults to returning three classifications containing the classification name and the probability. This can be overridden by specifying the number of classifications to return as a parameter.

5. When we want to create our Vue application, we use the following command:

```
vue create <<applicationname>>
```

Since we want to create TypeScript applications, we choose to manually select features and, on the features screen, we make sure that we choose TypeScript as our option.

6. When we create a class in a `.vue` file, we use `@Component` to mark it as a component that can be registered in Vue.

Chapter 10

1. JavaScript and C# both trace their syntax roots back to C, so they largely follow similar language paradigms such as using { } to denote the scope of an operation. Since all JavaScript is valid TypeScript, this means that TypeScript has exactly the same style here.

2. The method that starts our program is the `static Main` method. It looks like this:

```
public static void Main(string[] args)
{
    CreateWebHostBuilder(args).Build().Run();
}
```

3. ASP.NET Core uses a rewritten .NET version that removes the constraint that it can only run on the Windows platform. This means that the reach of ASP.NET has greatly increased because it can now run on Linux platforms, as well as on Windows.

4. Discog limits the number of requests that can be issued from a single IP. For authenticated requests, Discog limits the rate of requests to 60 per minute. For unauthenticated requests, for most cases, the number of requests that can be sent is 25 per minute. The number of requests is monitored using a moving window.

Other Books You May Enjoy

If you enjoyed this book, you may be interested in these other books by Packt:

Hands-On RESTful Web Services with TypeScript 3
Biharck Muniz Araújo

ISBN: 9781789956276

- Explore various methods to plan your services in a scalable way
- Understand how to handle different request types and the response status code
- Get to grips with securing web services
- Delve into error handling and logging your web services for improved debugging
- Uncover the microservices architecture and GraphQL
- Create automated CI/CD pipelines for release and deployment strategies

Mastering TypeScript 3 - Third Edition
Nathan Rozentals

ISBN: 9781789536706

- Gain insights into core and advanced TypeScript language features
- Integrate existing JavaScript libraries and third-party frameworks using declaration files
- Target popular JavaScript frameworks, such as Angular, React, and more
- Create test suites for your application with Jasmine and Selenium
- Organize your application code using modules, AMD loaders, and SystemJS
- Explore advanced object-oriented design principles
- Compare the various MVC implementations in Aurelia, Angular, React, and more

Leave a review - let other readers know what you think

Please share your thoughts on this book with others by leaving a review on the site that you bought it from. If you purchased the book from Amazon, please leave us an honest review on this book's Amazon page. This is vital so that other potential readers can see and use your unbiased opinion to make purchasing decisions, we can understand what our customers think about our products, and our authors can see your feedback on the title that they have worked with Packt to create. It will only take a few minutes of your time, but is valuable to other potential customers, our authors, and Packt. Thank you!

Index

Printed in Great Britain
by Amazon